The History of Beer and Brewing in Chicago, 1833–1978

The History of Beer and Brewing in Chicago 1833–1978

ENJOY!

by
Bob Skilnik

BOB SKILNIK

ISBN 1-880654-16-4.

Library of Congress Catalogue Card No. 99-60642.

Front cover design based upon:
Ben Shahn
"Destroying Wine: Federal Agents Pouring Wine Down Sewer"
Gouache, *circa* 1934.
Courtesy of the Museum of the City of New York.
Back cover design includes images from the collection of Fil Graff (Edelweiss cans)
and Phil Pospychala (Fox Deluxe tin sign).

Contents

Preface

"... [Business] historyans is like doctors. They are always lookin' f'r symptoms. Those iv them that writes about [the business climate] of their own times examines th' tongue an' feels th' [economic] pulse an' makes a wrong dygnosis. Th' other kind iv [business] histhry is a post-mortem examination. It tells ye what a [business] died iv. But I'd like to know what it lived iv."

With apologies to the memory of journalist and political satirist
Finley Peter Dunne and his alter ego, Mr. Dooley

Why breweries? Why bother writing about this long forgotten local industry? As a kid growing up in the predominately Irish neighborhood of Bridgeport during the 1950s and early '60s, there were two distinctive smells I'll always remember, the putrid fumes of the nearby Chicago Stockyards and the balancing sweet malt aroma from our neighborhood breweries. Living just blocks away from both, the aroma of the breweries was, understandably, more appealing.

My summer Sundays often started with an early morning trip with my father to the Ambrosia Brewing Company to pick up a twenty-five pound block of ice from the brewery ice house for a picnic or family outing. I can still recall the grainy smell of malt and the clouds of steam that seemed to foam out of the brick stacks of the old brewery. As it condensed, tiny droplets of sweet *wort* would settle on my Dad's old Kaiser. The imposing red façade structure on 37th Place and Halsted, just across the street from the 11th Ward Democratic office, was a familiar neighborhood sight and smell.

The Canadian Ace Brewery at 39th and Emerald holds similar childhood memories. In my youth little did I know that the brewery once belonged to gangster Johnny Torrio, later passed on to the control of Al Capone and, eventually, Frank Nitti. During National Prohibition, it was known as the Manhattan Brewery, supplying much of the thirsty South Side with illegal brew.

Interestingly, these two successful neighborhood breweries were atypical in their ownership and location. From the beginning, breweries had often demonstrated an ethnic secularism, typical of early Chicago neighborhoods. Almost every early immigrant group had its own schools, church and brewery. The initial growth of German-owned breweries on *die Nord Seite* of Chicago typified this phenomenon; early breweries were built by Germans for Germans. As other ethnic groups settled in Chicago and reverted to the protection of clannish isolation, they developed their own breweries. The Michael Keeley, O'Donnell & Duer and Cooke breweries served the South Side Irish; White Eagle Brewery, the Poles; and Atlas and Pilsen, the Bohemians and Czechs. But for every example of this ethnic solidarity, one can cite dozens of anomalies. The Canadian Ace Brewery, and in its earlier existence as the Manhattan Brewery, was owned by Jews. The Ambrosia Brewery had been profitably operated before the turn of the century by a determined German woman, Magdalena Junk, a rare exception in a male-dominated trade. At the time, the enterprise was operated under the rather unfortunate name of the Junk Brewery.

But now they're gone. The Ambrosia Brewery (later the Atlantic Brewing Company's plant 2), was torn down around 1965. Part of the Canadian Ace Brewery is now home to a slaughter and packing house. A few years ago, I tried to find some information about the old Chicago brewing industry, but most books of local history were useless. It was almost as though the industry had never existed. That is why this book was written.

This study mixes a general history of Chicago breweries with a number of local events starting in 1833, when William Haas and Konrad Sulzer established a small brewery for a grateful population of almost two hundred, and continuing until 1978, when the brewing industry in Chicago ceased to exist. No other work details the history or influence of the once great Chicago brewing industry or the effects that the brewery owners, products and policies had on the inhabitants and events of the city. It is not meant to be an exhaustive study, but does attempt to consolidate much of what is known of Chicago's breweries into one colorful and easily readable work.

I could have assembled and published a series of tables with the annual facts and figures detailing the rise and fall of the local brewing industry. I have chosen, instead, to intermingle instances of how the breweries and their owners have contributed to the economic, social and political development of the Windy City, feeling that this approach would be more interesting than the history of the breweries themselves.

To give a representative survey of the 145 plus year history of beer and brewing in Chicago, I followed a simple research tenet: if an event affected the local brewing industry or the relationship of beer with the citizens of Chicago, it was considered for possible inclusion in the book. No doubt some will find examples and events omitted, but representative examples had to be selected. On the other hand, in order to do justice to the brewers' positive and negative contributions to the industry and the city, I have included persons, activities and episodes perhaps considered inconsequential by some readers, but essential for an understanding of the rise and fall of the brewing industry in Chicago.

Research for this book was often challenging, limited by the lack of concise, readily available information for an industry that once was an important element of city life. That local historians have chosen to neglect the political, economic, cultural and social importance of the Chicago brewing industry or failed to document the positive and negative contributions of local brewery owners is what I found most amazing during my research for this book. Upon completion of this work, I'm still baffled by this historical oversight.

Geographically, I have defined the territorial boundaries of old Chicago as they exist today. In 1889, the townships of Hyde Park, Jefferson, Lake and Lake View were swallowed up by Chicago, tripling the size of the city. This land grab and earlier expansions and annexations makes the argument of what really was the true territory of Chicago, as discussed in *The History of Beer & Brewing in Chicago*, a nagging, but probably valid one. By using the contemporary city borders, I am following the lead of brewing industry researchers, Donald Bull, Manfred Friedrich and Robert Gottschalk, co-authors of *American Breweries* (1984). An excerpt from their detailed list of past and present American breweries appears as the list of Chicago breweries in the Appendix of this book.

The brewers of Chicago were political figures, entrepreneurs, philanthropists, millionaires, socialites and scoundrels. By the early 1890s, the Americanized second and third generation of brewing families had been absorbed into the city's elite society. The marriage of Adeline Huck, daughter of brewery owner and grain trader Louis Huck, to Marshall Field, Jr. before the turn of the century, was one of social significance. The brewing community was no longer perceived as a rough and tumble group of mostly German immigrants, but as a group who wielded wealth and power. Early editions of Chicago social registers list the names of brewers Huck, Seipp, Wacker, Bemis and others, included with the more familiar names of Chicago businessmen such as McCormick, Field, Swift and Pullman. However, the turbulent years of World War I, when the brewers' allegiance to the Stars and Stripes was questioned, followed by almost four years when the local brewing fraternity was willing to subvert the goals of National Prohibition, wiped out much of the prestige and respect the pioneer brewing families had striven so hard to achieve.

Prior to National Prohibition, the industry's relationship to Chicago's fiscal well-being was unparalleled; its economic influence far exceeded that of other local concerns. Chicago breweries, with their many affiliated saloon outlets, contributed over 25% of the city of Chicago's yearly revenue in the form of brewery permits and saloon licensing fees. For years, most local politicians had understood this fiscal dependency and had acted accordingly, side-stepping the festering issue of saloon reform. The loss of this annual windfall during the first years of Prohibition had even prompted a desperate Chicago City Council to petition Congress in 1923 to remove the congressional ban on light beers and wines, noting in the petition that the city had already lost $32,000,000 of anticipated revenue in the first four years of National Prohibition. Not only did city revenues suffer as a consequence of the *Noble Experiment*, but so did the many local peripheral trades such as those of the malt, cooperage and architectural firms that had long enjoyed the encompassing success of the brewing industry. It's almost understandable that so many brewery owners and once law-abiding citizens were willing to ignore the restrictions of the Eighteenth Amendment and the Volstead Act; for some, it was a matter of economic survival.

With many of the restrictions of National Prohibition lifted on the brewing industry in April of 1933, the question remains: why did the local brewing industry later fail? As we shall see, Chicago was an ideal centralized location for the production and national distribution of beer. Blessed with an abundance of water from Lake Michigan and positioned in the center of the grain industry and railroad commerce, Chicago brewers used only two of these assets to further their industry. The local brewing industry, as a whole, never demonstrated the aggressive initiative of the smaller-sized Milwaukee and St. Louis breweries in the exporting of their products. Milwaukee brewer Val Blatz established a downtown depot in Chicago *before* the Civil War, decades before Chicago's Golden Era of brewing during the 1880s. In the overly saturated, smaller-sized markets of Milwaukee and St. Louis, exporting surplus beer meant continued sales; more importantly, it meant survival. In time, export sales would mean regional, and later, national dominance of the beer market.

There were notable exceptions to this export apathy as demonstrated by the progressive Conrad Seipp and K.G. Schmidt breweries. The wealthy and politically connected Seipp had aggressively attacked the Chicago market after the devastation of the Great Fire of 1871 had wiped out the many older breweries located in and about the downtown area. Seipp's brewery, located south of the fire's origin, remained unmolested as the conflagration spread in a northerly direction. Soon rewarded with a huge increase in local sales, the Conrad Seipp Brewery was able to afford the considerable start up costs of an export operation which included bottling their products and shipping to the Western mining camps and as far south as Cuba.

Content in what appeared to be a large and ever growing market in Chicago, the belated efforts of a few smaller local breweries to ship to outside markets before the twentieth century were often hampered by the earlier inroads made by the far-sighted Schlitz, Miller, Phil Best (later Pabst) and Anheuser-Busch concerns. While the out-of-town brewers were initially forced to expand their businesses beyond their own small markets, the Chicago brewers stood passively by as the aggressive shipping brewers literally poured their products into the huge Chicago market. Weakened by the costs of modernization, ill conceived and poorly managed foreign buyouts by English investors, increased local competition, market saturation and the resultant price wars of the 1890s, Chicago's brewing industry proved no match for the successful shipping brewers whose markets increased with the demise of every short-sighted, family-operated neighborhood brewery.

National Prohibition obviously played a major role in fostering the end of the local industry. With the advent of Repeal, the Chicago brewers found themselves confronting many of the same problems they had faced during the pre-Prohibition era. But with the end of Prohibition, there were additional obstacles which hastened the industry's demise. Brand loyalty had become non-existent in Chicago; to the average beer drinker, whether it was brewed as a non- alcoholic near beer and later needled with alcohol to bring up its strength or it was a clandestinely brewed full strength drink, beer had simply become beer during National Prohibition.

For many of the families that owned the smaller neighborhood breweries, plants idled for almost fourteen years were deemed too expensive to modernize. Of the thirty-seven Chicago breweries that closed with the advent of Prohibition or were forced to close in the succeeding years, only twenty-four went back into production when the manufacture of beer was again legalized in 1933. Of these surviving breweries, most were now controlled by new owners. Those families that had abandoned the industry soon distanced themselves and succeeding generations from the stigma of brewery ownership.

The arrival of canned beer in 1935, hearty customer acceptance of this convenient new product and the negative connotations of the post-Prohibition taverns proved to be too much for a number of the remaining small breweries that had barely been surviving from their on-premise draft sales alone. Beer drinking was no longer the exclusive domain of the new post-Prohibition taverns. It was now a pleasure or day's end reward to be consumed at home, conveniently enjoyed in the company of family and friends. The key to successfully exploiting the take-out market during the years before World War II was now advertising. Once again, the local industry was no match for the deep pockets of the larger shipping brewers. Hard choices had to be made. Either compete with the well financed advertising efforts of the nationals or use the less costly method of price cutting as an alternative strategy. But attempts by local brewers to lower costs, maintain a reasonable profit margin and retain their place in the Chicago market often failed. Cost cutting measures were poorly planned and product quality deteriorated. Imploring end tags in newspaper ads by Monarch Brewery to "Be loyal to your community!" only emphasized how desperate the situation had become. The shipping brewers were slowly winning the generations-long battle for supremacy in the Chicago market. In the years just after World War II, it would become obvious that the Chicago brewing industry was destined to fail.

Brewing has always been a romantic industry. One hundred years ago, local breweries had familiar names and strong personalities who guided the everyday operation of the plants. Today, faceless corporations and conglomerates run national beer businesses; the heart and soul of these institutions have seemingly ceased to exist. Less than one decade after the closing of the last commercial brewery in Chicago in 1978, a movement to reestablish a local brewing industry has begun. Small in nature, in most instances limiting themselves to the city and suburbs, brewpubs and microbreweries have emerged to provide a new generation of Chicago beer drinkers with new choices. Their occasional *art over science* approach to brewing is interesting and reminiscent of early brewing efforts in the young city of Chicago. In the monopolistic shadow of the national brands, their efforts are commendable and their local appeal is growing as they reintroduce the Chicago beer drinking public to the tastes and styles of beers long forgotten.

Prozit!
Bob Skilnik
January 1, 1999

Foreword

The topic of *The History of Beer & Brewing in Chicago, 1833-1978* is one that many of us take for granted...beer and its history. Beer is man's oldest and most pleasurable beverage, dating back to ancient Babylon and Egypt. That part of history has been well recorded, but its role in the evolution of American culture has been largely ignored.

During the nineteenth century, brewers and their products were major forces in our young country's struggle to assimilate a growing immigrant population, expand trade and industry and settle the West. By the turn of the century, the American brewing industry had become one of money and power. A seemingly ever expanding customer base helped amplify the American dream of building industrial dynasties through hard work and sacrifice. For hundreds of immigrant brewers, most often German, the New World was truly the land of opportunity. The rewards of the brewing trade gave them the upward mobility to become influential politicians, civic leaders, philanthropists and industry giants.

The recorded history of brewing in America has, until this book, often taken a one man, one brewery approach. Given the similar backgrounds of most pre-Prohibition brewers, these stories are almost all predictable. Such is the case of most books and articles I have reviewed as the Associate Editor of the *American Breweriana Journal*.

The History of Beer & Brewing in Chicago, 1833-1978 is decidedly different; it's extremely readable! With an eye towards the varied interests of historians, Breweriana enthusiasts and even the casual reader, the author weaves a seemingly regional tale that is more than an entertaining and informative story. It's one of the first works about the American brewing trade that recognizes the broad historical spectrum of human endeavor, economic influence and the inseparable topics of society, politics and religion and the influence the trade had on all these social elements. In this context, the book is more than a history of beer and brewing in Chicago; it symbolizes the grander epic of American history using Chicago as its setting.

Having been asked to write this foreword, I was, of course, obliged to read the work. The reward for me was a book that reads more like historical fiction, but all its accounts are true. I was absorbed for several nights as I read a detailed story of suspense, forceful personalities and conflict. Like a good novel, the book will take you back to the teeming ethnic neighborhoods of the turn of the century, the devastating Great Chicago Fire, the wide open speakeasies of the city's Roaring Twenties and the Chicago brewing industry's desperate struggles to survive its own follies. A truly great read.

Stanley J. Galloway
Executive Director
American Breweriana Association, Inc.
Pueblo, Colorado
January 4, 1999

Chapter 1

Chicago's Pioneer Breweries, 1833–1860

"The work required for the production of one brew of beer was exceedingly protracted and difficult."
One Hundred Years of Brewing

Early Chicago

Prior to 1833, Chicago's sparse population of little more than two hundred could legally quench their thirst at either Elijah Wentworth's Wolf Point Tavern or Samuel Miller's Fork's Tavern. The two primitive establishments were located in the immediate vicinity of Fort Dearborn at the north/south branch of the Chicago River. The owners held the first liquor licenses issued by the young county of Cook. For their appreciative customers, the innkeepers brewed their own primitive style of ale on site to supplement the rare shipment of beer from the East. It sold for 6¼ cents a pint.[1]

Into this dreary environment in 1833 arrived one Charles Butler, a New York financier and successful Wall Street lawyer. Butler had been in communication for the last year with a General Scott who had toured the territory west of Lake Michigan after the Black Hawk War. Scott was impressed with the area and gave the opinion that Chicago would one day be an important town.[2] Butler soon made arrangements to visit the area, often referred to by New Yorkers rather encompassingly as "the West," looking for investment possibilities. After an arduous journey from Buffalo, New York, through Detroit, South Bend and Michigan City, Indiana, Butler later wrote of his first impressions of Chicago, as he approached the area from the sand dunes of the southern region:

> I approached Chicago in the afternoon of a beautiful day, the 2d of August, (1833); the sun setting in a cloudless sky. On my left lay the prairie, bounded only by the distant horizon like a vast expanse of ocean; on my right, in the summer stillness, lay Lake Michigan. I had never seen anything more beautiful or captivating in nature. There was an entire absence of animal life, nothing visible in the way of human habitation or to indicate the presence of man, and yet it was a scene full of life . . . I approached Chicago in these closing hours of day, 'So calm, so clear, so bright'—and this was the realization of the objective point of my journey.[3]

But after being momentarily swept up in the emotion of the moment, Butler took a harder view of Chicago as he drew closer:

> . . . A small settlement, a few hundred people all told, who had come together mostly within the last year or two. The houses, with one or two exceptions, were of the cheapest and most primitive character for human habitation . . .[4]

After making several discouraging personal tours of the area around the fork of the Chicago River and to the immediate north, Butler inexplicably decided to plunge $100,000 of his family funds into speculative Chicago real estate. He was especially encouraged by Chicago's location on Lake Michigan and its potential as an eventual trading center. The recent release by Congress of federal funds for the dredging of the city's natural harbor by a young engineer named Jefferson Davis and his crew helped enhance Butler's decision. Somewhat comfortable with his investment decision but anxious to return to his financial activities in New York, he contacted his brother-in-law, William B. Ogden, to oversee the results of his purchase and left Chicago.

Ogden eventually arrived in Chicago in 1835 to check on Butler's land investments. Unlike Butler, Ogden was appalled at what he saw, since the purchased land consisted mostly of swamp and bog. Butler had chosen Ogden because of his experiences in the investment and money houses back home and his past savvy handling of real estate transactions on the East Coast. After his initial shock at conditions in Chicago, Ogden wrote Butler of his concern for the real estate investment, preparing him for the eventuality of a huge loss. After further consultation with Butler by mail soliciting his approval, Ogden moved quickly, platting the land into saleable lots and commissioning the sale of all the remaining land he now managed. With only one-third of his holdings auctioned off, he quickly regained the $100,000 purchase price, picked up an additional return of $150,000 and stopped the auction. Chicago, Ogden finally determined, had investment potential.[5]

Haas and Sulzer

In 1833, soon after Butler had made his fateful land purchase, Germanic immigrants William Haas and Konrad (Andrew) Sulzer arrived in Chicago from Watertown, New York with $3000, a load of malt, one hundred and fifty barrels of ale and all the necessary equipment for construction of Chicago's first full-scale commercial brewery.[6] During these early years, living conditions in Chicago were exceedingly primitive; the town was inhabited by soldiers, traders and adventurers. The land within easy walking distance of Fort Dearborn was surrounded by the wigwams of Indian tribes whose braves still presented a threat to the intruding settlers. Just twenty-one short years ago, most of the garrison at the fort had been wiped out by an Indian attack; the massacre taking place in the area known today as 18th and the Lake. The fort was eventually rebuilt and new settlers warily arrived to stake their claims on land near the new fort. Why Haas and Sulzer chose Chicago for the site of their endeavor is unknown. Any number of towns or cities in the more civilized eastern portion of the country would certainly have been more attractive, less dangerous and, quite possibly, more profitable for men of a less adventurous bent. But like Charles Butler, the brewers decided to invest their time and money in this unknown market.[7]

They soon erected a small brewery on a 100 x 200 foot lot purchased from the land holdings of Butler.[8] The Haas & Sulzer Brewery was an immediate success. First year production was approximately 600 barrels (31 gallons per barrel) of ale shared amongst the growing town's population of two hundred. As small as the brewery's output might appear today, it was a determined brewer who could annually produce three to four hundred barrels of beer during the 1830s.

A description of early brewing details the difficult work involved in the process:

> The work required for the production of one brew of beer was exceedingly protracted and difficult. The hauling, dipping, pumping, breaking, stirring and boiling were tiresome work for the laborers, indeed, requiring 15 to 17 working hours every day, and making the brewer's occupation one of hard toil and almost unbearable labor.[9]

Brew kettles of six or eight barrels were common, limiting production. With primitive and non-mechanized equipment, anything could go wrong. There were artesian wells and cellars to be dug and malt to be ground by hand. Fires to boil the sweet wort could often be unpredictable, sometimes destroying the small plant. Even after surmounting these considerable challenges, the fermentation could go bad, leaving the brewer with undrinkable stock.

William Ogden, Brewer

For Haas and Sulzer, skill, determination and a little luck paid off. Three years after start up, with the business firmly established and operating at peak capacity, Sulzer sold his profitable brewery interest to William Ogden. As a new co-owner with Haas, Ogden financed the erection of a larger structure at Pine (now north Michigan Avenue) and Chicago Avenue to house a new brewery capable of keeping up with the increased demand for their ale. Ale imported from the East Coast had become very expensive, allowing the brewers to enjoy a captive, non-competitive market for their products. As the only full-scale brewery in Chicago, the Haas & Sulzer Brewery thrived and continued to expand.[10]

After selling his stake in the brewery to Ogden, Sulzer remained in Chicago. He purchased one hundred acres of property in the area now known as Lake View, in the vicinity of Clark and Montrose (formerly known as Sulzer Road), from the ever-obliging Ogden. The land was considered marsh, but Sulzer was quite successful here, making a living as a gentleman farmer and renowned floriculturist.[11]

William Lill

In 1839, William Lill, an English immigrant, bought out part of the brewery interest from Haas who later moved to Austin, Texas. Although Ogden had no brewing experience, leaving these matters in the more experienced hands of Haas and Lill, he did take firm control of the brewery's finances. An example can be found in a letter dated October 12, 1839 from Ogden to one Alex Logan:

> Sir:
> I learn from Mr. Haas that you owe the firm of Wm. Haas & Co., composed of Mr. Haas and myself about $107 + interest for which we hold note in our book . . . must have money . . . otherwise we shall have to send the demand to a lawyer for collection.[12]

During the mid-1830s, the financial position of many small businesses in the Chicago area had changed for the worse. Wild speculation on land made poor men millionaires overnight; unforeseen events could later bring economic ruin. The financial situation of the brewery firm of Wm. Haas & Company was no different than that of most of the few small businesses in the area. In an attempt to improve the financial stability of the brewery, Ogden made a careful study of the company's accounts receivable. Although his correspondence during the time indicates his grudging acceptance of write-offs of many of the firm's delinquent smaller accounts, he did his best to doggedly pursue whatever due funds he could:

> . . . By the Bye what has become of Haas & Co. judgment against E.D. Perry left with you, can anything be got upon it . . .[13]

he wrote to one of his agents.

Ogden also assumed responsibility for procuring supplies for the brewery, including hops for future beer production.

> . . . I want none other than a perfectly certain article if after I get them here I should find they are mostly bad from any cause, I could not replenish my stock through the winter my brewery would necessarily stop . . .[14]

With Ogden's tight control over accounts receivable and the acquisition of quality supplies for production, the brewery successfully weathered the financial storms of its early operation.

Lill & Diversey

Michael Diversey, an immigrant from Alsace-Lorraine who arrived in Chicago in 1832, helped operate a dairy out of the Haas brewery. This arrangement was quite common in these early years with both operations sharing the use of stored ice for their products. The dairy operation supplemented lost income for the brewery during the non-brewing summer season. Diversey eventually bought out Ogden's interest in the brewery around 1841. The brewery became known, appropriately, as Lill & Diversey after Haas severed all ties to the operation. Ogden, first mayor of Chicago in 1837 and entrepreneurial genius, would later lead the building of the Illinois & Michigan Canal, persuade Cyrus McCormick to build his farm machinery plant in Chicago and organize the construction of a sprawling railroad system in and out of Chicago.[15]

In 1854, after dabbling in the distillation of pure and cologne spirits, Lill and Diversey started advertising as brewers of ale and porter. Sales of their flagship brew, Lill's Cream Ale, were so good, that by 1857 the partners had invested the sizable amount of over $250,000 in their brewery.[16] The Lill & Diversey Brewery, sometimes known as The Chicago Brewery, was now considered the largest brewery west of the Atlantic seaboard. Renovated and enlarged in 1866, their plant was a formidable structure, four stories tall with an imposing tower soaring an additional three stories above the main structure. The brewery now covered two acres and employed fifty to seventy-five men. Located on the southeast corner of Pine (Michigan Avenue) and Chicago Avenue, it would overshadow the nearby Water Tower Pumping Station, built a year later.[17]

Charitable Contributions

Michael Diversey shared much of his wealth with the German community of Chicago. He helped establish a German school in the so-called "Dutch Settlement" on the North Side, as well as the Catholic churches St. Joseph and St. Peter in 1846, St. Michael in 1852, and the German daily newspaper, *Der Nationaldemokrat*. With his partner Lill, he donated five acres of land to the McCormick Theological Seminary. In addition to his many charitable works, Diversey also held the office of alderman in the predominately German Ward Six in 1844.[18]

Competing Chicago Breweries

Following the success of Lill and Diversey, numerous smaller breweries were established in Chicago including the James Carney Brewery on South Water Street in 1840 and Jacob Gauch's Brewery, located on Indiana Street in 1845. Peter Schuettler, son-in-law of brewer Jacob Gauch, perhaps disillusioned with his budding career as an apprentice brewer, placed a notice in the *Chicago Democrat* of August 13, 1845, offering his share of the brewery for sale and giving notice of the dissolution of his partnership with

Gauch. Schuettler used the proceeds of the sale to become a premier manufacturer of covered wagons for the U.S. Army, built for its later exploration and expansion to the Western states. He was also quite successful providing brewers with horse drawn beer wagons for local deliveries. Chicago folklore talks of his ghost still making occasional appearances at his former home at Aberdeen and Adams. Eyewitnesses claim that Schuettler's spirit seems to make a futile search for something in the rooms and corridors, indicating perhaps, that in heaven, there really is no beer.[19]

Some breweries, such as the Reiser & Portmann Brewery, or the John B. Miller Brewery, shut down within a year or two of start-up. Other local breweries merged or reorganized, many for the better, such as the rapidly expanding Conrad Seipp Brewery.[20]

Enterprising individuals began to bottle beer during this expansion period, including Michael Keeley, who bottled ale and porter. This was not a common practice as beer was normally served as a draft beverage. For Keeley, the bottling business would prove profitable. He would become a successful brewer in later years.

The demand for beer in early Chicago proved insatiable. On January 1, 1857, an annual report in the *Democratic Press* showed a total production of beer and ale in Chicago of 16,270 barrels for 1856. Total value of the breweries was estimated at $130,160, and they employed thirty-three workers. The report also made note of the growth of the new Conrad Seipp Brewery. A score of smaller, unrecorded breweries surely added to these figures.

John A. Huck Brewery and Lager Beer

The most significant new brewery established during this pioneering period of the Chicago brewing industry was the John A. Huck Brewery, the first true lager beer brewery in Chicago. Founded in 1847 by John Huck and John Schneider, the operation was guided, in part, by William Ogden who sold the land for the brewery to the partners and, with his experience as a former brewery owner, operated as a silent partner. For Ogden, it appears that beer and brewing was in his blood. Schneider eventually sold out to Huck in 1850 and went to seek his fortune in California.[21]

Lager beer differed from the more familiar ale. It was made from a slower acting, bottom-fermenting yeast rather from the top-fermenting ale yeast. For optimum quality and drinkability, it was necessary to store it in cool underground caverns through the winter for drinking in the spring and summer. Ale, on the other hand, fermented out in one to two weeks, and was ready for enjoyment.

Initial reactions by American-born residents to the German-styled lager beer were unenthusiastic. To these so-called "nativists," many with a distrust and suspicion of anything foreign, ale seemed to represent the status quo, and the influence of their English background. Lager beer represented the unfamiliar, the foreign, the Germans. The Germans, however, saw lager beer not only as a taste of home but as a social lubricant and

John A. Huck was Chicago's first lager brewer. From The Western Brewer, *February, 1878.*

By 1871, the John A. Huck Brewery was a substantial enterprise. From One Hundred Years of Brewing (1903) 233.

a healthful drink of moderation, to be enjoyed with friends and family. To this end, John Huck established the first beer garden in Chicago. Business was so good that he expanded his operation in 1855 at the corner of Banks and North State Street, the area later known as Ogden's Grove.[22]

Chicago's First Brewpub

By all indications, the brewing of beer in Chicago during the city's early history was a reasonably profitable venture. Almost anyone who could handle the start-up cost of a small brewery and establish a local distribution network could count on an ever-increasing customer base. In 1858, John Hoerber razed his combination saloon and boarding house to accommodate new city building and street grade regulations. During the modification of his site, he built a small brewery underneath his establishment, providing his patrons above with freshly brewed beer. In doing so, Hoerber established Chicago's first brewpub, beating the now defunct Sieben's brewpub on West Ontario by about one hundred and thirty years.[23]

Milwaukee Competition

In 1856, an additional 25,025 barrels of beer, almost all from Milwaukee, were imported to Chicago to keep up with the growing demand of the city's more than

During the hot summer of 1854 and after the Great Fire of 1871, Milwaukee brewers like Jos. Schlitz, established a market for their beers in Chicago. Shown is a typical delivery wagon. From The Western Brewer, July, 1887.

80,000 residents. A mere 1,319 barrels were delivered by Chicago breweries for export.[24] Milwaukee's fledgling breweries began to expand into the lucrative Chicago market during the early 1850s. One boost to sales for Milwaukee brewers was the exceptionally hot summer of 1854, when the Chicago supply of lager beer was completely exhausted. Less than ten years after its introduction by John Huck, lager beer now accounted for most of the beer consumed in the city. With summer being a non-brewing season, the lager drinkers of Chicago, mostly German, were beginning to panic at the thought of no more beer during the hot season. Hospitable Milwaukee brewers were quick to meet the needs of Chicago, shipping enough beer to satisfy the thirst of thousands until the resumption of local brewing in the fall.[25]

In 1855, Milwaukee's efforts at exporting beer to the city were further aided by the completion of the Chicago & North Western Railway linking Chicago to Milwaukee. In 1857, Phil Best & Company (later Pabst) took advantage of this new connection and opened a shipping business on Randolph Street to further facilitate the sale of their products. The Val Blatz and Joseph Schlitz companies would soon follow. With direct rail connections to the growing city and its proximity of less than ninety miles, Chicago would soon become the key market for Milwaukee brewers.

By 1860, there were thirty-two breweries in Chicago attempting to serve the growing population of almost 110,000 and its demand for fresh beer. In less than thirty years, Chicago was on its way to becoming a brewing Mecca.[26]

Notes

1. A. T. Andreas. *History of Cook County*, Vol. I. (New York, NY: Arno Press reprint, 1975) p. 116.

2. A. T. Andreas. *History of Cook County Illinois.* (Chicago, IL: A.T. Andreas, Publisher, 1884) pp. 129–131. This information was provided to Andreas in a letter written to him by Charles Butler in 1881.

3. *Ibid.*

4. *Ibid.*

5. David Lowe. *Lost Chicago.* (Boston, MA: Houghton Mifflin Company, 1975) p. 16; Finis Farr. *Chicago, A Personal History of America's Most American City.* (New Rochelle, NY: Arlington House, 1973) pp. 38–39.

6. There is some dispute as to whether the brewers arrived in 1833 or 1836. If, however, Sulzer and Haas did indeed purchase the land for the brewery from Ogden, it would have been after 1835 when Ogden arrived in Chicago to check on the family land holdings. I have used 1833 as the year of their arrival since the brewery changed hands so often in the late 1830s that 1836 makes little sense as the first year of operation.

7. I. D. Guyer. *History of Chicago. Its Commercial and Manufacturing Interests and Industry.* (Chicago, IL: Church, Goodwin & Cushing, 1862) p. 40; A. T. Andreas, *op. cit*, p. 564; *Chicago Sun-Times*, Aug. 16, 1953.

8. Stanley W. Baron. *Brewed in America. A History of Beer and Ale in the United States.* (New York, NY: Arno Press, 1972) p.164.

9. *One Hundred Years of Brewing.* (Chicago and New York, H.S.Rich, 1903) p. 86.

10. Baron, *op. cit.* p. 164; *Chicago Sun-Times*, August 16, 1953.

11. Rudolph Hofmeister. *The Germans of Chicago.* (Champaign, IL: Stipes Publishing Company, 1976) p. 134.

12. Manuscript Collection of William B. Ogden, William B Ogden, Letter Book, Ogden to A. Logan, October 12, 1839, Chicago Historical Society.

13. *Ibid.*, Ogden to J.A. Hoes, November 13, 1840.

14. *Ibid.*, Ogden to Townsend, July 15, 1839.

15. Letter to the author from Valerie Turner, February 5, 1999. According to Ms. Turner of Chicago, a descendant of Diversey, the correct spelling of the brewer's last name is DIVERSY. The added "e" seems to be a result of his own inconsistency of signature.

16. *One Hundred Years of Brewing*, *op. cit.* p. 202; Andreas, *op. cit.*, p. 331.

17. William Leonard. *The Lill Story in the History of Chicago.* (Chicago, IL: Lill Coal & Oil Co., 1958) pp. 7–8.

18. Hofmeister, *op. cit.* pp. 100–101.

19. *Chicago Sun-Times*, October 31, 1997.

20. Donald Bull, Manfred Friedrich,and Robert Gottschalk. *American Breweries.* (Trumbull, CT: Bullworks, 1984) pp. 57–68.

21. *One Hundred Years Of Brewing*, *op. cit.* p. 232.

22. *Ibid.*, p. 232. Perry Duis in *The Saloon: Public Drinking In Chicago and Boston, 1880–1920* claims that Valentin Busch and Michael Brand were responsible for bringing lager yeast to Chicago in 1854. According to *One Hundred Years of Brewing*, Busch began an ale brewery in Chicago in 1851. In 1853, Busch took on Brand as a partner in their Blue Island location and their branch in Chicago. The same source, however, states that John A. Huck and his partner, John Schneider founded the first lager brewery in Chicago in 1847. By 1854, lager beer in Chicago had already become the preferred drink of German-Americans. According to the *Milwaukee Sentinel* of September 12, 1854, because of the hot summer of the same year, Chicago ran out of this unique style of beer, prompting Milwaukee brewers to export their surplus stock to thirsty Chicagoans. Timewise, it would seem highly unlikely that Busch and Brand could have introduced lager beer to Chicagoans and gained widespread acceptance for their product in a period of just months.

23. *One Hundred Years of Brewing*, *op. cit.* p. 329.

24. Andreas, *op. cit*, pp. 575–576.

25. *Milwaukee Sentinel*, September 12, 1854.

26. Bull, et. al., *op. cit.*, pp. 57–68; Andreas, *op. cit.*, p. 370.

Chapter 2

The Lager Beer Riot, 1855

"Oh, lager beer!
It makes good cheer,
And proves the poor man's wealth;
It cools the body through and through,
And regulates the health."
author unknown

Economic Difficulties

During the early years of Chicago's development, the city's growth was tenuous, at best. The Financial Panic of 1837 had ruined many investors who had bought land in the area at wildly inflated prices, only to find the speculative bottom fall out. A lack of hard currency, high inflation and the introduction of President Jackson's *Specie Circular* had caused such a tightening of the money market that banks throughout the United States suspended business. Illinois was virtually bankrupt.

William B. Ogden, benefactor of early Chicago brewers and the city's first mayor, used the money of a group of wealthy New York investors and his own calming influence and leadership to allay the fears of Chicago's early businessmen, many of whom were now saddled with crippling debt. Responding to his leadership, Chicago's business community began to recover, offering jobs to thousands of newly-arrived Irish and German immigrants. After much personal lobbying, Ogden persuaded Cyrus McCormick to move his farm implement plant to Chicago in 1847. He urged building of the Illinois & Michigan Canal, dug chiefly by Irish immigrants and opened in 1848, which allowed passage from the Mississippi to Lake Michigan. Congress, during this period, freed up much needed federal funds for port improvements, greatly increasing Lake Michigan commerce to the city. Construction of the Galena & Chicago Union Railroad and the Illinois Central Railroad, along with track laid towards Michigan and Indiana, made Chicago, by the 1850s, the most important railroad hub in the Midwest.

The Rise of Immigration

In response to the abundance of jobs available in the growing city and the economic stability that these positions offered, a steady stream of foreigners was drawn to Chicago. By 1850, more than half of the Chicago population of 28,269 was foreign-born, the Irish comprising about 21%, the Germans, 17%.[1] The lot of the German immigrants in the New World was, for the most part, less trying than that of the Irish. Some of these new German immigrants were university educated or accomplished tradesmen, many having fled the 1848 Revolution in Germany. A later study of the educational and trade backgrounds of Chicago's early German immigrants confirms that almost sixty-two percent of these immigrants were either professionals, white-collar workers or skilled craftsmen. These advantages are indicated by the quickness in which they were able to establish themselves in the local brewing trade and successfully conduct their business in the English-speaking New World so soon after their arrival. [2]

Some of Chicago's early brewers and future members of brewing peripheral trades were included in this wave of German immigration. Conrad Seipp had wisely left his homeland after serving as a Hessian guard during the 1848 Revolution. Arriving in Chicago soon thereafter, Seipp established himself as the owner of a successful downtown hotel. After selling his profitable hotel in 1851, he entered the brewing trade, and later became one of the most famous brewers in Chicago history. Robert Schmid, who studied architecture in Berlin, arrived in Chicago and began working with the famous architectural firm of Van Osdel and Olmsted before leaving for an independent position

A view of Clark Street near Madison about the time of the Lager Beer Riot in 1855 includes a lager beer saloon (second building from the left). From The History of Cook County, 232.

as a designer of breweries. As the malting trade developed in Chicago in response to the growing number of breweries and distilleries in the area, positions were quickly filled with German immigrants who had worked in the trade as maltsters back home. The Irish, on the other hand, were less fortunate. They were forced to flee a feudal land system, crop failures and near starvation with nothing more than the shirts on their backs.

During this early wave of immigration, the German brewers brought to Chicago the technical knowledge and appreciation for lager beer, the golden colored, highly carbonated, smooth tasting brew, heightened in taste by the use of bottom-fermenting yeast and a long, cool secondary fermentation. Up until the mid-1840s, when one spoke of beer in the United States, one meant the sometimes dark, highly-hopped, low carbonated malted liquor called ale which utilized a more primitive top-fermenting yeast. The knowledge and understanding of the secrets of lager brewing, along with the importation of the lager beer yeast to the United States in the early 1840s and the Germans' appreciation of its smooth, familiar taste, helps explain the preponderance of early Chicago breweries owned and operated by Germans for Germans.[3]

This new peculiar drink was initially shunned by much of the non-German population. Although ale was the only alternative malted beverage and a familiar drink of native-born Americans, whiskey was the drink of choice. The distillation of whiskey from corn was an economic way of using up a bulky and perishable surplus harvest. In this liquid form, corn whiskey was not only used as a pleasant diversion but also as a portable trade bartering tool, especially in the rural areas where money, scrip or bank notes were often unavailable.

The Rise of Nativism in Chicago

The enjoyment of lager beer drinking, along with a host of other alien customs, habits and taste, eventually brought the Chicago German population into increasingly hostile situations with native-born Yankee Americans. Some of this anti-German sentiment was brought upon the newly arrived immigrants by the Germans themselves and their uncomplimentary criticisms of American customs and institutions. Ironically, after failing to bring about social and political changes during the 1848 German Revolution, these often well educated expatriates clearly expected to bring about sweeping changes in the United States, a feat that they were unable to achieve in the *Vaterland*. One observer described their attitude in Eugen Seeger's *Chicago, The Wonder City*:

> On Sundays they were in the habit of marching through the streets of the city to the strain of blaring bands, preferring to parade past crowded churches on their way to the picnic grounds, where they amused themselves to their hearts' content while guzzling enormous quantities of beer. In short, with more 'courage and vigor' than diplomatic consideration, the German lifestyle was demonstrated in order to show the Yankees once and for all what it means to be a 'free German of backbone' and then they enthusiastically assured each other that it was 'just like in Germany'.[4]

The Irish were also not immune to the scorn of the American-born citizenry. Looked upon as minions of the Pope, who preached that religious laws were above civil laws, the Irish papists also began to feel the hostile wrath of the American-born, so-called "nativists." Beginning in 1853, the *Chicago Tribune* writers began a jingoistic attack on the Catholic (read: Irish) population of Chicago. Another popular publication, *The Literary Budget*, also allied itself with the views of the nativists. Soon, the xenophobic philosophy of nativism began to come together. In Chicago, the members of the Native American Party, sometimes known as the Know-Nothing Party, began forming a fragile coalition of abolitionists, nativists and *teetotalers*, eventually connecting drunkenness with the German and Irish immigrants.[5]

Levi Boone

In 1855, the local Know-Nothing Party chose former city physician Doctor Levi Boone as candidate for mayor of Chicago, along with a host of other politically like-minded candidates for key city offices. Much of Chicago's population, ironically including a goodly number of immigrant Germans, appeared to have found something they liked in Boone's candidacy, ignoring the party's knot-holed political planks that sometimes ran contrary to their own interests and beliefs.

The dichotomy of the stormy political situation during Boone's mayoral campaign can be seen in the inherent prejudices of many of Boone's supporters amongst the local population. The Germans, as a rule, were strict abolitionists. German Protestants from the northern states of the fatherland, however, were suspicious of southern Bavarian Catholics and the papist Irish, as were most nativists. The teetotalers were against the consumption of alcohol as practiced by the "whiskey sodden" Irish and "lager beer swilling" Germans. Leading this unbelievable coalition were the American-born nativists. The intertwining philosophies of nativism and prohibition would continue to surface in Chicago politics for the next sixty-five years.

It was an early example of Chicago coalition politics at its worst. With hate and prejudice as the common denominator, the Know-Nothings were swept into office on March 6, 1855, giving Levi Boone the mandate he needed.

A week later, in his inaugural address, Boone unveiled his program, including his opinion on saloon licensing and Sunday closings of saloons.

> . . . I would therefore recommend the Council to refuse to license the sale of intoxicating liquors after the first day of April . . . Should the Council differ with me upon the propriety of licensing, I would then advise another alternative, that is, to grant licenses to such persons as desire to take them at the maximum price fixed by the (city) charter, that is $300 per year . . . I wish to bespeak your active co-operation in closing all places where liquor is sold upon the Sabbath day . . .

Refuting accusations made in the local press that he had been a "Know Nothing candidate" he went on, nonetheless, with a theme central to the ideology of nativism.

> I cannot be blind to the existence in our midst of a powerful politico-religious organization, all its members owing, and its chief officers bound under an oath of allegiance to the temporal, as well as the spiritual supremacy of a foreign despot . . .[6]

On March 26, the Committee on Licenses of the City Council set the annual liquor fee at $300, setting off a flood of petitions to the Council from local saloonkeepers to reduce the licensing fee, but to no avail. Three weeks later, the Council adopted a resolution by the Grand Jury of the Recorder's Court to prevent the sale of liquor on Sunday, effectively closing down all saloons on the Sabbath.[7] Of the 675 saloons in the city, native-born Americans owned only 50. The remainder of the watering holes were owned by German and Irish immigrants. The immigrant owners of the city saloons realized that these rulings by Boone and his City Council were directed against their establishments and not those which were American-owned, indicating to them that the crackdown was not necessarily a sign of reform or temperance.

Few of the affected saloonkeepers were willing or able to pay the new high license fee. It should be noted, though, that many of the saloonkeepers had been derelict in securing a license even at the old $50 fee. A neutral observer would have had to admit that some sort of regulation of the saloons for the growing city was necessary. Gambling, prostitution and public drunkenness were on the rise in the wild young city, especially in the unlicensed dives. But the mostly foreign-born saloonkeepers felt that the liquor license increase was part of a concerted campaign by local nativists to exclude them from the benefits of the American free enterprise system.[8]

The truth was probably a blending of both sides' opinions. As a result of the strict licensing enforcement, some saloon proprietors soon went out of business. Others continued doing business, ignoring the new fee and the Sunday closing law. Approximately 80 native-born American police officers were sworn in to ensure that all current liquor licenses were in order and that the rarely-enforced, state-mandated Sunday closing blue law would be observed. In the weeks that followed the license increase, two hundred saloonkeepers were arrested for non-payment of the new license fee or for staying open on Sundays. The Germans were especially vocal about the arrests and hit hardest by the crackdown. They argued that the blue law was a violation of their "personal rights" and an infringement on a traditional Teutonic practice of enjoying beer on Sundays.

In the meantime, American bartenders at the more respectable establishments such as the Tremont House and the Young America, established watering holes of the Know-Nothing constituency, simply directed patrons to a side door for their familiar Sunday constitutional of American whiskey, ignoring the foreign-tasting lager beer and the restrictions of the Sunday blue law.

The Germans were incensed at this double standard of enforcement and began to organize against it. German brewers and their patrons gathered at North Market Hall, pledged $5 each and formed a society to combat the high liquor license fee. John

Huck, owner of the John A. Huck Brewery, took on the leadership of the pro-beer society.[9]

The motives of Huck and the other Chicago brewers were pecuniary as well as based on genuine indignation. Enforcing the Sunday blue law had meant closing Huck's beer garden on its busy family day. In addition to the loss of Sunday sales, the brewers were also fearful of losing valuable retail outlets, legal or not, in which to sell their beer.

The Lager Beer Riot

A test trial of thirty-three of the violators was scheduled for April 20, 1855, in the courtroom of Judge Henry Rucker. Shortly before the trial, both sides elected to choose one defendant for trial, the others agreeing to abide by whatever ruling the court chose. On April 20, Judge Rucker was delayed out of town and sent word to reschedule the trial for the following day. The next morning, fortified by one more day of brooding and the offerings of the numerous lager establishments located up and down Randolph Street, a large crowd of Germans armed themselves and marched upon the Cook County Courthouse. So many supporters in the crowd accompanied the defendants into the small courtroom that Judge Rucker had to ask them to leave. Those that complied angrily milled about outside the courthouse, blocking the thoroughfare. Some fifty police agents then descended upon the unruly crowd. Confused and disorganized, the crowd began to fall back.

While the brewery and saloon interests were marshaling their forces, Mayor Boone quickly swore in an additional force of one hundred and fifty policemen. About three o'clock that afternoon, the Germans, accompanied by Irish saloon owners and their patrons, now numbering an unruly mob of six hundred, made their way down Clark Street to the bridge spanning the Chicago River. Swarming across, they met a solid phalanx of police forces. With a shout of "Pick out the stars!" shots were fired. Someone in the crowd of rioters discharged a shotgun at Officer George Hunt, hitting him in the left arm. With the perpetrator was Peter Martens, a German cigar maker who fired his revolver at Hunt. Attempting to flee, Martens was shot in the back by a deputized citizen. Martens died three days later of his wounds in a cell in the county jail. Hunt's injury was so severe that his arm had to be amputated the next day.

A young Alan Pinkerton was in the midst of the fray, dragging the wounded and whatever prisoners he could into the courthouse. With the addition of an Irish military group known as the Montgomery Guards, the all-American Chicago Light Guards and a battery of two small cannon, the riot was finally suppressed. At least sixty of the rioters were arrested.

Although only one death was officially recorded, it was said that a number of mysterious funerals in the German community resulted from the riot. A review of the list of those in custody attested to the fact that most of the rioters were indeed German. A lesser number of Irish names could be found as well. Of the sixty arrested, fourteen were brought to trial. Boone would continue the struggle, later vetoing an order by the nervous city council to dismiss all suits against those violating the liquor license ordinance.

Eventually, two perpetrators named Halleman and Farrell were convicted of rioting. Accusing two hapless Irishmen from among the hundreds of German protesters indicated perhaps a fear by Boone and his administration of further German disturbances. The two men were granted new trials but they were never held and the men were eventually released.[10]

Boone's Recollections

In a *Chicago Times* interview some twenty-two years later, a reporter noted Boone's interpretation of the events of 1855. "Doctor Boone . . . took occasion to remark that his actions at the time were considerably misunderstood, as he had never taken occasion to correct false impressions. (He) stated . . . what he did he did conscientiously, as he believed it was for the good of the whole community, and not on fanatical grounds. He also told of his belief that the business in the hands of the better class of saloon keepers, who, when the temperance law should go into force, could be rationally dealt with."[11]

But the damage had been done. The intensity of the riot and the clumsy treatment of the brewers and the German and Irish saloonkeepers and their patrons, affected the fragile coalition that Boone had patched together. The party's alliance with the drys added to its woes. With the voters' rejection of a state prohibition law in June of 1855, and a mayoral term of only one short year, Boone's government became a lame duck administration and faded away after the next year's election.

The first assault on the personal rights of imbibers by teetotalers in Chicago had ended in favor of the wets and the German beer and Irish whiskey drinking communities. The nativists' disturbing attitude towards foreigners and the influence of the prohibitionist movement in Chicago would be only temporarily suppressed, while the larger questions of slavery and state secession loomed on the country's horizon.

Notes

1. Bessie Louise Pierce. *A History of Chicago*, Vol. 2. (London: Alfred A. Knopf, 1940) pp. 13, 17.

2. *German Workers in Industrial Chicago, 1850–1910: A Comparative Perspective*. Hartmut Keil and John B. Jentz, editors. (DeKalb, IL: Northern Illinois University Press, 1983), p. 23.

3. *One Hundred Years of Brewing*, pp. 207–253.

4. Eugen Seeger. *Chicago, The Wonder City*. (Chicago, IL: 1893) p. 109.

5. Richard Wilson Renner. "In a Perfect Ferment: Chicago, The Know-Nothings, and the Riot for Lager Beer." *Chicago History* 5 (1976) pp. 161–163.

6. *Inaugural Addresses of The Mayors of Chicago, 1840–1995, Inaugural Address of Mayor Levi Boone, March 13, 1855.* Shah Tiwana, Ellen O'Brien, and Lyle Benedict, editors. Municipal Reference Collection, Chicago Public Library, 1998, pp. 5–6.

7. *Chicago City Council Proceedings File, 1833–1871.* Illinois State Archives. File numbers 0073 A, 0093 A, March 26, 1855; 0149 A, April 2, 1855; 0150 A, April 4, 1855; 0220 A, April 16, 1855.

8. *Chicago Daily Democrat.* January 26, 1849, June 26, 1850, January 21, 1854.

9. Renner, *op. cit.* p. 165.

10. Virgil W. Peterson. *Barbarians in Our Midst.* (Atlantic, Little, Brown Books, 1952), p. 21; *Chicago City Council Proceedings File, 1833–1871.* File number 1133 A, September 10, 1855.

11. *The Chicago Times*, August 5, 1877. This account gives a biased, but thoughtful account of the riot. Most of the account of the riot is from this article. But also see M. L. Ahern. *The Political History of Chicago.* (Chicago, IL: Donohue & Henneberry, 1886), pp. 31–32; and *Chicago Tribune*, April 21–27, 1855.

Circus celebrity Tom Thumb perches on a Schoenhofen barrel. The sign is dated 1898.
Courtesy of Fil Graff.

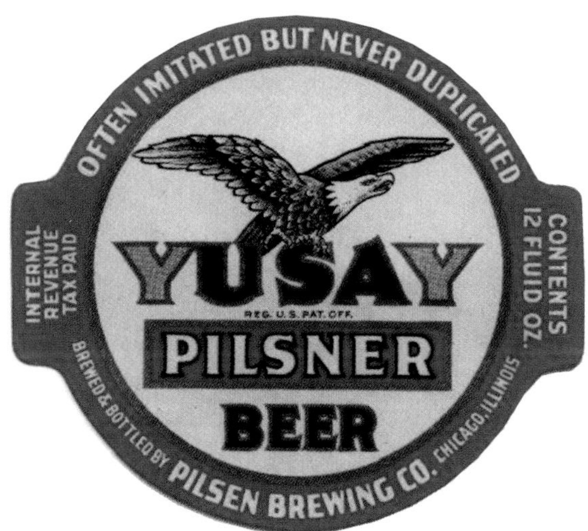

The patriotic eagle perches atop the "Yusay" name. The label is circa 1936-1950.
Courtesy of Bob Kay

Springtime brings Bock beer. Breweries used goats ("bock" means ram in German) to advertise this brew. Lithograph courtesy of Bob Brockmann.

Along with the brands listed on her skirt, the rose-bearing lady carries a bottle of Peter Hand Brewery's Malt Elixir.

Lithograph courtesy of Bob Kay.

The Independent Brewing Association used this flower-covered lady on lithographs and metal trays promoting their Prima beer.
Courtesy of Bob Kay.

Trays could show the owner's daughters as does this pair from the Conrad Seipp Brewery, or a mischievous kid who promotes the McAvoy Brewery's Malt-Marrow brand. The Seipp trays are courtesy of Bob Brockmann, and the McAvoy tray is courtesy of Fil Graff.

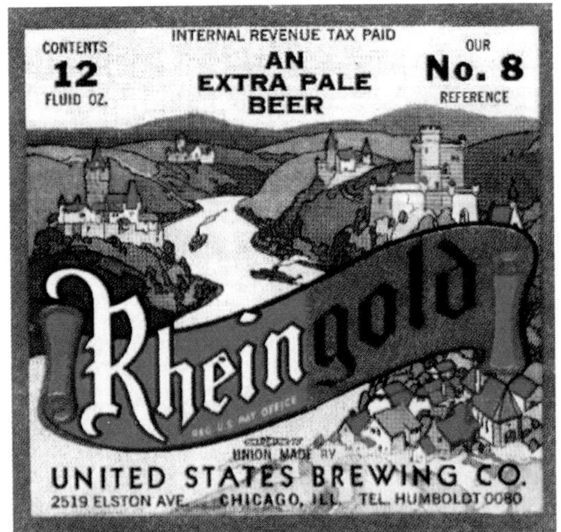

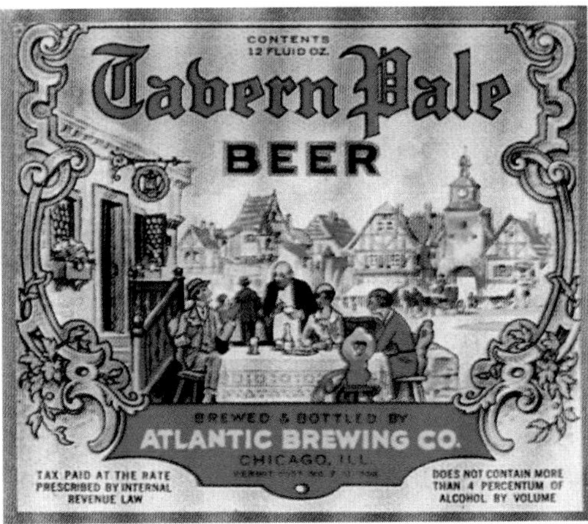

Whether the brand name suggested a race track, the Bavarian alps, an Old World square, or castles along the Rhine river, labels also had to carry the brewery's name, bottle contents, and, depending on the product year, a tax paid notice. Labels for Rheingold (1936–50), English Lad Ale (1936) and Tavern Pale beer (circa 1933) are courtesy of Bob Kay. The Alps Brau label (1974–1978) is from the author's collection.

With the exception of the Export Lager beer (1908–1914) all of these labels began to appear on bottles after Repeal took place in 1933.

Courtesy of Bob Kay.

Two elegant ladies appeared on signs for Chicago breweries. Prima's lass is a pre-Prohibition concept while Monarch's dates from the 1950s. Courtesy of Fil Graff and Phil Pospychala.

Chapter 3

Chicago's Developing Brewery Trade, 1860–1885

"It literally exploded."

Edward G. Uihlein, describing sales of Schlitz beer in Chicago after the Great Fire

Civil War Years

At first glance, the growth of Chicago's beer trade during the Civil War and the immediate post-bellum years appears to have been slow and unremarkable, a reflection perhaps, of the country's hesitant movements both during and after the nationwide upheaval. The imposition of an excise tax of one dollar per barrel of beer and a federal licensing fee of fifty to one hundred dollars per brewery, imposed in 1862 by the recently introduced Internal Revenue legislation, forced the Chicago brewers to adjust the wholesale price of their product to seven dollars per barrel.[1] With the beer tax proceeds used to help finance the struggling Northern government during the Civil War, the German-born brewers grudgingly complied, not wanting to rekindle any lingering nativist feelings by being perceived as negligent in their patriotic duty to their new country.

Of the twenty-three new breweries that opened in Chicago during this difficult period, a number of them went out of business after only a few years of existence such as the Chicago Ale & Malt Company (1861–1867), the N. P. Svenson Brewery (1866–1867) and the John Behringer Brewery (1862–1865).[2] One can only speculate as to why these breweries and others failed while so many more succeeded and even expanded, but a number of ideas come to mind. The lager drinking German population of Chicago avoided the products of most of the ale producers, limiting their market. Not surprisingly, Americans and other ethnic groups began to take a pronounced liking to lager beer, especially after a wartime excise tax was also imposed on the once cheaper priced distilled liquors. The significantly higher based whiskey tax drastically changed the drinking habits of the everyday man, turning him from the high priced whiskey to the lower priced lager beer. German lager was becoming the affordable drink of the working-class.[3] Brewers took note of this shift in the drink preferences of their customers, emphasized the debilitating effects of distilled products, and declared beer "the drink of moderation." This distinction between distilled and fermented products, promoted by the brewing industry until the beginning of National Prohibition, would eventually lead to a schism between the liquor and brewing industries.

Competition from the better established concerns, under capitalization, and poor management practices surely added to the financial demise of other firms. Brewery destruction by fire was also common in the early brewing trade, often wiping out not only the brewery but also the funds necessary to rebuild it.

Growth and Consolidation of Early Breweries

Continuing consolidations, mergers and outright buyouts of a number of breweries during the post-bellum period strengthened the position of a number of local breweries, readying them for the boom years of the 1880s. A few representative examples are noted here;

Seipp & Lehman. Conrad Seipp, a German immigrant, began his brewing career in Chicago in 1854, after buying the small brewery of Mathias Best. Seipp arrived in Chicago in 1849, where he first started a small, highly successful hotel at the corner of Washington and Wells. In 1851, he staked a claim on eighty acres of farmland near what is now 79th and Jeffery Avenue. Soon after he purchased the Best Brewery, a fire destroyed it. Undaunted, Seipp proceeded to build a new brewery on Twenty-seventh Street, near the Lake. A man of apparent frugality, he and his family lived on the second floor of the newly constructed brewery. In 1858, Seipp formed a partnership with Frederick Lehman. With the additional capital from his new partner, the brewery was greatly enlarged to meet the increasing demand for their popular products.

Lehman died in 1872 following a carriage accident. During their partnership, the brewery grew at an amazing rate, selling 48,437 barrels of beer in 1868, having outpaced production at Lill's Chicago Brewery by 17,505 barrels.[4]

Downer, Bemis & Company. Towards the end of 1860 or early in 1861, Corydon Downer and H. V. Bemis built a small ale brewery at Sixteenth Street and the Lake. Shortly thereafter, Downer retired from the business. In 1864, Bemis built another brewery on South Park Avenue. One year later, local politician John A. McAvoy bought a position in the brewery. In 1866, the company of Downer & Bemis was formed, retaining the name of Corydon Downer. From 1865 on, the output of the new brewery was devoted exclusively to the production of lager beer, reflecting an understanding by the owners of the increasing size of the lager beer market. Critics (mostly German brewers) were sure that the brewery would fail in the endeavor since the general opinion of most of the brewing industry was that only Germans could brew true lager beer. McAvoy, a native of

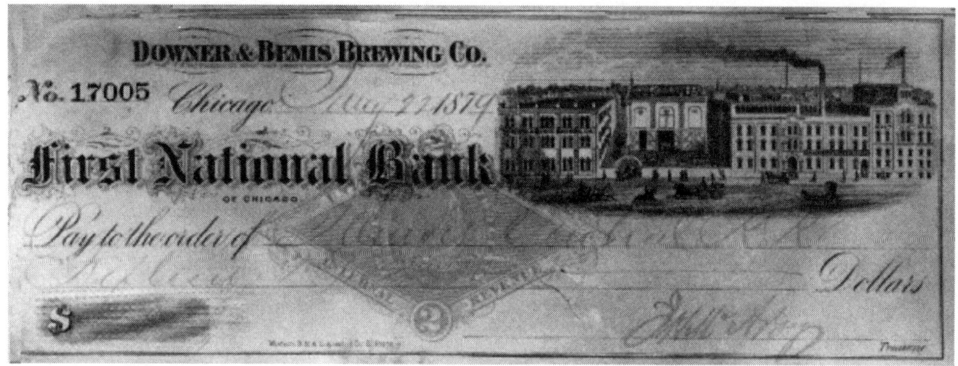

Cancelled check from the Downer & Bemis Brewing Company, 1879. Courtesy of Stan Galloway.

Newry, Ireland, and Bemis, born in Center Almond, New York, proved them wrong selling 3500 barrels of beer in 1865 and increasing production to 28,851 barrels by 1869. Apparently not wishing to tempt fate, Bemis and McAvoy did hire a German-born brewer at a later date.[5]

Jacob Rehm & Company. Jacob Rehm, a native of Alsace, began his long career in brewing in 1859 as an employee of Lill & Diversey. During his tenure at the brewery, he somehow found time to serve as Chicago Superintendent of Police in 1862 and Cook County Treasurer in 1863. Prior to his brewing career, he also served as a police officer in 1851; Street Commissioner in 1855; and City Marshal in 1857 and 1858. In 1865, Rehm left Lill & Diversey and started the Jacob Rehm & Company Brewery on West Twelfth Street. In 1866, Rehm took on Frank Bartholomae as partner but sold out his position two years later so the brewery was renamed Bartholomae & Company. Rehm soon became a partner of Frederick Wacker in the operation of a successful malting business on Elm Street.[6]

These consolidations, with a further strengthening of market position by such giants as Lill & Diversey and the John A. Huck Brewing Company, along with the success of recent start-ups such as Sand's Ale Brewing Company and Busch & Brand, increased beer production in 1869 in Chicago to a recorded output of 246,212 barrels. Numerous smaller beweries probably pushed this figure to well over 300,000 barrels. In less than forty years, Chicago's production of beer had increased over 900%, an apparent joy to Chicago's growing population of 298,977.[7]

But not everyone was happy with the success of the local brewers. Chicago's more independently-minded saloonkeepers began to complain and organize against the perceived high prices the brewers were charging them per barrel. Price increases by the brewers were customarily absorbed by the saloonkeepers who felt there would be resistance from their customers if the saloonkeepers passed on the wholesale increase on a barrel of beer to them. At the time, it was pointless for retailers to shop another local brewery for a better price per barrel since the members of the local brewing association had agreed to fix prices on a barrel of beer. There were also charges by saloonkeepers that barrels of beer delivered by local breweries were short of their full capacity.[8]

Tired of a drain on their profits, some saloon owners fought back and started the Chicago Union Brewing Company in 1868. With an investment of $250,000, the two story brick building was soon producing 100 barrels of beer a day for some of Chicago's more independently-minded saloonkeepers. But it was hard to see why the saloonkeepers wanted to enter in the brewery trade. At an average pull of over five hundred, seven ounce glasses of nickel beer per 31 gallon barrel, their profits were much more respectable than those of the brewers with their beer priced at around $6 a barrel.[9]

The Chicago Fire

The Great Chicago Fire of October, 1871, radically changed the face of the brewing industry in Chicago. This account of the fire by Edward G. Uihlein, an agent for the Jos. Schlitz and Company Brewery, is included in his memoirs:

> The Chicago fire occurred October 9, 1871. I was located with my little factory on West Chicago Avenue and did not have to suffer but the event was of such magnitude that I can not but say a few words about it.
>
> The fire started about 8:30 Sunday evening and apparently it took in a very short time such dimensions that I and my friend Grundlach concluded to go & see it thinking it was somewhere around Madison Street & Clinton. Walking along it proved to be near Canal & Polk Sts. We crossed the bridge when the Fire in less than ten minutes spread across the river taking its course in a north easterly direction. We hurried along Wabash only to find that Monroe, Adams, Washington were reached by the fire and if we undertook to proceed further north we would absolutely be cut off & would perish. So we turned South again and found our way via 12th Str. bridge and reached home, 436 Milwaukee Avenue, about two o'clock. Reports came, the Courthouse gone the Waterworks on Chicago Avenue on fire. Hundreds perished in the LaSalle Str. Tunnel so that part of the Southside and the whole Northside to Lincoln Park was doomed. Although all the neighboring towns & Cities including Milwaukee, Joliet, Peoria, Galesburg etc. sent fire apparatus of all kinds, nothing could check the elements in their fury. All they could do was to defend the Westside where the river gave a good opportunity to help. On the Southside south of Harrison whole blocks were blown up with Dynamite to check the fire going further south with fairly good success. On Tuesday a rain set in and the limits of Lincoln Park helped along considerable. Well it is not my intention to give a history of the fire but simply mention that I had witnessed all of it.[10]

Lost in the fire, with estimated damages, were the following breweries:

Lill & Diversey	$500,000
J.A. Huck	$400,000
Sand's Brewing Company	$335,000

Busch & Brand	$250,000
Buffalo Brewery a.k.a. Miller & Son	$150,000
Schmidt, Katz & Company	$ 60,000
Metz & Stege	$ 80,000
Doyle Bros. & Company	$ 45,000
Mloeler Bros. (Mueller Bros?)	$ 20,000
K. G. Schmidt	$ 90,000
George Hiller	$ 35,000
Schmidt & Bender	$ 25,000
Mitinet & Puoupfel	$ 12,000
John Behringer	$ 15,000
J. Miller	$ 8,000
William Bowman	$ 5,000
George Wagner	$ 5,000
Haas & Powell	n/a
Joseph Jerusalem	n/a
Total	$ 2,035,000+[11]

The Sand's Brewing Company burned during the Great Fire of 1871 and never reopened. Courtesy of the Harold Washington Library.

Brewer William Lill had just finished his first evening dinner in his new $40,000 home when he was forced to leave as the flames approached his property. Brewer John Huck not only lost his brewery, but also suffered the dubious distinction of also losing his house in the fire—the last structure in the city to succumb to the flames.[12] Production at the Downer & Bemis Brewery was temporarily interrupted when the water supply from Lake Michigan was cut off by the destruction of the city waterworks pumping station. Within three days, Bemis and his men laid a temporary line directly to the Lake. Besides meeting the needs of the brewery, Bemis furnished water to the surrounding community at no charge.[13] The fortunes of Michael Keeley, whose continued success at bottling had made him a wealthy man, were wiped out with the destruction of his bottling plant at Harrison and Canal.

Only brewers Busch and Brand, Jerusalem and K. G. Schmidt resumed production at a later date, with Brand's plant being up and running in less than three months. The fiery disaster narrowed the playing field, allowing the Seipp & Lehman Brewery to easily maintain its position as Chicago's most productive brewery. It also helped to increase the market share of the surviving smaller breweries, something that might have eluded them otherwise.

Neighboring Milwaukee breweries took advantage of the city's misfortune and increased their efforts to secure an even larger share of the Chicago market. The Jos. Schlitz and Co. Brewery seized the moment in Chicago but went one step further, utilizing Chicago's strategic freighting position to expand its business throughout the United States. Their business in Chicago after the fire "literally exploded," wrote Edward G. Uihlein. He noted in his memoirs that "orders came in so quickly that it was impossible to fill them all."[14] Schlitz became "The Beer That Made Milwaukee Famous", but Chicago was the city that made it so. Brewery owner Joseph Schlitz only had a short time to enjoy the rewards of his company's expansion into Chicago and beyond. In May, 1875, he boarded the "Schiller" in New York for a visit to Germany. Of the 800 passengers aboard, less than half were rescued when the cruise ship sank at sea. Joseph Schlitz and his wife were among those lost.

Technological Advances

Despite early manufacturing and technical limitations, the brewing industry in the early 1870s in Chicago was a viable one having annual sales of over $2,000,000. In the 30 years after the Great Chicago Fire, the increasing production pace continued as a technological and manufacturing revolution took place in the brewing industry, much of it originating in Chicago. Many of the limitations that had plagued the brewing industry were being overcome by the discoveries and inventions of the Industrial Revolution and the adaptation of a number of these findings specific to the brewing industry. The result would eventually become a tumultuous brew of men, machines and natural ingredients.

Harvesting the ice necessary for keeping lager beer cold was a complicated process. This engraving shows ice being harvested from Lake Calumet in the 1890s. From Chicago Blue Book of Selected Names (1893).

Mechanical Refrigeration

Ice, transported from the huge facilities of the Knickerbocker Ice Company at Wolf Lake, Indiana; from the many lakes of neighboring Wisconsin; or sometimes harvested from nearby Lake Michigan when conditions allowed; was an essential item for the production of lager beer. Ice, carefully hoarded in caverns or weather-proofed buildings and covered with sawdust to slow its eventual melting, had made brewing a seasonal practice, limiting production to the cooler months of the year. Used not only to cool the boiling wort to a temperature conducive to the *pitching* of yeast, the ice was also indispensable in keeping the beer at temperatures low enough during the essential *kraeusening* and *lagering* stages. Ice was a rare, but fleeting, commodity, a necessary expense.

As noted earlier, a lack of sufficient ice in Chicago during the summer of 1854 and the subsequent inability of local brewers to brew needed lager beer quickly, gave Milwaukee brewers a foothold in the Chicago market which they never relinquished. Prices and availability of ice were quoted in the daily newspapers and various trade publications, the brewing trade being only one of a number of industries dependent on its use

One early and simple way to cool heated and pasteurized beer was to send it from the wooden kegs through coiled tubes placed in a bucket full of ice. From the tubes the beer flows into bottles. The system is like that used by today's home-brewers. From The Western Brewer, *March 1878.*

as a refrigerant. Ice was a necessary evil, hauled to the brewery by wagon and pushed, dragged and shoved into position by brewery workers at considerable expense.

In 1877, H. V. Bemis, co-owner of the Downer & Bemis Brewery, working with inventor Daniel Boyle, erected an ammonia compression machine in the brewery for mechanical refrigeration. Determined to perfect the adaptation of an ice machine to the process of making beer, Bemis worked upon the monstrous-sized unit, correcting and adjusting it until it became an unparalleled success and an example of the first adaptation of this sort of refrigeration in any brewery. The perfected Boyle Ice Machine weighed over fifty tons and supplied refrigeration for the entire brewery, cooling the lagering cellars and fermenting rooms and making ice water for the *baudelots*, used to cool the boiling wort. One immediate advantage of the use of *baudelots* was the elimination of floating conical shaped *schwimmers* to cool the boiling wort. These metal containers, packed with blocks of ice from nearby lakes, would occasionally leak into the sterile wort and change the character and taste of the finished product. More often than not, the contaminated leakage would spoil the brew. The acceptance of Boyle's machine by the brewing industry was overwhelming. Boyle shipped twenty-two refrigeration units in a short five month period to brewers throughout the United States.[15]

In 1880, the Fred. W. Wolf Company of Chicago obtained the patent rights to the Linde Ice Machine, introduced in Europe by Professor C. P. G. Linde of Munich, Germany. The Wacker & Birk Brewing & Malting Company of Chicago was the first brewery to install this type of refrigeration unit in the United States.[16]

These machines now allowed year-round brewing with the brewers no longer dependent on the natural production and harvesting of ice or its fluctuating price levels. Although the initial outlay for the installation of a mechanical refrigeration machine was significant, its savings occurred in many different forms. Dozens of ice cutters and handlers were no longer needed. Exact temperatures could now be maintained in the fermenting and lagering rooms. A typical fermentation room during this period of American brewing needed 20 feet of solid ice above the tanks to cool the room. The need for carefully constructed wood trusses to support the massive load of ice was always a problem. This danger could now be eliminated and would result in a better utilization of space in the brewery. The control of ambient temperature also eliminated the need for underground caverns. With the resultant lagering of beer now above ground, the beer no longer had to be pumped to the surface for kegging.[17]

Advances in Beer Stability

The development of an analytical laboratory for the isolation of viable yeast and the detection of wild yeast and putrefying bacteria became a recognized necessity for the production of clean tasting, longer lasting beer whether ale or lager. After publication of *Étude sur la Bière*, a revealing study of yeast in beer by Doctor Louis Pasteur in 1877, more Chicago brewers began to farm out samples of beer and yeast for testing and analysis to Doctor John E. Siebel's analytical laboratory, founded in 1872. In 1886, the Wahl-Henius Scientific Station was also founded for the clinical testing and analysis of beer. Initial resistance to "beer doctors" waned as even veteran Old World brewers became convinced of the merits of production and product analysis and the use of clean yeast for consistent quality of beer. Brewing as an art was giving way to the more reliable methodology of science.[18]

Research and analysis of beer was conducted in the Wahl-Henius *American Brewing Academy which was also home to the* American Brewers' Review. *From* American Brewers' Review, circa 1903.

Early Bottling Efforts

The practice of bottling pasteurized beer began to gain wider acceptance during the 1880s. Bottling would eventually offer hotels, restaurants and saloons the opportunity to present a representative choice of brands and styles of beer bought by the case, rather than relying on the more perishable and space consuming barrels with their accompanying dispensing equipment. The profit potential of the home market was becoming evident, waiting to be exploited by brewers, bottlers and distributors alike. Some brewers readily embraced this practice, establishing bottling departments near their breweries, but the outlay for bottling equipment was enormous. Counter-pressure bottling machines, capable of delivering beer charged with carbonic acid gas for foaming purposes and to prevent contact of beer with outside air, were supplemented with conveyors capable of carrying the bottles to capping or corking machines, sterilizing stations and finally, labelers. A recurring expense was the bottles themselves. Early efforts to induce customers to return the empty clear glass bottles to the breweries were suggested by raised letter admonitions on the containers that read "THIS BOTTLE NOT TO BE SOLD" or "PROPERTY OF (brewery name) CHICAGO." It would be years before the concept of deposits on the costly bottles and the wooden cases that contained them would be successfully utilized by the industry.

There were earlier attempts at bottling beer but they often met with limited success. Bottling in its earliest stages of practice consisted of filling washed bottles with a rubber hose attached to a keg. A cork was driven into the bottle by hand or a pressing machine. Wire held the cork in place and the bottle sometimes received a glued label. Carbonation was achieved by the practice of kraeusening, the introduction of young, actively fermenting beer to a batch of almost completely fermented beer. This unreliable practice often led to bottles blowing their corks or the bottles exploding during transit because of contamination and an uncontrollable secondary fermentation. Storage and handling abuse by the distributor or even by the customer further aggravated the situation.

Since the Civil War, beer had been taxed by the barrel. With the advent of large scale bottling practices, the Internal Revenue stepped in to ensure a proper taxation of the bottled product. These new government procedures for accurately assessing the proper tax on all beer that left the brewery created a further financial drain on those breweries that chose to bottle beer on their own, since bureaucratic standards and regulations demanded retooling and reconfiguration of their plants. Permission was initially given to the brewers by the I.R.S. to remove beer from the regular shipping barrels to bottling departments, but the departments had to be separate and distinct from the brewery, separated from the main plant by a public highway.

Under pressure from the brewing industry, led by Milwaukee's Captain Frederick Pabst, this impractical and restrictive practice was eventually modified by Congress to allow beer to be pumped from the brewery by pipelines to the bottling department under strict rules of construction and operation. Even this revised practice was an added expense, necessitating the excavation of a government tunnel from the brewery to the bottling plant. The beer was then pumped off into measuring tanks in the bottlery and the tax paid to an on-site revenue agent with tax stamps normally affixed to outgoing barrels.[19]

This tax revenue practice and the large outlay for all the machines and devices needed for bottling led to the existence of separate bottling businesses, independent of the breweries themselves. In this way, small local breweries could contract out their bottling needs and enter the growing bottled beer market with little or no additional cash outlay. This brewing niche became an important part of the brewing trade in the late 1880s and 1890s, temporarily allowing small and mid-sized breweries to continue operation without increasing capital expenditures on new bottling equipment, but the operating expense could prove detrimental to profits. For those small breweries willing to utilize the independent bottlers, the result was a wider selection of beer types and brands for retailers and consumers. But the practice of using independent bottling plants would eventually end. Competition and the need to tighten production expenses forced the brewers to make the critical choice between reverting to draft beer production, buying a bottling line or quitting the business of brewing.

Malting Improvements

By the 1870s, Chicago was the undisputed greatest grain market in the world. With numerous breweries in Chicago and distilleries in nearby Peoria, there was an acute need for malthouses in the immediate area. *Malting* is the controlled germination of barley during which enzymes are formed and the food reserves are sufficiently modified in the grain kernel so that they can be further hydrolyzed during the *mashing* process. From the mashing of malted barley come the sugars that feed the yeast, leaving carbon

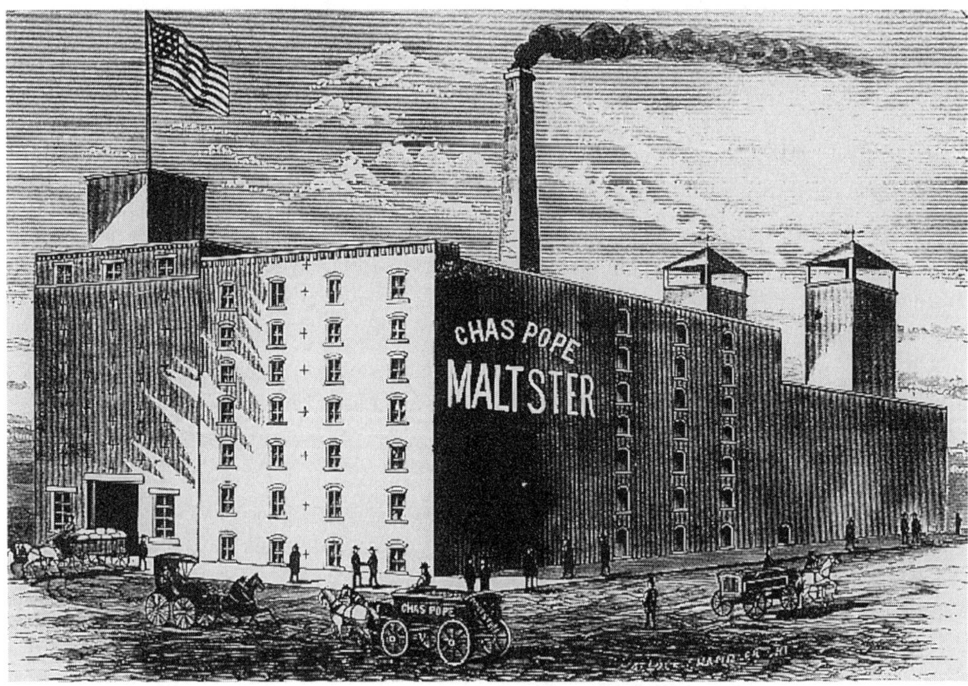

Charles Pope's firm was one of many that supplied malted barley to Chicago breweries. From The Western Brewer, *November, 1882.*

dioxide and alcohol behind. Initially soaked in steeping tanks until the proper moisture content is reached, the barley is then allowed to germinate under controlled conditions. Finally, the partially germinated barley is *kilned*, dried in a controlled current of hot air, stopping germination. The length of kilning determines the color and flavor intensity of the malt, analogous in practice to the roasting of coffee beans.

By the mid-1880s, there were twenty private malthouses in Chicago in addition to those vertically integrated with local breweries.[20] Malting techniques were now becoming more efficient. In 1882, Louis C. Huck, son of pioneer brewer John Huck, patented a system for air drying malt and ventilating malthouses. Using a huge fan, which ventilated the kiln and growing floors, and adding refrigeration to attemperate the air, he further modified his invention, adding the Saladin pneumatic malting system to his malthouse. This system controlled the temperature and moisture necessary for germination. The grain was stirred and turned by machine, ensuring a more efficient operation and a resultant quality product. The Saladin method is still widely used in the malting business today.[21]

Brewery Architecture

Chicago's predominance as a center for brewery architecture is well documented in the brewing trade journals from the 1870s on. Its central location gave Chicago designers a geographic advantage over East Coast architects in taking on projects in the Midwest and even in California. For architects there was plenty of work designing buildings for new lager breweries, for firms destroyed in the Great Fire of 1871, and for businesses that wanted to expand.

From the designs of German émigré architects Frederick Wolf, Frederick Baumann, Louis Lehle, August Maritzen, Wilhelm Griesser and others came ornate but equally functional breweries built in Chicago and throughout the United States. Wolf is probably recognized as the most notable Chicago figure in local brewery architecture. His designs were utilized by Schlitz in neighboring Milwaukee and by other breweries as far away as Canada.

What catches the eye of even the untrained observer is the use by these architects and industrial engineers of the German Romanesque Revival *Rundbogenstil* (rounded arch style) that can still be seen in the remains of the Schoenhofen Brewery office building on South Canal and the east wall of the Carl Corper Brewery on South Union. Round arched windows, crenellated rooflines, and corner towers were elements of the massive fortresses used for these late nineteenth century breweries. Their necessary size made a clear statement of the pride their owners took in their economic success while the decorative elements stressed a link with their European heritage. In contrast, the recently reconditioned Schoenhofen warehouse and powerhouse, now used as the operating plant of a water bottling operation, was designed in Prairie style by Hugh M. G. Garden,

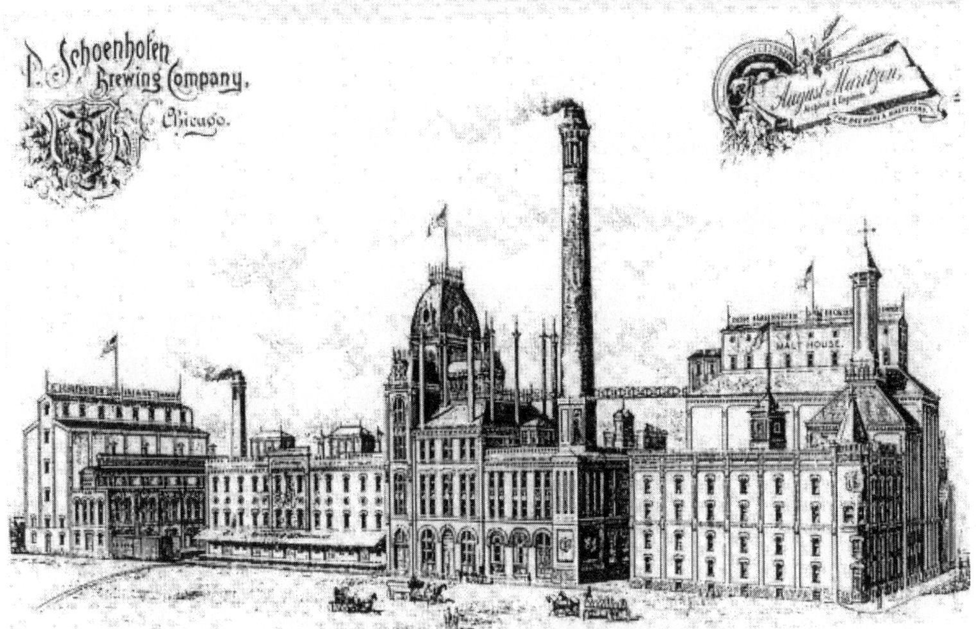

The size and grandeur of a turn-of-the-century brewery can be seen in August Maritzen's drawing for the Schoenhofen Brewery. From One Hundred Years of Brewing (1903), 325.

working for local architect Richard Schmidt in 1902.[22] This building stands as testimony to the evolving styles of a new generation of brewery architects.

Italianate and Greco-Roman designs were also used in Chicago brewery construction from 1870 to around 1900 as the recently destroyed Birk Brothers Brewery and the still standing Mutual Brewing Company showed. Later brewery structures lack the ornate style and maintain a functional industrial look, a reflection of the changing economic conditions of the local brewing industry after 1900. Functional now ruled over design.[23] A tour of Chicago breweries is included in the Epilogue of this book.

What these ornate brick buildings from the late 1870s to the turn of the century all had in common was the central concept of natural gravity flow in the brewing operation. By placing the raw brewing materials in the top floors of the brew house, usually distinguished from the rest of the plant by vertical towers, the boiling wort would flow down from the copper kettle to the hop-jack which strained the hot wort of the flavoring hops, and finally, to the cooling chambers of the baudelots, preparing the cooled wort for the introduction of the yeast. With each successive step in the brewing process, from lagering, cooling, filtering to carbonation, the product would continue to flow from floor to floor for a final stop at the kegging or racking department. By the mid-1880s, the enormous brewing kettles would often be stabilized with the interlacing support and structural features of the towers themselves. This dependent support technique probably explains why almost all of the brew house towers of the remaining brewery plants found throughout the city today have been removed. The kettles had been incorporated into the steel framing of the towers. Once the kettles had been removed for sale or melted down as scrap, the walls could soon have collapsed.

Professional Brewers' Organizations

Other subtle changes and events occurred that would have an effect on the local industry in years to come. In 1872, Doctor John E. Siebel, former Chief Chemist of Chicago began a laboratory in Chicago for analysis and prevention of beer spoiling pathogens. Siebel then focused his efforts on a brewing school in the city with his partner Michael Brand. Later Brand left, and Siebel developed the Zymotechnic Institute and later, the Siebel Institute of Technology, as a training ground for future brewers and industry leaders. The author is an alumnus of the Siebel Institute.[24]

The Chicago brewers realized the importance of organizing a professional association devoted to the technical aspects of brewing and the interests of the local brewing industry. In June of 1867 the Brewers Association of Chicago invited the United States Brewers Association to hold their national convention in Chicago, thus acknowledging the city's growing importance as a respected brewing center.[25]

Brewer Publications

Various brewery trade publications began operation in Chicago during the 1870s and 1880s, keeping the industry apprised of new technological findings and matters peculiar to the brewing and malting trades. The most successful and longest running publication was *The Western Brewer*, which began in 1876 and was published by J. M. Wing & Company. This German/English publication settled on an all-English format in 1882 after a questionnaire revealed that the majority of readers preferred the English language version. Originating in Chicago, *The Western Brewer* was a potpourri of scientific findings specific to brewing but regularly laced with an inner look at the social aspects of the brewing community, listing the births, deaths, weddings and frequent trips to Europe of the brewers and their families. Moving to New York after being purchased by the H.S. Rich & Company in 1887, the publication took a more national focus on the brewing industry, with recurring diatribes on the temperance and prohibition movements. It was published under this title until 1920. One of *The Western Brewer's* most often quoted issues was the supplement which appeared in 1903, known as *One Hundred Years of Brewing*. From June 20, 1920, until December of 1932, the publication was known as *The Beverage Journal*, reflecting the constraints of Prohibition. From January, 1933, to May, 1934 it was once again called *The Western Brewer*. From May of 1934 until its demise in 1960, it was called *The Brewer's Journal*.

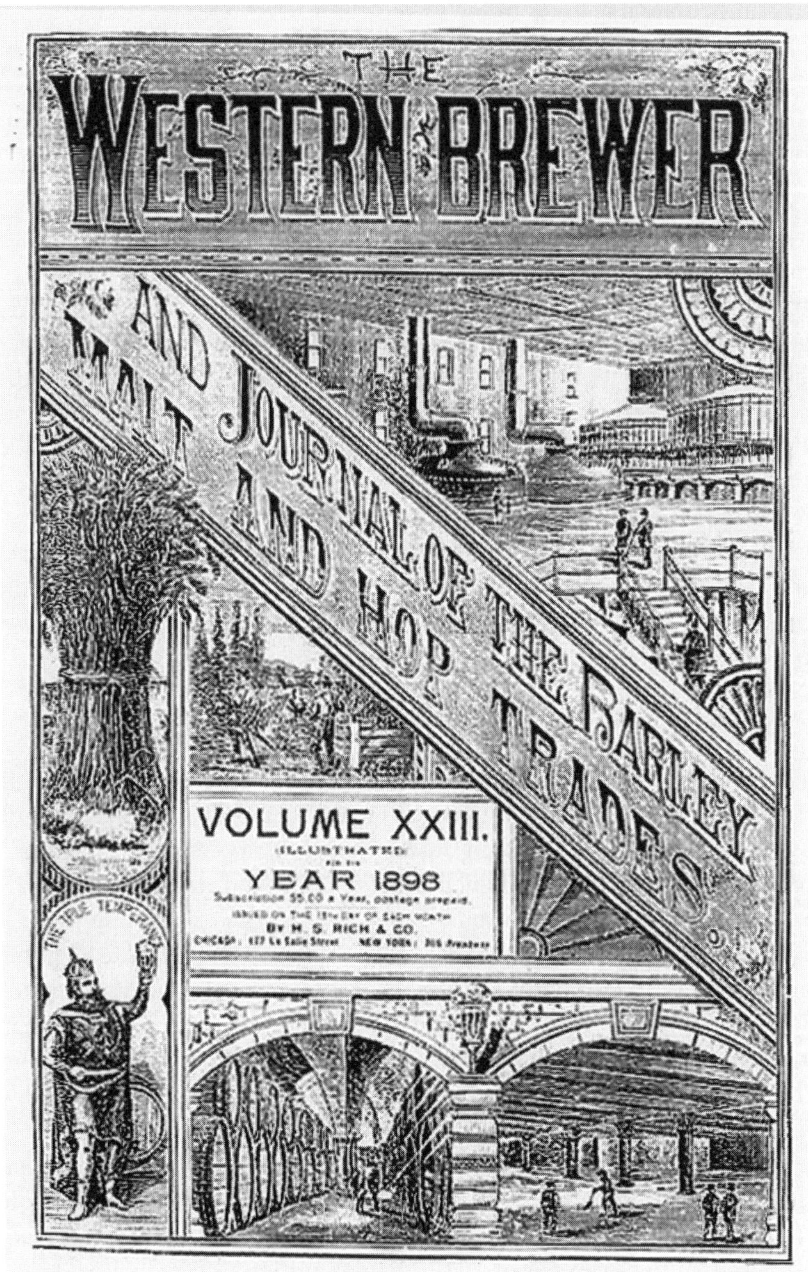

The pages of The Western Brewer were filled with news of the industry and the brewing community. Its volumes are still an important resource for breweriana collectors and historians. Shown is the inside cover from Vol. XXIII (1898) of The Western Brewer.

Other publications of note were the *Brauer und Malzer*, begun in 1881 by Eugene A. Sittig, eventually merging with *The Brewer and Maltster and Beverageur* which ceased publication in 1937. *Der Braumeister*, started in 1887, was the official organ of The Master Brewers Association. In 1891, the monthly publication was taken over by Doctors Max Henius and Robert Wahl and renamed the *American Brewers Review*. Like the early issues of *The Western Brewer*, it was published in Chicago and was particularly focused on the political scene in Chicago during the pre-Prohibition years. It ceased publication in 1939.[26]

The Origin of the Prohibition Party

Since the onset of the Civil War, the temperance movement in Chicago had lain dormant while the slavery question and most importantly, the very existence of the Union were tested. With the end of hostilities and a return to normalcy, reform and the more radical prohibition movement began to resurface.

For years the brewers had considered prohibitionists as no more than a nuisance. At the Seventh Annual Convention of the United States Brewers' Association, held in Chicago, the brewers changed their benign attitude and began to take a more serious stance with prohibitionists. A resolution was passed by national brewing leaders stating that "we will use all means to stay the progress of this fanatical party."[27]

Perhaps in response to this challenge from the brewers, the Prohibition Party was organized in Chicago, on September 1, 1869. Five hundred delegates from nineteen states were present for the party's initial sessions at Farwell Hall. The organization of a national prohibitionist party, capable of running a candidate in the upcoming presidential election, gave evidence that it was becoming a force that could organize in a fashion that had eluded earlier dry advocates.

But during the 1880s and 1890s, in spite of the devastation of the Great Fire, and the occasional annoyance of local prohibition and temperance efforts, Chicago's breweries would reach unprecedented levels of production, responding to population growth and an array of technological and manufacturing improvements. The Golden Age of brewing was about to begin in Chicago, but with it would come the elements of its decline.

Notes

1. Stanley W. Baron. *Brewed in America. A History of Beer and Ale in the United States.* (New York, NY: Arno Press, 1962) pp. 213–214.

2. Donald Bull, Manfred Friedrich, and Robert Gottschalk. *American Breweries.* (Trumbull, CT: Bullworks, 1984) pp. 59–67.

3. Bessie Louise Pierce. *A History of Chicago, Vol. II.* (London: Alfred A. Knopf, 1940), p. 89.

4. *John H. Weiss Papers [manuscript]*. A Biography of Conrad Seipp, 1900–1904, one volume, Chicago Historical Society; *One Hundred Years of Brewing.* (Chicago, IL: H.S.Rich, 1903) p. 422.

5. *Ibid*, pp. 321–322.

6. *Ibid.*, p. 416.

7. *Ibid.*, p. 422; A. T. Andreas. *History of Cook County Illinois.* (Chicago, IL: A.T.Andreas, 1884), figure for 1870, p. 370.

8. *Chicago City Council Proceedings Files*, 1833–1871, file number 1451 A, April 27, 1867.

9. *Chicago Tribune*, November 6, 1867; March 1,14, and 17, 1868; and January 26, 1869.

10. *A Memoir of Edward G. Uihlein*, translated by Rosina L. Lippi and Jill D. Carlisle, 1917, one box, Chicago Historical Society.

11. James W. Sheahan and George P. Upton. *The Great Conflagration, Chicago.* (Chicago, IL: Union Publishing, 1872) p. 141.

12. Herman Kogan and Robert Cromie. *The Great Fire, Chicago 1871.* (New York, NY: G.P. Putnam's Sons, 1971) p. 109; Leonard. *op. cit.*, p. 8.

13. *One Hundred Years of Brewing. op. cit.*, p.322.

14. Uihlein. *op. cit.*, p. 9,

15. *One Hundred Years of Brewing. op. cit.*, p.322.

16. John P. Arnold and Max Henius. *History of The Brewing Industry And Brewing Science In America.* (Chicago, IL: privately printed, 1933) p. 95.

17. Thomas Childs Cochran. *The Pabst Brewing Company.* (Westport, CT: Greenwood Press, 1975) pp. 107–110.

18. *Tenth Anniversary Reunion of Chicago.* (Westport, CT: Blakely Printing Co., 1901) p. 19; *The Brewers Digest*, April, 1947.

19. Cochran. *op. cit.*, pp. 126–127.

20. *One Hundred Years Of Brewing. op. cit.*, pp. 588–593.

21. John P. Arnold and Max Henius, *op. cit.*, pp. 106–107.

22. H. Allen Brooks. *The Prairie School.* (New York, NY: W. W. Norton Co., Inc. 1976) attributes his work to Garden who worked for Schmidt and later became his partner. See pp. 53–55.

23. For a more detailed discussion of Chicago brewery architecture, see Susan K. Appel. "Chicago and the Rise of Brewery Architecture," *Chicago History* 24 (Spring 1995) pp. 4–19.

24. Bessie Louise Pierce. *op. cit.*, Vol. III, p. 154; *The Brewers Digest*, April, 1947.

25. Pierce, *op. cit.*, Vol. II, p.89.

26. Pierce, *op. cit.*, Vol. III, p. 153.

27. *Record of the Seventh Brewers' Congress*, U.S. Brewers' Association, Incorporated, 1867, p. 10.

Chapter 4

Brewer Influence Grows, 1870–1900

> ". . . Chicago will soon stand ahead of her present position in brewing among the cities of this country."
>
> *Chicago Tribune*, 1880

New Breweries, Consolidations

An article published in the *Chicago Tribune* on January 1, 1880, gives a revealing look at the brewing industry in Chicago in the late 1870s. The local breweries during this time were capitalized at a combined value of over $12,000,000. Close to 340,000 barrels of beer were brewed in 1879 at a wholesale price of $8 per barrel. With the peripheral malting trade valued at $1,500,000, brewing was a huge, important business in Chicago. The city ranked sixth in national beer production, employing over one thousand workers in the numerous breweries scattered throughout the city.

Sales leader was the Conrad Seipp Brewing Company, located on Twenty-seventh Street near Lake Michigan, which brewed 108,347 barrels in 1879. Seipp was noted in the article as being "the only Chicago brewer who ships beer to any extent outside the city." Most renowned was his Salvator bottled beer which was heartily welcomed as far away as California. A testimonial from a Seipp customer in Colorado claimed that Seipp's beer "had done more to reform the mining districts of the West than all the moral agencies that have ever been sent there," replacing the more debilitating whiskies that had been the drink of choice amongst the miners. With a cash infusion from the buy-in of his partner Frederick Lehman in 1858 and having taken quick advantage of the devastation following the Chicago Fire in 1871, which weeded out nineteen local competitors, Seipp had the necessary capital to take on the high initial outlay for a bottling and export operation.

Ranked second was the Downer & Bemis Brewing Company at Twenty-fourth Street and South Park with a total production of 66,878 barrels in the same year.

Providing malted barley for the brewers were a number of malt houses including the George Bullen & Company, H.L. Huck, Charles L. Epps & Company, Charles Pope, the Northwestern, Binz & Pollock and Charles Sheer. These Chicago-based maltsters had taken advantage of their centrally located position and the city's vast network of railroads. With these nearby facilities, they were able to provide a savings in transportation costs over the distant East Coast malt houses.[1]

Start-up breweries included the Keeley Brewing Company, established in 1878; the Wacker & Birk Brewing and Malting Company, founded in 1882; the Junk Brewery, (1883); and the Cooke Brewing Company, started in 1885. The Non-Alcoholic Beer Company opened in 1893 on North Clybourne, apparently having tried to establish a niche market for reformers, temperance and prohibition advocates; the brewery closed the same year, indicating that, at least in Chicago, those who talked the talk didn't necessarily walk the walk.[2]

The enterprising Michael Keeley, whose bottling business had been destroyed in the Great Chicago Fire, was again in business soon after the disaster. In 1876, he left the liquor firm of Keeley & Kerwin and purchased the old F. Binz Brewery on Twenty-eighth Street which had a reputation for inferior products. First year's output was six thousand barrels of good quality beer and ale, increasing to ninety thousand by 1888. Keeley also distinguished himself by holding the position of President of the Milwaukee & Chicago Brewers Association in 1887, a rare honor in Chicago's brewing fraternity for a non-German.[3]

In 1882, Frederick Wacker, with his son Charles, and Jacob Birk, formed the Wacker & Birk Brewing and Malting Company. Birk, a successful harness maker and former owner of the old Wheeling House on Lake Street, had no experience in the brewing industry but his considerable business skills helped make his firm a success. Birk would go on in later years to form the Birk Brothers Brewing Company with his sons William and Edward.[4]

In a male-dominated industry, the name of Magdalena Junk stands out in the history of Chicago brewing. Married to Joseph Junk, a German immigrant from Salmrohr, she ably took control of her husband's brewery after his death in 1887. Faced with indebtedness from her husband's earlier financial difficulties, she soon cleared the business of all debt and expanded the plant on Thirty-seventh and Halsted in Bridgeport. Modernization of the brewery made it possible to increase production from 14,000 barrels in 1887 to 43,000 in 1900. Assisting Magdalena in the operation of the Junk Brewery were her sons Edward and Joseph, both popular figures in the local brewing fraternity.[5]

One of the few Irishmen to successfully enter the brewing trade in Chicago, John S. Cooke purchased the Chicago Union Brewing Company in 1885, founded earlier by P. O'Neil and an independent group of saloonkeepers. Starting with sales of only two barrels a day, Cooke quickly expanded brewery operations. Through hard work and per-

Frederick Wacker and Charles Birk established their brewing and malting company in 1882. From The Western Brewer, *circa 1889.*

severance, his family increased sales to 103,000 barrels in 1900. His sons George and Charles assisted him in the daily operations. Both sons took over brewery operations after Cooke's death in 1899.[6]

Milwaukee versus Chicago

Of the many local breweries in operation during this period, few made any real effort to export their products outside the Chicago area, the Conrad Seipp and the smaller K.G. Schmidt breweries being notable exceptions. Both breweries took advantage of the huge developing Western market, the Seipp brewery with its previously mentioned Salvator and the Schmidt brewery being particularly successful with its Budweiser brand.[7] The Chicago brewers' overall provincial view of exporting is, however, reflected in a comparison of beer production figures for 1879. For the first time ever, Milwaukee, with a population numbering a little over 115,000, surpassed Chicago's beer production, having brewed 411,245 barrels that year and shipped much of this beer to outside markets. Chicago brewers initially showed no alarm at this creeping trend. They were content to manufacture only 336,204 barrels for a population of about 503,000 and to dispose of most of it in the city. Milwaukee's

A. C. Kummer's saloon was an exclusive vendor of K. G. Schmidt beer as the sign on this "tied-house" indicates, 1916. Courtesy of the Ravenswood-Lake View Historical Society.

vigorous export efforts continued through the next few years. By 1884, Milwaukee beer production would almost double to 803,371 barrels with much of it destined to fill the steins and mugs of thirsty Chicagoans. During this same period, Chicago would meekly demonstrate a rise in beer production of less than 35,000 barrels from its 1879 barrelage.[8]

Before the advent of mechanical refrigeration, the abundance of ice and brewing water from nearby Lake Michigan, combined with an experienced labor force, almost exclusively German, and a geographical shipping advantage over Eastern brewers, gave Milwaukee and Chicago the enviable opportunity to expand their markets. Milwaukee brewers, however, with a much smaller local customer base and numerous local breweries competing for limited dollars, realized quite early the need to develop a viable export trade. They began shipping their products with a greater vigor than their Chicago brethren. The initial reason that Milwaukee brewers moved into the huge Chicago market in the mid-1850s was probably more defensive in nature than exploitive. The exportation of surplus beer to neighboring Chicago had meant survival and a relief valve for any Milwaukee brewery that had overestimated its home market demand. But as the country expanded to the Pacific, the Milwaukee brewers, now experienced in solving the problems and cost factors associated with shipping beer outside their market, realized the potential of national sales.

The expansion to the desolate West, where breweries were few, was soon accompanied by Milwaukee beer. The Milwaukee brewers were also rolling over much of the local competition in the Southern states where a lack of sufficient ice during the hot summer months limited production. This disadvantage was eagerly exploited by Northern railroad cars packed with fresh beer and cheap ice.

Having suffered through a lack of beer during the oppressive summer of 1854 and been saved by the eager to please Milwaukee brewers, the majority of Chicago breweries continued to concede the export market and its huge profit potential to Milwaukee. With extreme shortsightedness, the Chicago breweries used the excuse of high shipping rates to justify their lack of expansion into other markets ". . . and have left the outside trade to the Milwaukee brewers, who have made a specialty of that branch of the business," noted the *Chicago Tribune* in 1880.[9]

The Phil Best Company of Milwaukee led the invasion of Chicago selling 60,000 barrels of beer in Chicago in 1879, which was more than the combined output of mid-sized Chicago breweries Schmidt & Glade, M. Gottfried and the Fortune Brothers Brewing Company. By 1883, Best Brewing, with two branches and forty-five teams and drivers in Chicago, had a sales staff in Chicago almost as large as in hometown Milwaukee. The Jos. Schlitz Brewing Company also continued to expand their exports, shipping 35,000 barrels of beer to Chicago in 1879.[10]

While Chicago's brewers retired for the night, surrounded by fine possessions in their opulent mansions, perhaps dreaming of expanding beer sales to a bloc of new saloons on the other side of town or a nearby village, Milwaukee's brewers were supervising the night-time loading of specially fitted rubber-lined railroad cars packed with beer and ice that would quietly leave Milwaukee for transport to Chicago. Arriving in town early the next morning, the beer was rushed off to strategically located depots and ice houses throughout the city. No longer content with the restrictions of sales in Chicago, the Wisconsin brewing firms now used Chicago as a jumping off point for deliveries throughout the Midwest, the South and the rapidly growing West.

Although the beers of the above mentioned firms were brewed in Milwaukee, they still depended on brewery supplies such as barrels, wagons and copper boiling kettles which were made in Chicago. Even most of the malt used by the Wisconsin firms was purchased from the many malt houses in and about Chicago.

Increased competition from their northern neighbors, however, eventually became a matter of concern for Chicago brewers. Feeling the effects of market saturation and a slowing of beer sales in the city, they petitioned the City Council for relief from the invasion of out-of-town breweries in the form of a proposed substantially high priced license fee for non-Chicago breweries. The Council ignored their pleas for trade restric-

By 1883 Milwaukee brewer Phil Best had opened two depots with forty-five teams and wagon drivers to deliver his beer in Chicago. Courtesy of the Harold Washington Library.

tions and the invasion continued. Inexplicably, no viable, concerted effort was made by the Chicago breweries to invade the competing Milwaukee market. [11]

The Good Life

In spite of occasional events that challenged the maturing Chicago brewing industry, times were good for its brewer bosses during the 1870s and 1880s. Ornate residences, membership in exclusive clubs and diversification into other economic undertakings, especially the malt trade, demonstrated their new wealth and all the advantages acquired through their brewing efforts. The leading brewers and their second-generation families had begun to secure a social status equal to the respected Fields, Armours, Palmers and McCormicks. A look at *The Chicago Blue Book of Selected Names of Chicago and Suburban Towns* from the early 1890s and beyond reads like a "Who's Who" of Chicago brewers, listing the Hucks, Wackers, Seipps, Brands and other leading brewers and their families. The marriage of Albertine Huck, granddaughter of pioneer brewer John A. Huck, to Marshall Field, Jr. in 1892, was an event of social significance in Chicago demonstrating the respect and new financial standing the local brewing fraternity had finally achieved in the business and social communities. [12]

The brewing families, had acquired their considerable fortunes through hard work, determination and luck, sometimes just by being in the right place at the right time.

Their struggles were really no different than the struggles of other self-made millionaires in Chicago, and like the others, they were determined to enjoy, and on occasion, flaunt the trappings of their new wealth.

The Cardinal

Severing his connections with the brewing industry, H. V. Bemis sold his entire interest in the recently constructed Downer & Bemis Brewing Company to his partner and local politician, John H. McAvoy, in April of 1884 for the kingly sum of $750,000 cash. In a display of unlimited wealth and extravagance, Bemis used the proceeds of the brewery sale and opened the Hotel Richelieu in 1885 on Michigan Boulevard. A huge structure, much of it done in imported white marble, it rivaled the finest hotels of Europe. Over $500,000 was spent on appointments such as sculptures and elegant place settings. An art gallery was featured in the hotel exhibiting numerous works collected by Bemis during his frequent trips to Europe. The "Cardinal," as Bemis was referred to by friends and associates, imported a four-star chef with staff from Paris, making the kitchen, accompanied with the offerings from his wine cellar, famous.[13]

Although Bemis and his shrine to opulence entertained such local luminaries as George Pullman, Marshall Field, Mayor Carter H. Harrison and the visiting Buffalo Bill Cody, the Hotel Richelieu eventually proved too rich for the tastes and pocketbooks of most Chicagoans. It folded in 1893. The subsequent auction of its contents brought bidders from London, Paris, Vienna, Berlin and St. Petersburg.[14]

Brewer Philanthropists

Brewer families also became known as patrons of the arts and were active in numerous local charitable causes. In 1890, the Conrad Seipp family donated over $135,000 to sixteen charitable organizations. Francis J. Dewes paid for the Alexander von Humboldt monument dedicated in 1892. The Schoenhofen family also contributed to fourteen charitable organizations in 1893, totaling over $60,000. The Wackers and Seipps generously contributed towards the erection of the Schiller monument in Lincoln Park.[15]

Political Influence

Chicago brewers used their wealth and influence to secure a number of public offices during this Golden Era as the following table illustrates:

Rudolph Brand	City Treasurer 1881–1883
Michael Brand	Alderman 1872–1873
John A. Huck	Alderman 1859–1860
Louis C. Huck	County Treasurer 1875
Ernst Hummel	Legislator 1885–1887

John H. McAvoy	Alderman 1869–1870
Hermann Plautz	City Treasurer 1887–1889
Jacob Rehm	Chief of Police 1873–1875
W. C. Seipp	City Treasurer 1879–1881[16]

Sunday Closings, Part II

Having adapted themselves to American democracy and the Chicago political process, the brewers were now more organized and better prepared to protect their interests, especially from the growing reformist and temperance forces of the city.

In 1872, shortly after the Great Fire, a wave of reform swept through the city, organized by the *Committee of Seventy*, composed of leading and influential citizens and clergymen. Over 100,000 Chicagoans were out of work, many without shelter as a result of the recent conflagration. Crime and public drunkenness were on the rise.

Part of the reformers' demands was for a more vigilant regulation of saloons, and the perennial demand for enforcement of the Sunday blue law. Saloonkeepers and brewers, having heard the arguments before, protested that they were merely satisfying what the people wanted and that the problems of unemployment and housing, not the regulation of the city's drinking habits, should be the responsibility of elected officials.

Mayor Joseph Medill had attempted to mollify the demands of the committee in a personal meeting, agreeing with their objectives but noting the Herculean task in changing the habits of the drinking public, especially the Germans. The events of the Lager Beer Riot in 1855 had forcefully demonstrated that the German community in Chicago truly believed that drinking on Sunday was not a crime against morality as temperance forces had insisted. The issue, however, of the German community's Sunday enjoyment of beer went much deeper than the philosophical and religious issues of morals; it was seen by the Germans as an issue of the right to exercise the centuries old drinking traditions of their Germanic culture, mixed with the feeling that government officials were infringing upon their "personal liberties." But further pressure from Mancel Talcott, President of the Police Board and an avowed advocate of the Sunday law, forced Medill to order the enforcement of section 4, chapter 5 of the city ordinances to close Chicago saloons on Sunday.[17]

The Germans and Irish, recalling the events leading up to the Lager Beer Riot in 1855, felt the reform movement was simply another wave of nativism, organized by the old Know-Nothing forces in Chicago. Under pressure from the German and Irish bloc, Talcott eventually resigned as President of the Police Board but was replaced by Mayor Medill's appointee, Elmer Washburn. On April 28, Washburn reiterated the order that the Sunday closing law be enforced. Police Board Commissioner Mark Sheridan entered a protest to the records of the board meeting when the order was issued. "The right of the people to be secure in their persons, homes, papers and effects against unreasonable searches and seizures, shall not be violated," Sheridan proclaimed, expanding the argument far beyond Sunday closings. At one point during the meeting, Washburn and Sheridan almost came to blows, Sheridan once again claiming that the Sunday blue law violated personal rights as advocated by the Constitution. Sheridan had reason to empathize with the views of the local brewers and saloonkeepers; his father had been a brewer in his native Ireland.[18]

Mayor Medill, more or less washing his hands of the whole affair, notified the City Council that he would be gone from Chicago for an indefinite time, claiming poor health. He took an extended trip to Europe, hoping that the politically sensitive affair would somehow be rectified before his return. Lester L. Bond, sworn in on August 18, 1873, as acting mayor, continued Medill's policies in his absence. But the Germans and Irish were not ready to roll over.

The People's Party

Having experienced the disastrous consequences of Levi Boone's election in 1855 and the riotous results of their own earlier political naïveté, a coalition of brewers, distillers and saloonkeepers organized the People's Party, funded in part by Chicago brewers Peter Hand, Jacob Rehm, John McAvoy, F. J. Dewes, Michael Keeley and Michael Cassius McDonald, a well-known local gambler. The *Chicago Tribune* scoffed at this coalition of gambling and drink interests and began describing the organizers and their meetings as "Advocates of Free Whisky and Free Lager" and "The Beer Guzzlers' Meeting."

The Constitutionality of closing saloons on Sunday was once again argued by many Germans as one of personal rights for the individual. "The question is not whether I wish to drink a glass of lager-beer or wine, in company with friends or family, on Sunday, but whether any other man or set of men shall have the power to say I shall not," a sympathizer indignantly wrote the *Tribune*. Some Germans saw the closings as another nativist move directed towards their traditional Continental customs. Could native-born Americans dictate "You Germans shall not do so and so, and you Germans shall do so and so?" asked a speaker at one of the many political rallies on the North Side.

The new political party reached quick agreement on their political positions and searched for a mayoral candidate. One of the more prominent planks in the new party's platform declared that the Sunday blue law was "obnoxious" to a large portion of the people and should be rescinded. In an attempt to balance any future criticism from reformers, the platform conceded positions on the regulation of liquor licenses and the appointment of beverage inspectors but firmly reiterated the party's position on Sunday closings, declaring that law and order should be preserved, but "not at the expense of personal liberty."[19]

The Election of 1873

In the following city-wide election of 1873, Harvey Doolittle Colvin, the People's Party candidate for Mayor and his entire ticket, endorsed by the Liberal and Democratic Central and Executive Committee of Cook County, were swept into office. Colvin was no saint, known as a bit of a high roller and winkingly referred to by Chicago's sporting men as "Harvey." As expected, soon after the swearing in of Colvin and his ticket, the Sunday blue law in Chicago was repealed. During his inaugural address of December 1, 1873, Colvin reemphasized his feelings on the Sunday closing of saloons in Chicago. "If the Common Council, in its wisdom, and having undoubtedly full power upon the subject, should determine either to repeal or modify the Sunday prohibitions and Sunday . . . clauses in the license law, or to fully secure the religious exercises of a portion of our citizens from all disturbance, without interfering with the harmless enjoyments of other citizens, it will do no more than its duty toward the majority of the people of this city . . ."

Several other attempts were later made to resurrect the Sunday closing law, but were voted down by the City Council.[20]

In 1874, in a spirit of compromise, the City Council did pass a new, seemingly innocuous law requiring saloons to lock their front doors and draw the shades of their establishments on Sundays, leaving both the side and rear doors open to the public. The act placed a resultant premium on corner locations.[21]

The political strength and influence of the brewing community of Chicago had come a long way since the Lager Beer Riot of 1855. Their developing wealth now gave local brewers the prestige and political power that they had lacked during the Lager Beer Riot days. Recent events had ably demonstrated that they were not afraid to use it. Their victory, however, soon set up further abuses by some saloonkeepers who interpreted the election's results as free license to ignore municipal regulations on closing times, gambling and prostitution.

Unconcerned about the compounding problems of the city saloons, Chicago's brewers would soon begin a program of buying or controlling a majority of Chicago's saloons in order to increase beer sales. In doing so, they would become highly visible targets for the growing prohibition movement.

Notes

1. *Chicago Tribune*, January 1, 1880.

2. Donald Bull, Manfred Friedrich, Robert Gottschalk. *American Breweries*. (Trumbull, CT: Bullworks, 1984) pp. 57–68.

3. *One Hundred Years of Brewing*, pp. 488–495.

4. *Ibid.*, p. 488.

5. *Ibid.*, p. 492.

6. *Ibid.*, p. 495.

7. "Budweiser" was derived from the name of the town of Budejovice, in Bohemia. Early brewers argued that the name could be freely used to describe a particular style of beer, as the pilsner beer style is associated with the city of Pilsen.

8. *Chicago Tribune*, January 1, 1880; *The Western Brewer*, June, 1884; *The Western Brewer* uses a figure of 375,549 barrels of beer produced in Chicago in 1879.

9. *Chicago Tribune*, January 1, 1880.

10. Thomas C. Cochran. *The Pabst Brewing Company.* (Westport, CT: Greenwoood Press, 1975), p. 172.

11. Perry R. Duis. *The Saloon. Public Drinking in Chicago and Boston, 1880–1920.* (Urbana, IL: University of Illinois Press, 1983) p. 19.

12. Bessie Louise Pierce. *A History of Chicago.* (London: Alfred A. Knopf, 1940) Vol. II, p. 153; *The Chicago Blue Book of Selected Names of Chicago and Suburban Towns*, (Chicago, IL: The Chicago Directory Company, 1893–1915).

13. A. T. Andreas. *History of Chicago.* (New York, NY: Arno Press, 1975) pp. 355–356.

14. Carter H. Harrison. *Carter H. Harrison.* (Chicago, IL: Ralph Fletcher Seymour, Publisher, 1944), pp. 113–114.

15. Rudolph Hofmeister. *The Germans in Chicago.* (Champaign, IL: Stipes Publishing, 1976) p.119, 137.

16. Hofmeister, *op. cit.* p. 106; John Moses and Joseph Kirland. *History of Chicago.* (Chicago, IL: Munsell & Co., Publishers, 1895), pp. 133, 226, 253.

17. John J. Flinn. *History of the Chicago Police.* (Chicago, IL: Under the Auspices of the Police Book Fund, 1887) p. 138; *Chicago Tribune*, April 25–26, 1873, and May 28, 29, 1873.

18. Flinn. *op. cit.* pp. 142–143.

19. Flinn. *op. cit.* p. 145; Chicago Tribune, May 28–29, 1873; Ahern, pp. 34–37

20. Flinn, *op. cit.* pp.137–146; Herbert Asbury. *Gem of the Prairie.* (DeKalb, IL: Northern Illinois University Press, 1986), pp. 144–145; *Inaugural Addresses of the Mayors of Chicago, 1840–1995*, *Inaugural Address of Mayor Harvey Doolittle Colvin, December 1, 1873*, p. 5.

21. Perry R. Duis. *op cit.* pp. 175–178, 234.

Chapter 5

Unionization, 1886–1900

"We will not allow any interference
with our legitimate rights as owners
of breweries . . ."

Chicago brewery owners to union organizers

Working Conditions in Chicago Breweries

For many students of early American breweries, the idea of the brewing industry as a romantic one prevails. Indeed, the scenario of a struggling immigrant reaching the shores of a young United States, beating back adversity and eventually establishing a successful brewery has a certain Horatio Alger ring to it. For the workers who struggled to help the early brewer bosses achieve their dreams, however, the reality was disturbingly different.

The everyday conditions of brewery workmen in America were arduous. Long hours and poor pay were the norm. Beatings of employees by owners or their foremen were common. Brewery employees were susceptible to respiratory ailments, including tuberculosis. Rheumatic disease was reported as being higher among brewery workers than in the general population. Besides industrial diseases, there was always the threat of accidents causing disability and even death.[1]

Wages and Benefits

Compensation for brewery workers varied during the 1840s from an average of $4 to $12 per month, with the lower wage usually for those who boarded free or at a reduced rate either at the brewery or at a nearby saloon. In many instances, the saloon was under the control of the brewery. The average salary increased little by the 1860s. A ruling by the Internal Revenue Office in 1868, favorable to brewers nationwide, allowed the brewer bosses to include beer as part of the workers' wages. In cities where free beer was permitted, wages were paid at the lowest rate. This free beer privilege, or *Sternewirth*, would eventually become a common perk in American breweries, an inducement that not only kept the employees going during the grueling fourteen-hour workdays, but also served as a means of pacification. A numbed worker, wallowing in an alcoholic haze, was less likely to revolt against the harsh conditions surrounding him.

A movement by national brewer organizations to institute a system of issuing daily beer tokens to brewery workers, each token representing one-half liter of beer which could be turned in at the end of the day for cash if not used, was unsuccessful. This token system, known as the Frankfurt system, had been successfully implemented in Germany to combat the destructive problems of drunkenness on the job and chronic health problems related to alcoholism. There is no evidence that this approach was used by any brewery in Chicago or anywhere in the United States during this period.[2]

In the early 1880s, the average national wage of brewery workers started to fall, the result of a nationwide recession that had begun in the early to mid-1870s. Because of the local rebuilding efforts after the Great Fire of 1871, the effects of the recession in Chicago were less noticeable and somewhat later in coming, buffeting Chicago from the economic downturn until the end of the decade.

Labor Troubles

In July of 1877, a series of labor strikes took place in a number of Midwestern cities, including Chicago, as a result of a nationwide railroad strike and the hardships brought on by the recession. In Chicago, the unrest culminated in a bloody confrontation between police and a roving band of demonstrators on the near South Side. As the demonstrators massed at Archer and Halsted, a group of them left, marched east down Archer Avenue, stopped in front of various businesses and demanded that the workers leave their stations to join them in further protest. As they approached the M. Gottfried Brewery and hollered for the brewery employees to join them, the strikers were incensed to find that the employees would not only **not** join them, but had barricaded the entrance to the brewery. While a heated attack on the front side of the brewery took place, a loyal brewery employee slipped through the back entrance of the plant and summoned help at a nearby police station. After clashing with the police, thirteen of the one hundred or so demonstrators were subdued and finally arrested. The brewery was damaged slightly by the attack.[3]

The non-combative attitude of Chicago's brewery workers was similarly demonstrated throughout the city as walkouts and strikes of other trades prevailed. There were no recorded instances of any brewery workers leaving their posts in any of the breweries throughout Chicago during these days of civil unrest.

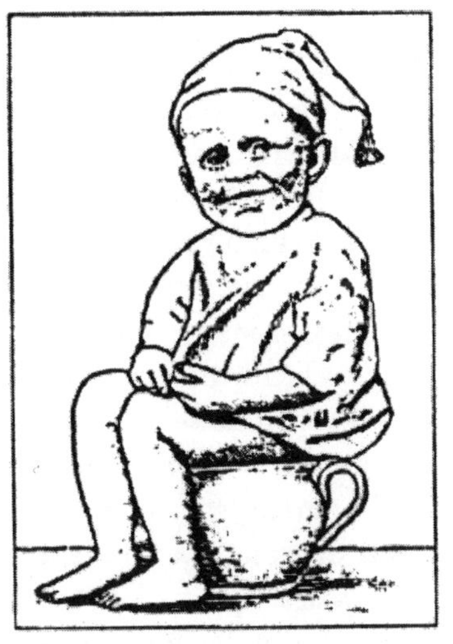

A pro-brewery workers' union cartoon from the 1880s. From the American Breweriana Journal, *November-December, 1996, 30.*

Brewery Workers Strike

In 1886, Chicago was rocked by another series of strikes that affected a number of trades in the city, this time including the local brewing industry. After watching the disastrous results of an earlier general strike by brewery workers in Milwaukee, and the calling out of the militia by the Wisconsin governor, the Chicago brewers made a quick settlement with the newly-formed Beer Brewers' and Maltsters' Union No. 1 in an effort to avoid any similar troubles in Chicago.[4] The agreement was considered liberal for the times, but was still an indication of the hard working conditions in Chicago's breweries during the latter part of the 19th century. Highlights of the agreement were:

10 hours regular work day
4 hours work on Sunday
Washhouse wages at $60 per month
Cellars, fermentation and malthouse wages at $65 per month
Foreman of malt house wages were $10–$15 more
First man in washhouse was $5 more

An interesting part of the labor agreement was the continuation of the *Sternewirth*. Beer was made available in quart-sized schooner glasses five times a day at 6, 9 and 11 a.m. and 2 and 4 p.m., with each break limited to "only" 3 glasses.[5]

Despite the apparent accord, Chicago brewery workers threatened another strike in the early months of 1888. Buoyed by a membership of 529 and with support from national union representatives, the brewery unions continued their demands for better wages and working conditions. In addition to these demands for improvements in working conditions, the national Central Labor Union also demanded recognition by the local brewers' associations and the right to dictate terms under which men could be employed and discharged in breweries throughout the United States.[6]

The Chicago brewer bosses, tired of dealing with union leaders whom they considered "... arrogant, intolerant and un-American ..." stood firm with a resolution signed on March 23 by thirty-four defiant local brewers. The harsh tone of the signed resolution infuriated the union leaders. The brewery owners had noted that the union was "organized by Oscar W. Neebe, one of the condemned anarchists (from the Haymarket Square incident), now serving time in Joliet . . ." Still smarting over the one day suspension of local brewing operations on the day the Haymarket Square "Anarchists" had been executed, the brewery owners felt the socialist leanings of the unions placed a stigma on an industry that had tried so hard to achieve respectability in Chicago. In a final warning, the coalition of brewers stated, "We will not allow any interference with our legitimate rights as owners of breweries or as citizens of the United States . . ."[7]

Caught in the socialistic fervor of the times, the workers walked out on the 1886 agreement on April 12, 1888, followed two days later by the maltsters. The brewery owners, in turn, declared a lockout. The ill-conceived and poorly organized strike was an obvious failure by the second day of the walkout. Many Braumeisters, occupying a quasi-managerial role and treated in many instances by brewery owners and workers alike as something akin to gods, refused to leave their positions. Although hoping that the workers would come back, the master brewers were willing to do little or nothing in support of the workers while leaving their own options open.

The Strike Collapses

Prepared for the possibility of a walkout, the owners had made earlier contingency arrangements with pensioned brewers and workers in Milwaukee to fill positions left by the strikers. Cots and meals were provided at the Tosetti, Seipp, Keeley, Fortune and Schoenhofen breweries for these scab workers as production continued in most of the breweries. Although a few breweries had been forced to shut down on the first day of the walkout, beer production was back on-line in all of the local breweries by the second day of the strike. The Chicago *Tribune* lambasted the ". . . Socialistic working brewers . . ." questioning why the ". . . beer-swilling anarchistic disciples have struck . . ." The newspaper's editorials went on to predict a short strike since their ". . . wide parched throats will begin to long for lager and these big stomachs (will) yearn for their favorite fluid."[8]

Reports during the next few days confirmed that every brewery in the city was still running at full capacity, ably managed by the scab workers. A feeble attempt at bravado occurred when the desperate strikers announced that they were now going to boycott beer made by breweries associated with the local brewers' association since the association had assisted in the hiring of scabs to operate the breweries where needed. Since many of the saloons in the city were either controlled or owned by the breweries, the threat was virtually meaningless.

In the ensuing weeks, those strikers who had walked out meekly returned to their jobs. The workers' union was exposed as nothing more than a paper tiger that haplessly stood by when the brewer bosses reneged on a number of previously agreed-upon concessions. On June 8, 1888, the strike was officially declared over.

A special conference of national union delegates was held in Chicago from July 15 through the 18th to discuss not only the state of the Chicago brewery workers' union but also that of twenty other similar unions throughout the country. With their cause weakened by brewery owners' resistance, intimidation and lockouts, the delegates reverted to petty bickering and accusations of incompetence at the national level.[9]

One important lesson was learned at the Chicago conference. That was the need to organize all the labor organizations involved in the brewing trade. As demonstrated in Chicago and in other labor strongholds, unskilled hands, combined with scab workers and the cooperation of auxiliary beer manufacturing companies could perform the daily functions of a brewery. Only through the coordinated efforts of the maltsters', coopers', drivers', brewers' and other brewery-affiliated unions, could the workers achieve their goals.

The struggle for better pay and working conditions would continue for years to come as the brewery owners returned to the former oppressive conditions that had been so common prior to the initial agreements. Devastated by the lockout in 1888 and the subsequent collapse of the brewery workers' strike, the Chicago brewery workers union wasn't reorganized until September 13, 1891. It was not until the early 1900s that the Chicago brewery owners, wounded by the beer price wars of the 1890s and increased local and outside competition, realized the economic necessity of making peace with all the brewery-related unions.[10]

An Eyewitness Account

Alfred Kolb, a young freelance writer who posed as a Chicago brewery worker and later returned to Germany to write about his experiences, described the dangerous conditions and numbness of mind and body that engulfed the average Chicago brewery employee. Kolb's eyewitness account was written sometime between the collapse of the 1888 agreement and the turn of the century. The Seipp brewery was probably the "T. brewery" Kolb described.

Conrad Seipp. From One Hundred Years of Brewing, (1903).

"The T. brewery is located on the South Side, . . . next to the entrance in a low wing was the bottling department . . . The beer is forced out of the vats by compressed air into the filling machines which do the bottling by themselves. Filled like this and then corked, the bottles are sterilized in a steam bath, and the better brands are then decorated with labels, wires, and tinfoil caps. The washing, brushing, rinsing, bottling, corking, wiring, and labeling was done by machines which were operated by young male or female workers . . ."

But while the bottling operation appeared an easy task, other jobs were more physically intensive, including the stacking and arranging of cumbersome kegs and wooden beer cases. ". . . I still remember handling wet barrels and heavy beer cases. Amongst the cases were many old ones riddled with glass splinters, splints, and nails. Within eight days my hands were covered with bloody cuts and cracks. My back had become stiff, my walk and posture clumsy and heavy . . . Once, right before quitting time, a heavy case full of empty bottles that I was supposed to bring into the basement slipped out of my tired arms . . . a small office penpusher with a four-inch stand-up collar passed by, turned up his nose and said: 'That guy's probably loaded! . . ."

As was the custom in breweries throughout the United States, most of the workers were German immigrants. ". . . My co-workers, about seventy of them, were without exception unskilled, younger people, mainly of German origin. And German was the language spoken among us . . . "

The *Sternewirth*, the daily ration of free beer, was, rather amazingly, a perk that this worker felt was not abused. ". . . beer was handed out at 9 and at 3 o'clock. Of course, everyone drank at other times also, whenever we got thirsty. As long as you didn't put your hands on stout or other good brands, the foreman looked in the other direction . . . this privilege was not at all abused . . . I hardly ever saw anyone tipsy, except maybe during overtime, when the men restored their dwindling strength with alcohol. . . ."

Overtime was a regular routine that every worker had to endure. ". . . Overtime night work was almost routine; usually until 9, sometimes to 10 in the evening. In that case a half-hour break was taken at 6 o'clock, which would have been all right if the lunch break had not been shortened accordingly. The total length of work was from 14 to 15 hours. We also worked on Sunday mornings from 6 to 12 o'clock . . ."

But the long hours and forced overtime, mixed with a lack of safety equipment, could take its toll on any worker who let down his guard. Death or disability was an everyday occurrence. But what was more frightening was the callousness that Kolb saw among his co-workers after any disaster. ". . . One day the machine operator was caught in the driving belt of a big steam engine and torn to pieces—no wonder, by the way, given the lack of any safety equipment . . . 'Too bad for him,' someone said, 'he was a good guy! Now he's had it!' Then someone else said: 'Eat and drink, guys, because soon we'll all have had it, and that's that.' The others remained quiet; they seemed to agree. . . ."

After the poorly executed brewery strike of 1888, wages continued to hold steady in the Chicago breweries. "We received the standard wages for Chicago's unskilled manual labor—for boys 50 cents, for women 75, for young men 1 dollar, for adults 1¼ dollars per day. Overtime was paid separately, but not at a higher rate . . . Brewers and maltsters earned 17 dollars a week and up. After a failed walkout, their union and the brewery administration agreed upon this sum as the minimum wage."

As a freelance writer, Alfred Kolb's experiences were tempered with the knowledge that he could return to his room, change his dirty work clothes and leave, an option that hundreds of brewery workers throughout Chicago could not envision. [11]

Notes

1. Herman Schlueter. *The Brewery Industry and the Brewery Workers' Movement in America*. (Cincinnati, Ohio: International Union of United Brewery Workers, 1910) pp. 256, 258.

2. *Ibid.*, pp. 94, 262–263.

3. *The Western Brewer*, August, 1877; John J. Flinn. *History of the Chicago Police*. (Chicago, IL: Under the Auspices of the Police Book Fund, 1887), p. 196.

4. Schlueter, *op. cit.* p. 129.

5. *The Western Brewer*, May, 1886; *Chicago Tribune*, April 13, 1888.

6. *Chicago Tribune*, April 13, 1888.

7. *The Western Brewer*, April, 1888; *Chicago Tribune*, April 13, 1888.

8. *Chicago Tribune*, April 14–25, 1888.

9. Schlueter, *op. cit.* pp. 167–170.

10. *Ibid.*, p. 167.

11. Alfred Kolb. *Als Arbeiter in Amerika. Unter deutsch-amerikanischen GrossStadt-Proletariern.* (Berlin, 5th Edition, 1909), pp. 74–79.

Chapter 6

The Syndicates, 1889–1900

"... they do not feel like taking part in the war at Chicago if it can be avoided."

Newspaper reporting on Milwaukee brewers reaction to a price war in Chicago during the 1890s

The British are Coming

During the late 1880s, with a widespread industrial depression limiting investment opportunities in Great Britain, English investors began to eye the profitable American beer industry. An unprecedented growth in beer sales in the United States during this period, buoyed by record levels of German immigration and enthusiastic acceptance by Americans of lager beer, appeared to make American breweries attractive targets for investors, ripe for English acquisition.

In 1889, the McAvoy Brewing Company and the Wacker & Birk Brewing and Malting Company were the first Chicago breweries to be acquired by an English-owned syndicate, the Chicago Breweries, Limited. Authorized capital was £600,000, of which £400,000 had been issued in shares of £10 each. The combined barrelage of this merger was 315,000 per year with total sales in 1890 of 206,000 barrels. Chicago's brewers saw this consolidation as an answer to a developing industry problem that they knew would eventually have to be faced by both local owners and brewers nationwide.[1]

The established American brewery owners were beginning to realize that new advances in the malting of barley, the bottling and pasteurization of beer and the inevitable installation of electricity and mechanized refrigeration in the breweries would require an enormous capital undertaking; the problem was, money for modernization was tight. In Chicago and other large brewing cities, competition now limited sales. Most of the breweries were producing beer well under capacity. By selling out to foreign investors, former owners would have the easy choices of pocketing a huge profit and perhaps staying on as consultants or managers, or simply taking the return on equity and leaving the impending problems of modernization and increasing competition to the new owners.

The Selling Continues

In July of 1889, the City Contract Company of London took stock in the Peter Schoenhofen Brewing Company, Limited, with an authorized capital of £400,000. In June of 1890, the English-owned City of Chicago Brewing and Malting Company, Limited captured about one-third of the existing shares of the Conrad Seipp Brewery and its subsidiary, the West Side Brewery, along with the F. J. Dewes Brewing Company (a.k.a. City Brewery Company, Chicago), the L. C. Huck Malting Company and the George Bullen Malting Company. The reported price of this new consolidation was $9,500,000 with $3,106,000 worth of bonds issued, to mature in 1910.[2]

In 1891, the Milwaukee and Chicago Breweries, Limited, another English conglomerate, merged with the previously formed American-owned syndicate, the United States Brewing Company. This merger included the Bartholomae & Leicht Brewing Company, the Ernst Brothers Brewing Company, the Bartholomae & Roesing Brewing and Malting Company, the K. G. Schmidt Brewing Company and the Val Blatz Brewing Company of Milwaukee. As noted in a prospectus in the *Chicago Tribune*, one believed advantage of combining these breweries was to increase the shipping and distribution efficiency of these Chicago breweries using Val Blatz Brewing Company's established distribution network.[3] The K.G. Schmidt Brewing Company had already dabbled in exporting their Budweiser brand to the western states and territories with success, but their foresightedness was the exception.[4] After years of neglecting the export market, it took an English syndicate, working through a Milwaukee brewery to develop a serious plan for the export of Chicago beer. Later results would prove that, for the most part, this plan was too little, too late.

Swept up by the wave of consolidations that were taking place around them, a group of American investors organized the American Malting and Elevator Company, buying a handful of local, independent malt houses that were providing malted barley and other cereal grains to nearby breweries.

The combined authorized capital of these mergers and consolidations was $11,716,000, an extraordinary sum for the times, and the total brewing capacity was estimated at 1,631,000 barrels annually, little more than half of the barrelage of all the breweries in Chicago.[5]

Investors Build More Breweries

American capitalists, some with little or no experience in the brewing trade, took note of the generous outlay of cash and securities used by the English to acquire these breweries and began to construct an additional eighteen breweries in Chicago during the period of the syndicates' greatest acquisition frenzy, from 1889 to 1900.[6] Some of these risk takers, with little or no experience in the brewing industry, hoped that English investors might acquire their breweries soon after construction, leaving them with a quick and generous profit. Other American brewery owners-to-be noted the high capitalization of the syndicated breweries and attempted to bypass the problem of huge start-up costs by establishing themselves with a minimal amount of leverage, if any at all. By 1894, Chicago had a total of fifty-three breweries. It ranked third in the nation in total number of brewing firms. Philadelphia and New York ranked number one and two respectively.[7]

The local brewers soon realized that Chicago, denied the export market and facing a stabilization in demand, could no longer support such a competitive environment.

Troubles for the Syndicates

The English taste for American breweries began to waiver as investors realized that the properties were overvalued. Blatz's dilapidated brewery in Milwaukee had been purchased for the kingly sum of $2,500,000. Within a year, it was necessary to pour an additional $400,000 into the plant for needed repairs. Coupled with the burden of overcapitalization, the syndicate's stock quotes fell. Dividends were lower than anticipated. English investment brokers offered one excuse after another—bad weather, poor barley harvest, weak economic conditions—but stiff competition from the numerous independent breweries and the other syndicates, mixed with the financial drain of stock and bond dividends were the real reasons for the syndicates' dismal performances.[8] Robbing Peter to pay Paul, they worked with little operating capital, trying desperately to meet preferred stock and bond dividends. To make matters worse, Irish-American saloonkeepers threatened to boycott any English-controlled breweries and turned to the independent Irish owned breweries for product.

Disturbed by the onslaught of foreign capital buying up local breweries, the Independent Brewing Association, composed of several wealthy and influential Chicago citizens, established a brewery in 1891. The organization's objectives were to operate a local brewery maintained ". . . by home capital and conducted on free principles, independent of any and all syndicates and pools." A similar effort in 1903 by a group of wealthy saloon owners inspired the formation of the Pilsen Brewing Company.[9]

Despite vigorous attempts by the syndicates and independents alike to boost sales, beer consumption in Chicago inexplicably started to taper off. Belated efforts by the local syndicates to increase the export trade offered no real chance in which to increase sales. Schlitz and Pabst in Milwaukee and Anheuser-Busch Brewing in St. Louis, well on their way to securing national markets, had already gained dominant positions, not only in the surrounding Midwest and South, but also in the developing western states. Iron-

The Independent Brewing Association opened its brewery in 1891. One of its saloons or tied-houses was located at Belmont and Lincoln. Courtesy of the Ravenswood-Lake View Historical Society.

ically, they used the vast railway shipping yards of Chicago as the hub for their expansion.

The Beer Wars in Chicago

With hopes of securing a larger market share and, if need be, squeezing the remaining independents out, the English-controlled breweries abruptly started to bring down the wholesale price of their beer.[10] Having anticipated such a move, the Chicago & Milwaukee Brewers' Association had joined together in 1890 to stabilize the now sinking barrel price at $6, a two dollar decrease.[11] Up until this cutthroat move by the English syndicates, any rivalry between brewers taking over each other's retail accounts had been quite civilized. If an aggressive brewer took a saloonkeeper from the account of a rival brewery, he was obliged to pay the rival brewery $3 per barrel for each barrel purchased by the retailer for a pre-determined period of time as compensation.[12]

This informal gentlemen's agreement, along with a number of more detailed pacts, soon fell apart as the syndicates brought the barrel price down to $4, with a 50 cent rebate, if necessary to effect a sale. The Manhattan Brewery was the first independent brewery to pull out of the fragile coalition of breweries hoping to stabilize the price per barrel. At this low retail level there was now less than one dollar profit per barrel. Adding to the local problems of price, smaller out-of-town breweries began to import beer to Chicago. Even at a price as low as $3 per barrel, these breweries found that their production and shipping costs were still low enough to make a profit. There was talk in the Chicago brewing community that prices would eventually fall to the inconceivable price of $2 a barrel.[13]

American-Styled Lager Beer

In an attempt to maintain some sort of profit on their beer, a number of brewers began to introduce the cheaper cereal grains of rice and corn to the brewing mash. This cost-cutting move ran contrary to the old German purity law, the *Reinheitsgebot*, which stated that beer was to be made only with water, hops, malted barley and yeast. But with an eye as much on survival as profit, the local breweries started to change the Old World character of Chicago's beer. The adulteration of the centuries old purity standard was the beginning of a new local beer, the American-styled lager, lighter in taste and character than its all malt predecessor. The addition of cereal grains not only maintained the bottom line but also helped to hinder the formation of 'chill haze,' an unsightly coagulation of protein from American six-row malted barley that can form when beer is cooled. With the growing acceptance of chilled beer in clear glass bottles, the customer would have no reason to question its drinkability.

Fears of the Milwaukee Brewers

The Milwaukee brewers, who had shipped 325,000 barrels of beer to Chicago in 1890, were forced to participate in this beer war, selling their products as low as $4 per barrel, $4 less than the going rate in Milwaukee.[14] Unwilling participants as they were, the Milwaukee brewers could not afford to pull out of this one time profitable market while the price war continued. Their biggest fear, whispered throughout the Milwaukee brewing community, was of a possible assault on their home grounds by the English-controlled Chicago breweries, possibly importing beer priced as low as $3.50 a barrel and bringing havoc to a previously unchallenged market. ". . . they do not feel like taking part in the war at Chicago if it can be avoided," the *Milwaukee Daily News* reported.[15] Their fears were unfounded as the Chicago brewers failed to take this aggressive sales initiative.

Tied-Houses

Price cutting was only part of the syndicates' plans to increase sales. In 1892, both the Chicago Brewing & Malting Company, Limited and the Milwaukee & Chicago Breweries, Limited, through their representatives, the City of Chicago Investment Company,

A former Schlitz tied-house is now the Southport Lanes & Billiards, on the North Side. Photograph by the author.

pooled over $6,000,000 for the purchase of saloons through which to exclusively sell their products.[16] By adopting this English practice of tied-houses, it was hoped that profits would rise as the syndicates seized control not only of the lagging beer market but also of the retailers themselves. Even Milwaukee tried this approach in Chicago. From 1897 to 1905 Edward G. Uihlein, buoyed by the takeover of the Jos. Schlitz Brewing Company by members of his family after the brewery's founder drowned, oversaw the building of fifty-seven Schlitz saloons in Chicago. Concrete reliefs of the Schlitz globe logo can still be found on the former tied-houses built by Schlitz at Ninety-second and Ewing and Thirty-fifth and Western on the South Side. Found at the North Side intersection of Damen and Belmont and at two locations on Southport Avenue are similar structures designed for Schlitz saloons.[17]

The World's Columbian Exposition of 1893

There remained one slim hope for Chicago breweries, one possible surge in beer sales that might give a needed respite while the local brewers, especially the syndicated firms, tried to stabilize the depressing conditions of the home market. That opportunity was the World's Columbian Exposition of 1893. For Chicago politicians and business leaders, this was their chance to introduce a new city that had literally risen from the ashes of the Great Fire of 1871. Chicago's syndicate brewers envisioned the millions of visitors to the city as a market to exploit. Improvements, though, would be fleeting, an artificial stimulus that would only delay the increasing effects of competition. The wholesale price for a barrel of beer was now around $4, leaving little more than $1 per barrel in profit.[18]

The syndicated breweries, concentrating more on survival than show, bypassed any participation in the exhibits of national and

Brewers' Pavilions were located in the Agriculture Building at the World's Columbian Exposition of 1893. The North Western Brewing Company's exhibit is shown here. From The Western Brewer, *November, 1893.*

The famous Linde Ice Machine for cooling purposes was brought to the United States by Fred W. Wolf of Chicago in the early 1880s. Wolf had a display of the Linde ice machinery at the World's Columbian Exposition of 1893. From The Western Brewer, *August, 1887.*

international breweries featured in the Agriculture Building. Only two independent Chicago breweries, the Cooke Brewing Company and the North-Western, used the Fair as a chance to demonstrate their brewing skills and the quality of their products, with both breweries winning awards for their beer in wood and bottles.[19]

The local peripheral brewing trades, with their expanding nationwide market, relatively independent of the struggling sales of the Chicago breweries, were better represented in the exposition hall of the Agriculture Building. The Geo. A. Weiss Malting & Elevator Company, Chicago Automatic Scale Company, Liquid Carbonic, the American Copper, Brass and Ironworks Company, and the Chas. Kaestner & Company, all displayed their wares. But the most impressive Chicago display in the event was that of the Fred Wolf Company with its Linde exhibit. The Linde machines had already shown their worth to the national brewing industry.

But Wolf was now moving away from the faltering brewing industry market with his products. In a joint effort with The Waukesha Hygeia Mineral Springs Company of Wisconsin a pipeline was laid from Wisconsin, carrying spring water to pressurized cooling tanks on the fairgrounds. Chilled to a temperature of 38° Fahrenheit by two 50 ton Linde refrigeration units, the spring water was pumped to 300 water fountains on the fairgrounds, providing over 60,000 gallons of water daily to the thousands of fairgoers. It was the first industrial demonstration of cooling water while in transit.

An analysis of beer sales, comparing the years from 1892 through the surge of sales from the World's Fair of 1893 to the returning normalcy of 1894, demonstrated the effects of local competition in Chicago. Overall consumption of beer in Chicago had leveled off. Of the market that remained, a larger portion was now being seized by the out-of-town brewers. There was, however, a slim hope for Chicago brewers. A second look at the production figures for 1894 showed an expected drop in sales from the inflated figure of 1893, but the barrelage in 1894 still showed an advance from 1892 sales of almost 400,000 barrels. A more aggressive strategy of expanding the number of saloons in Chicago would be the only recourse for local brewers.

CHICAGO BEER SALES IN BARRELS, 1892–1894

1892	1893	1894	Decrease 1893–1894
2,275,525	2,761,714	2,656,994	104,720

The Beer Wars Continue

One more attempt to end the beer wars took place during the fall of 1895. There was industry talk of forming a loose confederation of Chicago breweries to end undercutting of the price of a barrel of beer. It was proposed that the brewers would form a pool of over $1,000,000 by turning in two dollars per barrel for a certain period of time. This money would then be supplemented by an additional stipend of ten cents on the barrel. With a combined barrelage of over 4,000,000 per year, the ever increasing fund would be deposited in the Illinois Trust and Savings Bank and managed by a board of directors, elected by the brewers. From this fund, dividends would be issued to those breweries that cooperated in regulating the price of beer to a non-competitive level. Any brewery that broke ranks would lose access to the previously invested money and any future dividends. Like previous attempts at cooperation, this compromise never took effect as the brewers maintained a maverick attitude on pricing.[20]

Local Investors Consolidate

In 1898, one more consolidation of breweries took place in Chicago with the formation of the United Breweries Company, Chicago. With the support of the Chicago

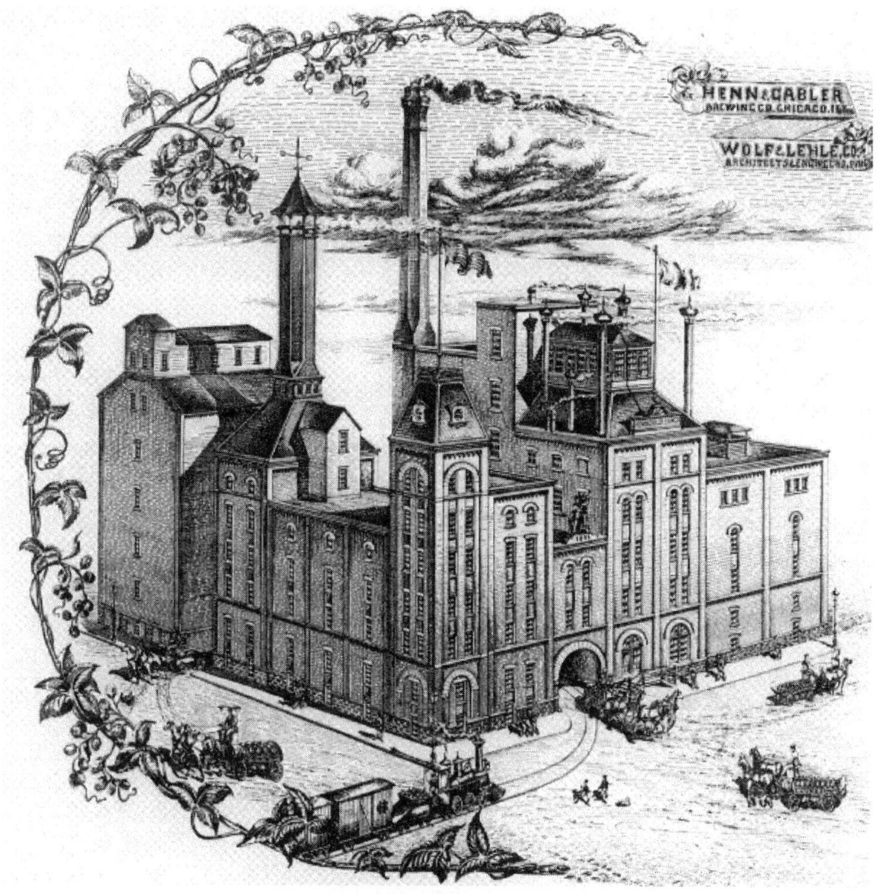

In Bridgeport the Henn & Gabler Brewing Company, shown in a drawing by Wolf & Lehle, circa 1890, later became part of the United Breweries syndicate. From The Western Brewer, *April, 1892.*

brewers association, a group of local liquor interests instituted the new syndicate, hoping to stabilize and even raise the price of a barrel of beer to that of pre-syndicate days. Involved in this merger were thirteen breweries, twelve in Chicago including the Chicago Brewing Company, Citizens Brewing Company, Carl Corper Brewing & Malting Company, Fecker Brewing Company, Henn & Gabler Brewing Company, Monarch Brewing Company, North Western Brewing Company, Phoenix Brewing Company, William Ruehl Brewing Company, M. Sieben, South Chicago Brewing Company, Star Brewing Company of Chicago and the Blue Island Brewing Company in neighboring Blue Island, Illinois. Contrary to the syndicate's original business plan, which called for the quick consolidation and closing of some of the breweries, administrators of plants targeted for closing managed to temporarily delay the inevitable, causing fiscal and prolonged legal nightmares for the syndicate's investors.[21]

Troubles Continue for the Syndicated Breweries

The troubles of the syndicated breweries seemed to go on and on, dissent even coming from within their own ranks. In 1892, during the early days of the syndication craze, William C. Seipp and Louis C. Huck, sons of pioneer brewers Conrad Seipp and John A. Huck, along with T.J. Lefens resigned their positions as managers of the Chicago Brewing and Malting Company. The official reason given for the mass resignation was that they had simply agreed to stay on only for a short time to aid in the smooth transfer of the newly formed syndicate to English control. Rumors abounded in the Chicago brewing community that they had been forced out because of dissatisfaction in London with their management of the floundering syndicate. The discharged brewers offered no explanation for the resignations, allowing the rumors to continue.[22]

In 1894, Leo Ernst, Vice-President and General Manager of the Chicago & Milwaukee Breweries announced that he, too, was leaving syndicate control and starting his own independent brewery, which was perceived as an affront to the English owners who he had served.[23]

Ernst Fecker, Jr., an independent brewer, held a realistic view of the brewing situation for the syndicates in Chicago. In an interview with a Chicago newspaper, he said:

> I venture the prediction that the English brewing companies will never again earn a dividend on their common stocks. The trouble is that old time prices cannot now be obtained and it is not likely that they can be obtained in the future. The price of beer is now $5 per barrel and the reduction from $6 a barrel, the price in effect last year, is enough to remove the possibility of dividends being earned on the common shares of the overcapitalized English companies and to make even the preferred shares uncertain.[24]

The independent breweries were also having a difficult time during the price wars, even with the fiscal advantage of being unencumbered with the crippling debt of the syndicates. "I know what I am talking about," Fecker confessed, "because I have a brewery of my own. I am in no combination, have no stock to pay dividends on or bonds requiring a certain amount of interest money to be set aside and I find it difficult to earn a moderate return on the cold cash invested."

With local breweries producing well below capacity, Fecker understood the problems of competition, the demands of anxious investors and a sudden drop off in cash flow which the syndicates were now facing. The problems of falling output had been reported by the local press. The *Herald American* newspaper called the situation "appalling."

Fecker predicted that the drop in production, coupled with the demands by investors for dividend returns, would soon be disastrous for the syndicates. "There is no chance nowadays for brewery combinations to earn money on watered securities. Only the other day I heard that one of these English breweries, which paid 7 per cent on its common stock last fall, was trying to borrow money for the purpose of paying interest on its bonds."

The independent brewer continued with his inside analysis of the syndicates' problems of production, ". . . I have talked with several big brewers, and they tell me that their output is falling 30 to 35 per cent as compared to last year (1893). The original *Chicago Herald American* statement that the falling off was 55 per cent was more nearly correct than the compilation of the syndicate stock manipulators."

With continued local competition and no hope in sight for his independent brewing operation, Fecker gave in to the overtures of the locally organized, American-owned, United Breweries Company, Chicago in 1898. He sold just in time; his former brewery was subsequently closed in 1901 as part of a cost-cutting measure by the American syndicate. Two years later, the American brewery syndicate filed for bankruptcy protection.[25]

With beer prices already lowered during the local beer wars to unprecedented levels, the U. S. Government slapped a $2 a barrel tax on beer to help finance the Spanish-American War, cutting deeply into what was left of brewing profits.[26] Finally, in 1899, English courts ruled that English firms operating in foreign lands were to be taxed at the same rate as those operating on English soil, erasing a tax advantage the English syndicates had enjoyed for years.[27]

No further attempts were made by English investors to purchase breweries in Chicago, but the damage was done. The beer wars, syndication, the cost of modernization and the Spanish-American war tax had crippled the Chicago brewing industry.

Notes

1. John E. George. "The Saloon Question in Chicago." *Economic Studies* 2 (American Economic Association,) 1897, p. 69.

2. *Ibid.*, p. 69.

3. *Chicago Tribune*, March 4, 1891.

4. The early use of the name *Budweiser* was not exclusive to Anheuser-Busch. Philip Van Munching, *Beer Blast*. (New York, NY: Times Books, 1997) p. 16, claims that even Miller and Schlitz both used the name at one time. DuBois Brewing of DuBois, Pennsylvania, continued to brew DuBois *Budweiser* until 1970 when the Pennsylvania Supreme Court ordered them to stop.

5. John E. George. *op. cit.*, p. 70.

6. Donald Bull, Manfred Friedrich and Robert Gottschalk. *American Breweries*. (Trumbull, CT: Bullworks, 1984) pp. 57–68.

7. John E. George. *op. cit.*, p. 68.

8. *The Western Brewer*, Vol. XVII, June–September, 1892.

9. *The Western Brewer*, December, 1891; *The First Fifty Years of the Pilsen Brewing Company, 1903–1953*, Chicago, company pamphlet, 1953.

10. John E. George. *op. cit.*, pp. 71–72.

11. *The Western Brewer*, September, 1890.

12. John E. George. *op. cit.*, p. 72.

13. *The Western Brewer*, March and May, 1892; *Chicago Herald American*, April 3, 1894.

14. *The Milwaukee Daily News*, July 12, 1890.

15. *The Milwaukee Daily News*, *Ibid.*

16. John E. George. *op. cit.*, p.73.

17. Perry Duis. *The Saloon. Public Drinking in Chicago and Boston, 1880 1920*. (Urbana, IL: University of Illinois Press, 1983), pp. 41–42.

18. Duis, *op. cit.*, p. 38.

19. *The Western Brewer*, November, 1893.

20. *The Western Brewer*, September, 1895.

21. *One Hundred Years of Brewing*. (Chicago, IL: H. S. Rich, 1903) p. 505.

22. *The Western Brewer*, June, 1892.

23. *The Western Brewer*, May, 1894.

24. The Fecker interview appeared in *The Chicago Herald American*, April 3, 1894. Additional comments appeared in the same newspaper on April 10, 1894.

25. Bull, *et. al.*, p. 60.

26. Bull, *et. al.*, p. 9.

27. Duis, *op. cit.*, p. 39.

Chapter 7

The Saloons, 1875–1910

"We could set our own prices . . ."
Edward G. Uihlein, Schlitz sales representative in Chicago

Placing the Beer

For years, brewers had followed a policy of *placing* beer with retailers. More than 90% of beer sales during the early 1880s was draft. Because of the high cost of draft equipment, the availability of only one or two taps in any given saloon and the perishability of non-pasteurized draft beer, it was necessary for brewery representatives to aggressively convince retailers to take on their product rather than that of their competitors. Any slow moving, bad tasting or contaminated product or one priced too high could be replaced by a vigilant competitor with the thrifty consent of a saloonkeeper looking at the bottom line. Competition was intense with savvy retailers pitting one brewery salesman against another for the best possible deal. Bar displays, coasters, matches and other promotional items would sometimes be thrown in to sweeten a deal. Money, though, was the key inducement. Beer sales reps would often be obliged to use an allocated sales expense called *spendings* to treat a prospective client's customers at the bar, even if the customers were drinking a rival product. After buying a beer or two, the *beer drummer* might convince the saloon crowd to give his product a try, pressuring the saloonkeeper to switch brands to keep his customers happy. This actually wasn't too difficult a sales pitch to successfully accomplish. Brand loyalty was in an embryonic stage; for most customers, beer was beer. It merely had to be affordable and fresh. This same practice of buying rounds for the house would even apply to established accounts, plus an additional obligation on the drummer that might also include discounts or rebates to the saloonkeeper on the barrel price, coupled with favorable credit terms for continued purchases.[1]

The Harper High License Act

A more dependent relationship between brewers and saloonkeepers started to take place after the Illinois General Assembly passed the Harper High License Act in 1883, effective on January 1, 1884. In a bow to one more wave of temperance and reform, state legislators raised the price of a liquor license in Illinois, hoping that a higher liquor license fee would force out the lower class dives and slow any further growth of saloons throughout the state. With a license fee of $150 for a beer license and $500 for a beer and liquor license (later changed to one flat fee of $500 for all), some saloonkeepers turned to the breweries for financial assistance in securing a liquor license. In return, the brewers demanded that the retailers exclusively purchase and serve their beer, adding a service charge to each barrel in compensation for the license fee. Of course, if a competing brewer came along and was willing to buy the license and offer an even better deal on their product, the saloonkeeper might consider replacing the original beer supplier. This dog-eat-dog practice was a constant source of frustration for brewery representatives and owners alike, but fostered a competitive environment.[2]

Saloons Increase in Number in Chicago

The English syndicates and their tied-house concept raised the level of retailer dependency to the extreme. The sales and marketing campaigns of syndicate breweries in the early 1890s consisted of a concerted program to increase the consumption of beer in three ways: 1) by organizing holding companies to purchase saloon sites and properties, corner locations with their front and side entrances being the most favored, 2) by establishing cheaply furnished saloons and placing in them agents to sell their beer, the furnishings secured by chattel mortgages, and 3) by signing the saloonkeepers' surety bonds and advancing money for liquor licensing and any other permit fees.[3]

Many of the independently owned local breweries had already utilized the signing of surety bonds for saloonkeepers as a way to gain some control over retail outlets. A look at the saloon license register for the area of Lake View from the period of 1883 through 1886 shows the names of local brewers Virgil M. Brand, William C. Seipp and Otto Ernst listed as sureties for a number of saloons.[4]

With this syndicate program of expansion, which would be copied by many of the remaining independent breweries, any would-be entrepreneur with only $50 to $75 could open a saloon at a brewery-owned or leased site, have it furnished with brewery-owned stock and equipment, be licensed with brewery money and then obligated to purchase beer at whatever price the brewery demanded. Thus the apt term for such a saloon was "tied-house."

Brewery-owned bar equipment, leased to the enterprising businessman, could be extensive. An agreement and lease made between Southwest Side saloonkeeper Piotr Adamezyk and the Manhattan Brewery, an independent brewery located northeast of the

Before the Great Fire the Sand's Ale Brewing Company sold its pale cream ale at the Green Room Saloon, next to the McVicker's Theatre, at State and Madison Avenues. From Prominent Citizens and Industries of Chicago. *Chicago: W. P. Dunn Company* (1901), 17.

Chicago Stockyards, detailed the necessary equipment for a typical mid-sized neighborhood saloon start-up:

> 40' Bar, 24' Bbar (backbar) . . . Footrail, 24' Mirror, IceBox, Office partition w door, 6 Tables, 4 doz Chairs, Ice Box, Basement, stove w pipes . . . Urinal Closet, one cash register.

In return for the use of these brewery items, Adamezyk agreed to ". . . purchase all beer in his saloon from said first party (Manhattan) . . ." The benefit of a small start-up cost for a saloon was negated by a total dependency on the terms and pricing structure of the controlling brewery.[5]

Saloons would often forgo the use of tables and chairs in their establishments. But in many of the neighborhood bars, like Adamezyk's Back-of-the-Yards business, wives would sometimes accompany their husbands to the traditionally male-dominated saloon for a Sunday drink or two, a practice that was accepted in the ethnic enclaves; women could not, however, stand at the bar. Thus, there had to be chairs for female customers.

Despite the restricting arrangements of choosing only one beer purveyor for product, almost anyone could now have the opportunity to run a saloon. The signed exclusivity agreement, however, kept saloonkeepers from pitting one brewery against the other for liquor license fees, surety bonds or favorable credit terms as had been the earlier practice. With this ease of entry into saloon ownership, the number of saloons proliferated. By 1877, before the tied-house practice was widely in effect, only one thousand and seventeen saloon licenses had been issued by the city. By 1895, there were six thousand five hundred and twenty-two legally licensed saloons operating in Chicago. The 1884 increase in the liquor license fee and the subsequent assistance from the breweries in securing licenses for saloonkeepers, later coupled with the tied-house practice, had the overall effect of increasing, rather than decreasing, the number of saloons in the city.[6]

The sharp increase in the number of city saloons appeared to give the sales results that local brewers had anticipated. The *Brewers' Journal*, using figures provided by the syndicates, reported that sales of beer from the beginning of the syndicates' reign in 1889 through 1894 had more than doubled, totaling 2,656,994 barrels in 1894. These figures would later become questionable as industry insiders began claiming that the syndicates' production figures were being inflated in order to mollify nervous investors.[7]

Saloon Failures

The mortality rate of the tied-house saloons, though, was high. If the saloonkeeper failed to make payments on his rent or product, his bar would be promptly seized by the brewery, including all chattels such as saloon fixtures, glasses and stock. "It is understood that said second party has no interest in said property," was a typical part of a

Chicago, ______________ 190

Mr. ______________

____

____

I hereby agree to save and keep you harmless from any and all loss or damage by reason of the execution by you of a certain agreement in writing, bearing even date herewith, provided however, that during the period mentioned in said agreement, you will at all times use, sell or give away no other Domestic Draught Beer or Beers in and about your place of business in the City of Chicago, excepting the Domestic Draught Beer or Beers, made and manufactured by me, and provided further that you will at all times promptly pay for any and all such Beer and Beers furnished by me, at current prices.

____

(Form 4)

A sample contract to be completed by an independent saloon owner wishing to do business with a brewery. Courtesy of Larry Anderson.

A former Schlitz tied-house is now doing business as Schuba's on Southport Avenue. Photograph by the author.

brewery/saloon lease agreement. If business soured for the hapless saloonkeeper, someone else might be behind the bar the next day, hoping to achieve better results than his luckless predecessor.[8] "Independent" saloon ownership was quickly seen as an illusion, but there was no lack of willing applicants for saloon positions.

This harsh business practice, with the occasional annoyance of an interrupted cash flow to the breweries from the openings and closings of their poorest performing bars, was balanced with the Darwinian effect of survival. Only the most productive saloonkeepers survived and sometimes even prospered. The majority of the breweries hoped that by continuing this practice of eventually replacing poor performing retailers with those with more business acumen, the situation would stabilize.

Schlitz' Tied-house Policy

In his memoirs, Edward G. Uihlein of Schlitz shows a different interpretation of the tied-house policy and their Chicago saloon outlets:

> For our own purposes we often invested funds by financing our customers. In this manner we not only reached higher sale figures, but we also insured our clients against the competition. We could set our own prices, but of course we never took unfair advantage of this situation. When we rented to a merchant who handled our products exclusively we were very sure of his reputation and his compliance with all laws and ordinances. A respectable merchant need not fear an increase in his rent unless an increase in taxes or cost of maintenance made it necessary. Needless to say, our policies were not highly regarded by the competition. However, after some time, when we had achieved a reputation for keeping our contracts and the most inconsequential of promises we had no problem renting all available space. The final result was the respect of the whole business sector in Chicago.[9]

Uihlein makes no reference to what the Schlitz tied-house policy was when a saloon-keeper failed to satisfactorily perform.

The Free Lunch

In an effort to increase their chances of survival, the saloonkeepers looked for endless ways to increase their patronage, the free lunch being the most popular. Beginning

Customers at a typical Chicago saloon of the early 1900s stood, as tables were seldom provided. Courtesy of the Harold Washington Library.

with the simple but effective practice of giving one heated oyster with every nickel beer, a Chicago phenomenon, the free lunch blossomed to a dinner of meats, beans, boiled potatoes, pigs' feet, sauerkraut and bread. This spread might cost the average saloon owner $2 to $3 daily. In the downtown area, some of the more opulent saloons could spend $30 to $40 with a food bill consisting of 150–200 pounds of meat, 1½ to 2 bushels of potatoes, 50 loaves of bread, 35 pounds of beans, 45 dozen eggs, 10 dozen ears of corn and $1.50 to $2 worth of vegetables. Up to five men would be employed at the lunch counter.[10]

But in the poorer neighborhoods, the free lunch held a higher significance. "I believe it is true that all the charity organizations in Chicago combined are feeding fewer people than the saloons," Royal Melendy, a researcher for the Chicago Commons settlement house determined after a study of the practice.[11]

The whole idea of the free lunch, however, was to encourage the customers to buy beer. By charging a nickel for a seven ounce glass, sometimes inscribed with the brewery's logo or name, a saloonkeeper could realize a profit of over $20 per barrel of beer. The more successful saloons could run through three or more 31 gallon barrels during lunch.

Dance Halls

Other saloon owners resorted to less honorable undertakings including prostitution and gambling. In the immediate area of City Hall were so-called family resorts where men could meet women of loose character, to drink and party, often past the legal closing time. The West Side was noted for the concert saloons which would offer a stage performance for free. After performing, the women artistes would leave the stage and circulate throughout the hall, persuading the men to buy them drinks. Prostitution was not uncommon.[12]

Reformer Samuel P. Wilson appears to have had an intimate knowledge of Chicago's dance halls and concert saloons. In his 1910 expose, *"Chicago" and its Cess-pools of Infamy*, the author described the goings-on in a typical concert saloon, calling it ". . . the worst feature of the social evil (saloons)."

> The dance halls are often handsome places, but were simply rendezvous of street walkers, and men who came to seek their company. The principal establishment of this kind was the infamous Apollo theatre and dance hall . . . We enter through a lobby into a barroom, back of which is the dance hall. The place was furnished with tables, and chairs are scattered about the sides of the first floor, but the central space is kept clear for dancing. The galleries are also provided with tables and chairs. At the back is a dimly lighted space, fitted up like a garden, where those who desire may sit and drink. The place was always well filled. The women present were the inmates of the neighboring house of ill-fame, and street walkers. Each one is a prostitute, and each one is intent upon luring some man into her chamber . . . The air is heavy with tobacco smoke. Men and

> women are constantly passing in and out; drinking is going on in every part of the hall. In spite of its brilliancy and splendor, the place is but one of the numerous gateways to hell, with which Chicago abounds.
>
> Men meet abandoned women here, and accompany them to their houses, risking disease, robbery, and even death, with a recklessness that is appalling.[13]

Slot Machines

During the mid-1890s, nickel-in-the-slot machines started showing up in Chicago saloons. Originally developed in Germany to dispense postage stamps, gum and cigarettes, Yankee ingenuity modified a number of them to pay out money, a precursor to today's video-poker machines. By dropping a nickel in the slot located at the top of the machine, and allowing the coin to negotiate a maze of nail heads, a successful player could receive a pay-out if the nickel landed in the right slot at the bottom of the machine. Saloonkeepers could make up to $15 per day on these devices. These machines could still be found in some Chicago taverns up through the late 1950s. During the turn of the century period, pool tables would also become fixtures in local saloons, adding additional profit to the saloon owner's bottom line.[14]

German bier gartens, where families often enjoyed oompah bands, sandwiches and lager beer were still popular. Two of the more famous beer gardens were located in Ogden's Grove on Clybourne Avenue and Schuetzen-Park, which became Riverview Park in 1905–1906, at Western and Belmont.[15]

Beer Deliveries

Independent businessmen, bypassing the need for a liquor license and the subsequent dependency on the brewers for a license fee loan or grant, took to the streets. Using horse-drawn carriages, they loaded their saloons-on-wheels with bottled beer, cigars and sandwiches, peddling their wares at construction sites and work areas. This practice was openly endorsed by the brewers who didn't have to pay for liquor licenses nor for the added distribution costs of their products and were quite happy for any additional outlets through which to further beer sales.[16]

Saloon and Brewery Revenues

Although only a small percentage of these watering holes dabbled in unsavory and illegal practices, the reformers and prohibitionists looked upon all saloons as dens of inequity, with brewers as catalysts in the downfall of humanity. With pressure once again upon the city politicians to clean up the saloons, local officials were caught in the horns of a dilemma. As noted earlier, the 1883 increase in liquor license fees had the startling effect of increasing rather than decreasing the number of saloons in the city as brewers started to pick up the license expense. From the beginning of the new license requirements in 1883–1884 alone, the annual city revenues from liquor licenses rose from $385,964 to over $1 million, much of the money paid out by the brewers. The increased revenues from the surge in new licenses surely had an addictive effect on Chicago's politicians; from mid-1894 to mid-1895, one-tenth of all receipts to the city now came from saloon licenses, totaling $3,335,359 in 1894.

Mayor Carter H. Harrison, Jr. was aware of the political dilemma of balancing the demands of reform groups and nurturing this huge source of revenue. In a meeting with a group of leading Chicago brewers (among them Rudolph Brand, Charles H. Wacker, one of the Seipps, Adam Ortseifen, Theodore Oehne, Otto Tosetti, Virgil Brand, and representatives of Schlitz, Lemp, and Anheuser-Busch) during his first term as mayor, Harrison admonished them, asking the brewers to help curb the disreputable conditions that were being reported in the city saloons. His pleas were met with icy stares. Carter saw the cleaning up of the saloon industry as essential. If not, reformers using legal maneuvering might force prohibition or a restriction of the drink trade in Chicago. The brewers, with millions invested in saloon property and the continuing need to further sales, had much more to lose than the small businessmen who ran the saloons. Realistically, if the brewers lost, so would the city, and Harrison knew it. As they left the mayor's office, with Harrison's criticisms of their neglect in establishing control over their retail outlets still ringing in their ears, local brewer Theodore Oehne, seemingly oblivious to the cascading problems of Chicago's saloons, was heard to remark to the group, "Huh! So he's turning Temperenz!"

Harrison was wise enough to understand that he had to balance pressure on the local brewing community with political reality. He estimated that the powerful coalition of Chicago brewers, saloonkeepers and distillers was capable of controlling over fifty thousand votes, a political fact that could not be ignored.[17]

The economic effect of licensed drinking establishments on the entire city was becoming enormous. Total sales for city saloons in 1894 were around $70,000,000, beer accounting for $34,000,000 of the total. Expenditures by the saloons, excluding distilled liquors, were $9,750,000. Of the revenues to the city from the liquor licensing fees, two percent was allocated for the police pension fund and a maximum of $20,000 went to the Washingtonian House, a hospital for alcoholics.[18]

Corruption

With the semi-annual licensing fee windfall swelling city coffers, tempered by the growing demands of reformers that lawmakers do something about the conditions of saloons in Chicago, it became increasingly obvious to city officials that there was a need to gently regulate, or at least give the appearance of regulating and policing, the overwhelming number of saloons now operating in the city. In an effort to add seeming control over a wide open industry and still keep a steady flow of revenues pouring into the city treasury, the City Council passed a number of ordinances to appease reformers, including the regulation and enforcement of opening and closing hours of city saloons.

Abuse of these laws, not only by saloonkeepers but also by neighborhood policemen would occasionally come to public notice. The April 11, 1895 edition of the *Evening Post* reported on the operation of *blind pigs*, or unlicensed saloons, near Jackson Park during the World's Fair in 1893. "Probably the most sensational statement in the hands of reform organizations concerning the blackmailing practice of police, is made by a man who during the World's Fair conducted a saloon within the prohibited districts near Jackson Park. This person declared that he was assessed $1,200 a month for the privilege of continuing the illicit traffic . . . it was contribute so much or close up." At the time, there were about twenty-three blind pigs operating in the area, part of the recently annexed township of Hyde Park. The number halved when the prices to operate steadily rose. But the free wheeling practices of Chicago's saloons would continue with only sporadic hindrance by local politicians and the police department.

The crippling beer wars of the 1890s, increased competition from local and outside breweries and the imposition of the Spanish-American War tax on barreled beer would force the brewery owners to assume a "see no evil, hear no evil" attitude concerning the growing problems of the local saloons. Increased sales at any cost were necessary for the continued existence of the local brewing industry. Saloons, with all their problems, were the only hope for the Chicago brewers to maintain sales.

But by the turn of the century, the problems of Chicago's saloons would start to rest uncomfortably in the laps of the brewers. It would take at least another decade before they would acknowledge their part in having helped to create the problem. By then, the tail would be wagging the dog.

Notes

1. Thomas Childs Cochran. *The Pabst Brewing Company.* (Westport, CT: Greenwood Press, 1975) pp. 139–142.
2. Perry R. Duis. *The Saloon. Public Drinking in Chicago and Boston.* (Urbana, IL: University of Illinois Press, 1983) pp. 22–28. pp. 82–83.
3. John E. George. "The Saloon Question in Chicago," *Economic Studies* II (1897), p. 76 and Besssie Louise Pierce. *A History of Chicago.* Vol. III (London: Alfred A. Knopf, 1957) p. 151.
4. *Archives of Lakeview City,* 1872–1889, 7/0015/08–11, Northeastern University.
5. *Charles Schaffner Collection,* Agreement and Lease, Box 321, Chicago Historical Society.
6. *Chicago Times,* August 5, 1877; Duis, p. 83.
7. *Chicago Herald,* April 3, 1894.
8. *Charles Schaffner Collection, Ibid.*
9. *A Memoir of Edward G. Uihlein,* 1917. Translated by Rosina L. Lippi and Jill D. Carlisle. Chicago Historical Society.

10. Royal L. Melendy. "The Saloon in Chicago," *American Journal of Sociology* 6 (1900–1901) p. 296.

11. Royal L. Melendy. *Ibid.*, p. 297.

12. Herbert Asbury. *Gem of the Prairie.* (DeKalb, IL: Northern Illinois University Press, 1986), pp. 271–275; Duis, *op. cit.* pp. 237–238.

13. Samuel Paynter Wilson. *"Chicago" and its Cess-pools of Infamy.* (Chicago, IL: 1910) pp. 199–200.

14. *Chicago Herald*, April 1,1894.

15. Hartmut Keil. *German Workers' Culture In The United States 1850 to 1920.* (Washington, D.C. and London: Smithsonian Institution Press, 1988) pp. 48, 305; Royal L. Melendy, *Ibid.*, pp. 304–305.

16. Duis, p. 66.

17. For the acount of the mayor's meeting with the brewers and his estimate of their political power, see Carter H. Harrison. *Stormy Years. The Autobiography of Carter H. Harrison.* (Indianapolis, IN: The Bobbs-Merrill Company, 1935) pp. 340–341.

18. George, *op. cit.* pp 83, 88.

Chapter 8

Rebirth, 1900–1905

"a brewer love feast"

Brewer John H. Weiss describing a reconciliation dinner of leading Chicago brewers in 1901

The Industry Regroups

The stirrings of a rebirth in the Chicago brewing industry were unmistakable in the early 1900s. For the syndicate-owned and independent breweries alike, the beer price wars of the 1890s, coupled with an additional one dollar Spanish-American War tax on each barrel of beer, had had a crippling effect on Chicago breweries. Demands by local unions, along with the economic necessity of meeting the challenges of new technologies in the brewing field, had left many of the breweries in a precarious financial position. With survival as their chief objective, Chicago brewers began a campaign to reenergize the local industry. The obstacles to stabilization and possible growth were many, but surmountable.

In the early summer of 1900, the price of a barrel of beer in Chicago rose once again to $6.[1] Even with the price increase and the added profit it afforded the local brewers, the continuation of the war tax and sluggish sales problems started to take their toll on the City of Chicago Brewing and Malting Company, Limited. In July, the company failed to pay its midsummer dividend, citing the war tax.[2] The investors of the City Contract Company of London, who had earlier taken stock in the Peter Schoenhofen Brewing Company, Limited, had had enough of poor returns and the unsettling financial situation of their investments in Chicago. The Schoenhofen family, recognizing the desperation of the English investors, offered to buy the common shares of the minority stockholders at $2.40 per each $10 share and dissolve the English company. The investors were livid with the low offer but soon reached terms with the family.[3]

The United States Brewing Company during this time was having a protracted legal nightmare with one of their brewery managers. After paying $450,000 cash and stock for the Star Brewery on North Rockwell, Patrick Rice, who had been appointed as manager for a term of two years, refused to leave his post when his contract was not renewed. Realizing that his dismissal was a prelude to the cost-cutting measure of closing the brewery, Rice, along with his employees, actually barricaded the brewery entrance and retained physical control over the plant. After a series of suits and counter suits, the embattled Rice was finally evicted, allowing management to return to their initial plan of closing the brewery and further consolidating the assets of the syndicate. Not surprisingly, the siege and subsequent court battle drained the syndicate of much needed working capital.[4]

The War Tax

In April of 1900, a delegation of the United States Brewers Association, led by their president, Chicago brewer Rudolph Brand of Brand Brewing, appeared before the House Committee on Ways and Means to appeal for a reduction of the war tax, imposed on the brewing industry in June of 1898 to help finance the Spanish-American War. They argued that an extraction by the federal government of such a large portion of the selling price of an article (beer) was oppressive, unfair and un American.[5] In the face of unfavorable public opinion, the tax was reduced a disappointing forty cents a barrel. The cost of goods at the time for a medium sized brewery with capacity of about 75,000 barrels was still around $4.86 per barrel. With wholesale prices hovering around $6 a barrel, brewing was no longer a business of high profits and low overhead.[6]

Harmony in the Industry

There was a growing realization among local brewery owners that cooperation with competitors, union leaders, creditors and regulatory agencies was vital for continued existence. Truces among brewers were becoming the norm in the Chicago brewing community. Modern, reliable equipment, a solid capitalization of assets, a quality product and a strong management team were the tools to continuing, albeit moderate, profits. Those who ignored the signs of the times and continued with the old ways might soon be run out of business or absorbed by a leaner, more aggressive competitor. Recent experiences had proven so.[7]

Most of the brewery owners, though, had seen the writing on the wall; cooperation was the operative word, especially among competitors. A banquet for Chicago's leading brewery owners in 1901 at the home of Edward G. Uihlein, an officer of the Jos. Schlitz

Brewing Company in Chicago, was described by owner John H. Weiss of the Gottfried Brewery as a "brewer love feast." [8]

Preparing for the Future

In 1902, the war tax was finally eliminated, reducing the tax on a barrel of beer to the old $1 rate. Coupled with a steady increase in beer sales, this rise in the average profit per barrel brought about a flurry of renewed activity in the battered Chicago brewing industry. The Chicago & Milwaukee Breweries, Limited, the United Breweries Company, Chicago, and the Chicago Brewing & Malting Company, Limited took steps to reorganize, calling in old bonds, raising additional working capital and consolidating outstanding shares where necessary. Dividends were sharply curtailed, and, in some instances, eliminated, as the syndicates took a tough stand with nervous investors. In 1903, the Chicago Brewing & Malting Company authorized payment of its first dividend since 1897, proving the effectiveness of its reorganization plans.[9]

The non-syndicated breweries, led by the Peter Schoenhofen Brewing Company and the Independent Brewing Association, unburdened by the restrictive debt of the syndicates, began a campaign of expansion and modernization. The Schoenhofen Brewery installed the world's largest hop-jack in 1905 to filter their beers of the flavoring herb after leaving the copper. The huge device had a capacity of 800 barrels. The Carl Corper Brewing Company began expansion of their plant in Bridgeport at Forty-first and Union in 1903. The new structure was plain and unpretentious, unlike the style of the older breweries, reflecting the industry's new philosophy of efficiency and practicality. The bulk of the construction expenditures were reserved for the latest in modern brewing equipment.[10]

This period of belt-tightening and a refocusing of business goals by almost all the Chicago breweries began a revitalization of the local industry. Trade publications noted this new growth, citing an increase of capital stock in many of the breweries that had successfully weathered the beer wars of the 1890s and the war tax. Anheuser-Busch, Schlitz, Blatz and Pabst also noticed the pick-up in business and renewed their endless invasion of the Chicago market, building new depots and storage facilities throughout Chicago.

Effects on Related Trades

As the brewing industry in Chicago continued its growth, the auxiliary trades flourished as well. The Liquid Carbonic Company, A. Magnus Sons Company, the Saladin Pneumatic Malting Construction Company and the brewery architectural firm of Louis Lehle, along with scores of other companies integrated with the local brewing community, continued to meet the needs of breweries not only in Chicago, but throughout the country as well.

This front elevation and cutaway view of a lager brewery was drawn by Louis Lehle and published in One Hundred Years of Brewing (1903). *Note the statue of Gambrinus on the roof.*

Albert Schwill & Company began construction of the world's largest malting plant in South Chicago, a distinction formerly held by the Northwestern Malt & Grain Company. A twenty-four tank behemoth, with an annual capacity of 2,500,000 bushels of grain, the new plant was poised to supply the needs of the revitalized Chicago brewing community.[11]

Peace with the Local Unions

In 1904, in a further sign of harmony and cooperation, the Chicago Brewers' Association entered into contract negotiations with Brewers' & Maltsters' Union #18 and Brewery Laborers' Union #337 for a two year contract. After some posturing by both sides, the brewer bosses offered a one year extension of the previous contract. In a decidedly different tone from earlier years, they stressed their willingness to take up the matter of a new contract once business improved. After a quick counter offer by the unions, noting the obvious improvement of the brewers' financial situations, the Chicago Brewers' Association quickly made a contract with the Brewers and Maltsters' Union and the Brewery Laborers' Union. Both agreements were decidedly liberal in pay and benefits. A further concession established a seven man arbitration board consisting of three management and three union representatives with an impartial seventh member chosen by the two groups.[12]

The Weiss Beer Brewers of Chicago also made peace with their brewery workers, giving them practically the same terms as those offered to the lager brewers. A wasteful and potentially disastrous labor confrontation had been averted.

The beginning of the new century for Chicago's breweries was a keystone, bridging the incredible growth of the 1870s, '80s and '90s with the moderate, but profitable growth of the twentieth century. It certainly wasn't like the good old days but the local brewery owners had learned to adapt to a set of circumstances that had never challenged their fathers and grandfathers. Not only were they adapting, it appeared that business for Chicago brewery owners was once again thriving.

Notes

1. John Herbert Weiss Papers [manuscript], 1 Volume, 1900–1904, Chicago Historical Society.
2. *The Western Brewer*, July 1900.
3. *The Western Brewer*, July, 1900.
4. *The Western Brewer*, April , 1901 and Oct. 1902.
5. *The Western Brewer*, May, 1900, February, 1901 and March, 1901.
6. *The Western Brewer*, June, 1901.
7. John Herbert Weiss Papers, *Ibid.*

8. *Ibid.*, March 9, 1901.

9. *The Western Brewer*, January, 1903 and May, 1903; *American Brewers' Review*, September, 1903.

10. *American Brewers' Review*, September, 1903, October, 1903, and November, 1905.

11 *American Brewers' Review*, July, 1903.

12 *American Brewers' Review*, April, 1904.

Chapter 9

Early Prohibition Efforts, 1900–1917

"The saloons with their attractions,
and the bartenders, with their effusive
smiles, lure men to drink . . ."
The Saloon Problem and Reform, 1905

"The sum of the matter is, the people drink because they
wish to drink."
Rudolph Brand, Chicago brewer

The Anti-Saloon League

The undeniable connection between city saloons and the Chicago breweries went under strong attack by local reformers and prohibitionists during the early 1900s. Leading the broadsided assault was the Anti-Saloon League, founded by the Reverend Howard Hyde Russell of Ohio. Russell was a lawyer turned minister. After spending time at the Armour Mission in Chicago and noting the conditions in Chicago's many saloons, he returned to Ohio in 1893 and founded the Ohio Anti-Saloon League. The League's initial efforts in the late 1890s consisted of temperance pledge drives but were soon supplemented with sophisticated political and legislative efforts. Fueled by the financial support of rural Methodists, Bible Belt Baptists, Presbyterians, Congregationalists and several smaller fundamentalist sects, the Anti-Saloon League, now spearheaded by the efforts of Wayne Wheeler, the League's national lawyer, led forces to defeat the reelection of Governor M.T. Herrick of Ohio. Herrick had taken a strong stand against a *local option* campaign in the state, making him an easy target for the new, well financed aggressiveness of the League. Local option allowed petitioners in any precinct, ward, city or county to place a prohibition referendum on any ballot, a powerful tool for early prohibitionists. The League's well financed efforts defeated Herrick by almost 43,000 votes.[1]

Flushed with their first important political victory, Wheeler's forces moved on to larger cities, including Chicago. Their efforts began to exhibit a class and philosophical struggle between puritanical ruralists and the wicked inhabitants of the big city. Chicago was, to the small town mentality of League followers, a center of depravity close to the League's strongholds. It was a city of immigrants who spoke little or no English, where political graft, gambling and prostitution were common. These foreigners, felt the League's members, also brought their dangerous religious institutions with them including the seditious teachings of the papist Roman Catholic Church and the equally menacing philosophy of the Germanic Lutheran churches. A rural, small-minded perception took hold of the Anti-Saloon League that clearly reflected the xenophobic leanings shared by its membership.

Their central focus of attack upon arriving in Chicago was the brewery-controlled and independent saloons. Prohibitionists narrowed their aims and targeted Sunday saloon closings as their first objective in imposing their puritanical views on the big city heathens. In spite of a long standing state law ruling otherwise, saloons in Chicago traditionally remained open on Sundays. The Know-Nothing character of the prohibitionists' initial efforts was not lost on the German-American brewers, many of whom still had strong ties to Europe and recalled the old stories of Chicago's Lager Beer Riot of 1855 and the rebuffed 1873 efforts of Mayor Medill to close local saloons on Sundays.

Chicago city authorities initially resisted the growing pressures of the Anti-Saloon League and others like the Evanston, Illinois-based Women's Christian Temperance Union to do something about the social problems associated with the saloons and their breweries. Mayor Carter Harrison Jr.'s relationship with the Chicago brewing community had become extremely amiable, as had been his father's, despite a frothy beginning. Having mimicked the political savvy of his father during his five term mayoral reign, the younger Harrison would initially be accused by local reform groups of catering to the drink industry. In a sign of solidarity with Chicago's brewers, Harrison led the Grand March of the local brewmaster association's annual ball in 1903. He was attuned to the political strength of the brewers and distanced himself from reformers.[2] The mayor, often referred to by the German brewery owners as "Unser (our) Carter," knew that there was no political practicality in upsetting the considerable flow of tax revenue that poured into the city coffers from the activities of the breweries and their tied-houses.

The Brewers and their Saloon Connection

Nonetheless, political and community activists increased pressure on the brewers and city aldermen to clean up the local saloon industry. A special report by the Chicago City Council in 1904 detailed some of the violations that had led to revocations of liquor licenses in 1903:

> Allowing or conducting a gambling business on the saloon premises or as an annex to the saloon; permitting the saloon to be a resort and refuge for dissolute women, thieves, pickpockets, gamblers and confidence men; allowing men to be lured to the

At the intersection of Lincoln, Belmont and Ashland Avenues, the Independent Brewing Association's saloon selling Prima beer competed with the saloon selling the Schoenhofen Brewery's Edelweiss beer. Photograph circa 1916. Courtesy of *the Ravenswood-Lake View Historical Society.*

> saloon, drugged, robbed and assaulted; conducting depraving 'vaudeville' exhibitions in connection with saloon and allowing girls under age to appear; . . . being implicated in the collection of police 'protection' money from women in the street and being the landlord or renting agent of rooms used for immoral purposes. . . .[3]

Though damning in many ways, the report did go out of its way to acknowledge the important functions that many neighborhood saloons provided for working-class Chicagoans.

Feeling the public pressure to start a public relations campaign to disassociate themselves from the more disorderly saloons, the brewery owners' early efforts lacked focus, often taking one step forward and two steps back. In 1904, Mayor Harrison refused a liquor license for a saloon to be opened next to the Lyman Trumbull School on Division Street. An appellate court ruling, soon after Harrison's license refusal, decided that the Mayor of Chicago, in spite of his recent action, did not have the discretionary power to refuse a license for a saloon wanting to open next to a church or school. A number of local brewers soon made it known that they were ready to take advantage of this appellate ruling and establish saloons in the vicinity of local schools, prompting even the *American Brewers' Review* to question the sanity of such a move:

> No matter what may be the letter of the law, it is quite well understood that the people as a general thing are opposed to saloons near schools, as for fifteen years Chicago's mayors have acted upon that public sentiment . . . Will the brewers stir up a hornet's nest when there is no call for any more saloons to dispose of their product in a profitable manner? [4]

To make matters worse, yellow press charges that saloons and their owners were involved with murder, white slavery, prostitution, gambling and underage drinking became everyday fare in the local papers, further strengthening the resolve of reformers and prohibitionists while creating an increasingly uncomfortable position for Chicago's brewers.

Comfort Stations

For better or for worse, the everyday operations of many of the city saloons were inexplicably tied to the daily activities of the average Chicago citizen. Taking advantage of the new transit system, saloons started to spring up along major arterial routes, offering a brief respite between trolley or train transfers for increasingly mobile Chicagoans. The placement of saloons at busy intersections was a source of irritation to the dry forces but the saloons often were the only place where a traveler could find a toilet, warm up when cold or get a cool drink during the summer months. And if the weary traveler stopped for a beer, so much the better.

In a public relations coup for city brewers, the owners of the Schoenhofen Brewery opened a public comfort station in 1909 at Schoenhofen Park in conjunction with the city. The idea of public toilets and drinking fountains at trolley transfer points had been one originally suggested by reformers. This would allow commuters the option of using a comfort station rather than entering a saloon for relief and succumbing to the temptations of a cool draft beer. The brewery-maintained comfort station was built in a small triangular area located in front of the brewery. The concept was the idea of Joseph Theurer, Schoenhofen's president.

The original construction plan called for a fountain to be erected as the centerpiece of the park. When the fountain, which represented a stork family in repose, arrived for setup and display, the Municipal Art Commission rejected it, noting that the stork was "a foreign bird," common in the northern parts of Germany. Mayor Busse dismissed the commission's objection and gave the go ahead for the fountain's erection. Total cost for the comfort station was $5000, with the land, the disputed fountain, comfort facilities, and $2000 donated by the brewery. At any other time, the objection by the commission to Schoenhofen's fountain might have seemed merely an annoying bureaucratic occurrence, perhaps even a legitimate difference in aesthetic taste, but there was an anti-German sentiment behind the commission's move, a sentiment that would soon become an effective weapon in the burgeoning arsenal of local prohibitionist forces.[5]

Saloons and the Working-Class

But the saloons were more than just comfort stations. For the working-class and the newly arrived immigrants, saloons often acted as informal employment agencies, providing information about open positions in the nearby factories. In the many brewery-controlled or owned saloons, the brewers customarily supplied the necessary funds to cash the checks of appreciative workers who would respond with the purchase of a round or two of beer. Perry Duis, in his book, *The Saloon. Public Drinking in Boston and Chicago: 1880–1920*, reports of one saloon at 43rd and Ashland, directly west of the Stockyards, that cashed over $40,000 worth of paychecks each month for workers. The backroom of the neighborhood saloon in the ethnic enclaves was often used by local residents as a gathering place for weddings and after burial ceremonies, especially in the predominately Irish Back-of-the-Yards and Bridgeport communities. For the average workingman, often abused in an industrial non-union environment of debilitating twelve hour work days, the saloon could be a place of respite and solitude. "He don't want to go home," observed social satirist Finley Peter Dunne through his all-wise Mister Dooley. "There ought to be wan place where th' poor wurrukin'-man can escape being patted on the back," Dunne's mythical Irish barkeep observed. For all the bad that came from a few Chicago saloons, many of the others served important functions in the outlying neighborhoods and were fixtures in the lives of average Chicago citizens.[6]

In the minds of reformers, the evil of the saloon far outweighed any perceived benefits to the local population. Efforts in 1905 by Anti-Saloon League forces, joined by some opportunist local civic and religious leaders, to pressure Mayor Edward F. Dunne into closing saloons on Sundays, once again proved fruitless. The Mayor duly noted that the people of Chicago had decided that question by vote years ago. Surprisingly, the normally conservative *Chicago Tribune* commented favorably on the wisdom of Dunne's position. In the years that followed, the newspaper would continue to assume a wet attitude in its editorials.[7]

In December of the same year, the *American Brewers' Review* wrote of the Anti-Saloon League's increasing efforts to support local option bills, recognizing the League's ultimate goal. It warned, "By taking a little at a time they expect to accomplish . . . prohibition. . ." The editorial labeled the League "the most dangerous enemy the brewing trade ever had."[8] A later unmasking of the true nature of the League's intent would prove the editorial prophetic, for it would soon be demonstrated in Chicago and the rest of the country that the intent of the Anti-Saloon League was much more than the mere implementation of saloon closings on Sundays.

Some members of the local brewing community were fighting back in their own small ways. *The Western Brewer* reported that Adam Ortseifen, president of the Chicago Breweries, Ltd., had begun a letter-writing campaign to refute mounting arguments sent to city newspapers by prohibitionist organizations advocating saloon closings, arguments that had previously gone unchallenged. In the face of the growing strength of local prohibitionist forces, this sporadic and uncoordinated effort by a few local brewers would prove ineffectual.

Liquor License Fee Increased

By January of 1906, the efforts of reformers to shut down or limit the number of saloons in Chicago had finally stirred the political sensitivities of some local politicians. Following this reform trend, the Chicago newspapers began a series of articles suggesting the doubling of the current $500 liquor license fee. The *Chicago Record-Herald* of February 3, 1906 headlined the "huge array of sentiment for saloon permits at $1000" and suggested that the increase in revenue could be used to hire additional policemen. Any alderman who voted against the increase was warned that he would be "... condemned at the polls ..."

Initially, it seemed that brewers would naturally suffer from any sort of license fee increase. Their ownership of citywide saloons was strong and any license increase would directly affect them. However, the whole campaign was actually led by wet Chicago aldermen and the local brewery and liquor interests to prevent the more conservative Illinois General Assembly from increasing the liquor license fee much more than the proposed $1000. Illusions of saloon reform in Chicago did have a price and the local brewers were willing to pay it. The fee increase also served the dual purpose of temporarily appeasing the prohibitionist forces who had become more vocal and efficient in their latest round of anti-drink efforts.[9]

The $1000 liquor license fee passed the City Council and went into effect on May 1, 1906. 1,354 of Chicago's 7600 saloons closed soon thereafter, mostly in the poorer neighborhoods. Things looked worse for the brewers and their retail outlets a few months later when alderman Daniel Harkin, representing one of the more affluent wards, introduced an ordinance freezing the number of liquor licenses to a ratio of 500 citizens per permit. When the ordinance took effect, license number 7,353 would be the last license issued under the new ratio limit. The next license could not be issued until the city's population had doubled.[10]

As with the Harper High License Act of 1883, the poorly conceived Harkin Law had a much different effect on the number of liquor licenses than the lawmakers had intended. Because of the finite number of licenses available, a Chicago liquor license now had a premium value of around $150 over cost. The Chicago brewers took advantage of this unintended phenomenon and quickly applied for additional licenses before the law went into effect on July 31, 1906. This temporary loophole pushed the number of outstanding licenses to 8,097, or one for every 239 men, women and children in the city.[11] The local brewers also purchased many of the 900 or so licenses now available in the premium market, transferred to them by independent saloon owners unable or unwilling to pay the $1000 fee.

Brewery control over Chicago's saloons was now overwhelming. There could be no mistake or denial; any problems associated with Chicago's saloons would clearly be the responsibility of the city brewers.

The uncomfortable issue of saloon reform was brought up in an Illinois State Brewers' Association meeting in early 1906. Rather than paint the situation in a pessimistic light, the brewers concurred that some practical measures certainly were needed to resolve the situation. A moment after the initial discussion had begun, however, Charles Vopicka of Atlas Brewing motioned to continue the ineffectual committee on saloon regulations and control for another year and quickly moved on to other business. The swiftness of the gathering in affirming the motion proved to be nothing more than lip service from the brewers to a problem that was becoming unmanageable. The problem, however, must have gnawed on the consciences of some of the more enlightened participants in the I.B.A. meeting. A representative of the Conrad Seipp Brewery later conceded that ten percent of the saloons in Chicago, almost 800 of them, were "objectionable." [12]

For the growing financial needs of the city of Chicago, the implementation of the liquor license fee increase and the brewers' frenzy to purchase additional licenses resulted in a revenue windfall. In just one day, the receipts of the license office reached $478,500. Final receipts for the semi-annual liquor license fee of $500 eventually totaled over $3,500,000.[13]

Bottled Beer Consumption Increases

As the overall number of saloons initially diminished, then surged again in Chicago after the institution of the $1000 license fee, a new pattern of beer drinking began to unfold behind the closed doors of Chicago's homes and tenements. Beer sales dramatically increased, bolstered by the convenience of bottled beer, allowing men *and* women to now drink in the privacy of their homes. Heretofore, the practice of women drinking in saloons was frowned upon. If properly escorted by a husband or gentleman, a respectable woman could make use of the discreet family entrance located on the side of select corner saloons and then take her refreshments at a table with her escort, but this was the exception rather than the rule.

With the availability of bottled beer, it now became quite practical for the man of the house to pick up a case or two of beer from his local saloon or, in most instances, purchase beer directly from the neighborhood brewery. The brewers used this steady increase in bottled beer consumption and the corresponding decrease in liquor sales as proof of their perennial argument that beer was a recognized temperance drink, a "drink of moderation."[14] Their argument that beer was a benign, healthful refreshment unlike the stronger, debilitating liquor, would eventually drive a wedge between the distillers and the brewers at a time when unity against prohibitionists should have been paramount.

Horse drawn wagons delivered bottled beer to customers who telephoned breweries from their homes. Here the wagon is delivering Gambrinus beer. Courtesy of the American Breweriana Journal, *September-October, 1997, 30.*

The rising consumption of bottled beer was also alarmingly noted by reform groups. In an attempt to stir up public opinion against the city government's blind acceptance of its segregated areas of vice, such as the near South Side's notorious Levee District, a number of startling claims were made by reformers. These claims managed to bring the existence of the vice districts to the front pages of the local newspapers and the attention of the average Chicagoan. The reformers' investigation also suggested a link between the brewers and prostitution in the Levee District, fueled by an embarrassing estimate that over 27,000,000 bottles of beer had been served by the madams of the Levee's numerous whore houses during the preceding year.[15]

Dry Referendum

Enraged by the unexpected outcome of the new high license fee and the Harkin ordinance, the Illinois chapter of the Anti-Saloon League pushed through a bill in the state legislature to establish home rule in Chicago in 1907. This measure, it was hoped by prohibitionists, would be the instrument to further the cause of local option and ultimately, city-wide prohibition. In the meantime, Mayor Busse rebuked another delegation from the Sunday Closing League, declaring "If the saloons of Chicago are closed on Sunday, it must be without my aid . . ."[16]

Eventual passing of home rule and the implementation of local option did dry up neighborhood saloons in some wards as aldermen bowed to the wishes of their constituents. As a further demonstration of their resolve, anti-drink forces organized a prohibition march in Chicago on September 26, 1908. Newspapers estimated that 6000 to 10,000 people marched; prohibition supporters, naturally, claimed a higher figure. Whatever the number, local politicians were once again forced to take notice of the increasing strength of the prohibitionist bloc.[17]

In March of 1909, in an address before the Chicago Section of the Society of Brewing Technology, Henry E. O. Heinemann, editor of the *American Brewers' Review*, spoke of the very real threat of prohibition and the drink question. "I cannot bring myself to look upon it (prohibition movement) as a mere passing wave." He reiterated an earlier warning from the editorial pages of the *A.B.R.* that the true purpose of the Anti-Saloon League was not to simply shut down the saloons on Sunday or limit their number, but to ultimately achieve "suppression of the entire drink traffic. "

Chicago brewers now had a real reason to worry. Bending to the wishes of their constituencies, two-thirds of Chicago's precincts were now dry as the result of local option. Fortunately for brewers and some saloonkeepers, the City Council allowed saloons in dry precincts to remain open along major commercial streets, still sparing the residential areas from the saloons. But if one wanted to get a drink in Chicago, one still could. In the working class community of Bridgeport, travelling south down Halsted Street from the northern border of the neighborhood, starting near the banks of the Chicago River to the southern end of the 4600 block, skirting the western edges of the Chicago Stockyards, 62 legally licensed saloons were open for business with no dearth of customers. The restrictions of local option banned the sale and consumption of alcohol in saloons; it did not, however, prohibit the act of drinking, as evidenced by Chicago crime statistics for 1908. Of the 68,220 total arrests for the year, 40,875 were for drunkenness-related occurrences.[18]

The warnings of the *American Brewers' Review* almost became a sobering reality in Chicago when a petition with 74,805 signatures was presented to the city election board in 1910 in support of a city-wide referendum on the prohibition question. But a careful examination of the signatures led to an estimate of at least 25,000 fraudulent entries on the petition. As a result, the election board decided to omit the question from the ballot.[19]

In spite of the celebratory posturing of the local brewers in blunting this latest attack by prohibitionists, a poem by Charles Frederic in the March, 1910 issue of the *Western Brewer* seemed to indicate a sense of resigned fatalism by some members of the local brewing community:

When Chicago goes dry,
As they say that it will,
When no more you and I
By our fire when it's chill
Our glasses may fill
And the winter defy,
What joy shall instill
When Chicago goes dry?

When Chicago goes dry,
And the summertime heat
Turns to brass in the sky
And to fire in the street,
When a-weary we meet
And for comfort we sigh
Then what solace shall greet
When Chicago goes dry?

When Chicago goes dry,
And the neighbors come in
Then a stein foaming high
Will, alas, be a sin.
We their friendship to win
With cold water must try,
But 'twill seem awful thin
When Chicago goes dry.

When Chicago goes dry
What a horrible thirst
Then will spread far and nigh
From the 'Steenth to the First!
Why, I think I will burst
And I know I will die—
Oh, I fear for the worst
When Chicago goes dry!

When Chicago goes dry,
As at present the scheme,
Then old State Street so spry,
Like Sahara will seem.
We will slumber and dream
While the business goes by—
For New York gets the cream
When Chicago goes dry.

When Chicago goes dry,
And no glasses may clink,
When we give a black eye
To the demon of drink,
We'll be longing, I think,
Something wetter to try—
For our business will shrink
When Chicago goes dry.

When Chicago goes dry,
What will other folks do?
Well, the world will not cry
And the world will not stew,
We will sink out of view
While the world hurries by
To some market that's new
When Chicago goes dry.

When Chicago goes dry,
Then the man with the grip
He will gives us a sigh
And will give us the slip
And, on railroad or ship,
To some haven will fly
Where his Beer he may sip
When Chicago goes dry.

When Chicago goes dry—
But a secret I've heard
That was told on the sly
By a wise little bird;
And he says it's absurd,
That the tricks folks will try
That have elsewhere occurred,
When Chicago goes dry.

When Chicago goes dry,
And the cupboard is bare
Folks will drink on the sly
What is now on the square.
And it's better, I swear,
In the open to buy
Than a mask thus to wear
When Chicago goes dry.

When Chicago goes *dry*
We shall owe such a debt
To those people who try
All our courses to set!
Yet I know we will sigh,
We who wanted it wet,
When Chicago goes *dry*—
But it hasn't—NOT YET![20]

Additional city-wide prohibition referendums were attempted in early 1911 and 1914, but these efforts also fell through.

Controversial Visits

Chicago wets had thus far shown stiff resistance to the increasing assaults by local prohibitionists. Arthur Burrage Farwell, leading the Chicago forces of the Anti-Saloon League, was looking for an influential figure to help further the local dry cause and strengthen their political position at home. Inexplicably, Farwell approached the visiting Samuel Gompers, president of the American Federation of Labor, and solicited his support of the "cause," suggesting he address a local meeting of the Anti-Saloon League.

Targeting Gompers for help was a naïve choice by Farwell. Unionism was sweeping the nation, buoyed by the millions of newly arrived ethnics, especially the hordes of lager loving Germans. Prohibitionists had already displayed xenophobic tendencies, not lost on the newly arrived foreign element. For the hundreds of thousands of foreign-born Chicagoans, prohibition equaled nativism.

Gompers knew where his support came from and brusquely refused Farwell's overture. The union leader noted that his travels throughout the country had demonstrated to him that prohibition was a failure. "I told Mr. Farwell that I could not consent to endorse local option and appear at the meeting because I am not in sympathy with the movement," he told Chicago reporters. Following the standard wet argument, he went on. "Proper regulation of the liquor traffic is much more effective than the abolishment of saloons under the local option or prohibition laws."

Speaking of his observations in the state of Maine, dry since 1851, Gompers pointed out the hypocrisy and futility of prohibition as he saw it. "There is not a city in Maine where you cannot go openly and get all the whiskey you want and all the beer you want. I have seen some drunken people in my life, but I have never seen drunks so drunkenly drunk as those in Maine."[21]

Rebuffed by Gompers and needing to make a show of strength in Chicago, the national forces of the Anti-Saloon League stepped into temporary control of the local league chapter. They used the planned attendance of Secretary of Agriculture, James Wilson in October of 1911 at the Second International Brewers' Congress in Chicago as a platform to dissuade President Taft from seemingly lending any sort of approval to the brewing industry. Taft received a written protest from Homer C. Stunts, First Assistant Corresponding Secretary of the Board of Foreign Missions of the New York Methodist Episcopal Church in early September. "I hope you will find it in your power to induce him (Wilson) to refrain from relating his name, in any official relationship, to that liquor organization . . . As I see it, such a step would be giving an entirely needless amount of comfort to the brewing interests . . ."[22] The Department of Agriculture nervously reported to the President that it was receiving 50 to 60 letters a day in protest of Secretary Wilson's scheduled appearance at the brewing convention. Despite the pressure from the League, Taft ignored the campaign and Wilson participated as the honorary president of the Brewers' Congress. Secretary of Agriculture Wilson later reported to Taft that "my judgment is that the best has been done that could be done, and there where a friend to you may have been lost I am well satisfied one, if not more, has been gained." As to threats by the Anti-Saloon League to retaliate against Taft's stand at the polling place, Wilson was of the opinion that "(they) do not vote the Republican ticket anyway, and some do not vote the Democratic ticket. They vote the Prohibition ticket. These people are the noisiest."[23] Taft was defeated in the next presidential election.

Bottled versus Draft

Rebuffed in their persistent attempts to close city saloons on Sundays, local prohibitionists did manage to score a small victory in 1913 when the *Chicago American* and the *Record-Herald* newspapers refused to accept further advertising from beer and liquor interests.[24] Newspaper advertising had become an important vehicle for the local brewers since the turn of the century. Milwaukee's aggressive Pabst had led the way in utilizing the local press to push their products. The brewers made an end run around this move by stepping up an ad campaign of outdoor billboard signs and ads in the smaller ethnic newspapers.

The Peter Schoenhofen Brewing Company began running a series of light-hearted, one panel cartoons in the Chicago *Abendpost* newspaper, with the implied message that things went better with their Edelweiss Beer. Milwaukee's Jos. Schlitz Brewing Company took a more serious approach in their German newspaper ads, hammering out the message that their beer, bottled since 1911 in amber bottles, was far superior in taste and more healthful than rival brands still using clear bottles. But it was Anheuser-Busch that took the sophisticated approach of catering to the different ethnic groups that lived in Chicago. In their "*National Hero Series*," AB's ads featured glowing tributes to William Wallace—"Scotland's Great Patriot," and his struggles against ". . . England's tyrannous rule," and days later praised Leif Ericsson, "The Discoverer of America," and the ". . . liberty-loving sons and daughters of Sweden, Norway and Denmark." After AB's demographically-niched appeals to these various Chicago tribes, the brewery ads would all end with a nod to the sensibilities of ". . . these great lovers of Personal Liberty" and harshly criticize any attempts by anyone to enforce ". . . Prohibitory Laws . . ." While every rival brewery seemed to skirt the issue, the Busch family wasn't afraid to take a strong public stand on prohibition.

Both local and out-of-town breweries also increased the delivery of bottled beer from the brewery or depot, direct to the customer's front door, even to city precincts that had voted themselves dry. In these wards, delivery from the local brewery to a home in a dry precinct was perfectly legal. Those moralists who publicly decried the dangers of saloons in their own neighborhoods could still settle back at the end of the day with a cool beer at home, all the while digressing on the "saloon problem." All it took was a telephoned order to the local brewery for a case or two of bottled beer. The result was a further weakening of saloon sales as the majority of sales of bottled beer now came directly from the breweries.

Despite the fact that business in the local saloon industry was slowing down, total consumption of beer in Chicago continued to increase.[25] The saloonkeepers stood helplessly by as the brewers siphoned off their declining profits with increased off-premise sales. As retail saloon sales continued to tumble, so did the liquor license premium, dropping from a high of $2800 to zero in 1915.[26]

Saloons were not the only business suffering from the effects of bottled beer sales. Smaller breweries that failed or could not afford to establish bottling lines could only watch as bottled beer gained in popularity and their draft sales further declined. The slim profit margins of brewing now discouraged the use of independent bottling outfits. Between 1910 and 1918, twelve small to mid-sized breweries closed in Chicago as bottled beer continued to gain greater acceptance.[27]

Thompson's Betrayal

Throughout the years of continuing assault by the Anti-Saloon League and other local prohibitionist forces on the local drink trade, the United Societies for Local Self-Government, led by local politician Anton Cermak, had spearheaded the drive to beat back their efforts. The United Societies had helped defeat earlier city-wide referendums advocating prohibition by demanding a close inspection of signatures on submitted petitions by prohibitionists. They claimed responsibility for the election of a wet Cook County State's Attorney and had continuously fought off any efforts to impose the Sunday closing law. The organization was a buttress against Anti-Saloon League efforts and was considered a powerful political force in Chicago politics.

In 1915, Republican mayoral candidate William Hale Thompson had agreed to sign a United Societies' pledge not to close saloons on Sundays in return for Cermak's and the United Societies' much needed support. Thompson's move infuriated local prohibitionists. After Thompson won the election, however, he began to have second thoughts about the pledge, especially after rumors prevailed that a grand jury was about to investigate his non-enforcement of the state-mandated Sunday closing of saloons. States Attorney Hoyne, a Cermak loyalist, had gone so far as to publicly admit that an indictment and possible impeachment of Thompson had been discussed by a reformist-led grand jury.

On October 4, 1915, Thompson and his entourage were headed by rail to the Panama Pacific Exposition in San Francisco when the City Collector read a startling mayoral proclamation to the City Council. By mayoral decree, beginning on October 9, 1915, all 7152 Chicago saloons would be closed on Sundays. Any attempt to ignore the order to close would be met with a fine not to exceed $200. More importantly, violators could also have their liquor license rescinded by Thompson. Cermak and his supporters were stunned. "I wish there were an election for mayor tomorrow and I were running against Thompson," said a seething Cermak.[28]

Thompson's Reasons for the Closings

En route to San Francisco, Thompson initially explained to reporters that he was simply following the advice of the City Corporation Counsel. "When the Corporation Counsel told me it was the law, why, then, I made the decision."[29] When former Mayor Carter Harrison, Jr. was asked his view of Thompson's order, he cited home rule, presuming that the people of Chicago wanted the saloons to stay open on Sunday. Edgar Tolman, who had served as Corporation Counsel under Harrison, was later asked by a reporter why he had not similarly advised Harrison in the matter of Sunday closings, Tolman declared that he had never given the issue any study while in office; no one had ever asked him to. F. Scott McBride, state superintendent of the Anti-Saloon League, naturally characterized the order as a great victory and added, "Chicago, I believe, will soon be totally dry."[30]

Sunday Closings, Part III

Cermak forwarded a copy of Thompson's signed pledge to keep the Chicago saloons open on Sunday to the *Chicago Tribune* for publication, hoping to discredit the mayor. Thompson admitted that he had indeed signed the pledge but stated once again that he had to enforce the law. The state law banning the Sunday opening of saloons had been passed in 1851. Aside from rebuked attempts to close them in 1855 and 1873, Chicago mayors had followed a benign policy of non-enforcement. In the last few years, however, the burgeoning efforts to close saloons on Sunday had become a festering political irritant, culminating with Thompson's order.

The validity of the mayor's action in 1915 had been legally established years earlier, but no Chicago mayor had acted upon it. In 1906, Reverend William A. Bartlett, pastor of the old First Congregational Church, initiated a lawsuit against then Mayor Dunne to enforce the state-mandated Sunday blue law and specifically attacked Alderman Michael "Hinky Dink" Kenna's saloon in his suit. The suit went to the state Supreme Court in 1909 where it was ruled that the Sunday closing law was indeed in effect in Chicago as it was throughout the entire state. The court also opined that enforcement of the law was the duty of the Mayor of Chicago.

Coinciding with Barlett's Sunday-closing campaign was one by the Chicago Law and Order League which had attacked the state charters of the Great Northern and Congress Hotels for violating the Sunday blue law. These suits were eventually dismissed but caused the voluntary closings of the bars of the Windemer, Palmer, Blackstone, Grand Pacific and Virginia Hotels on Sundays. Mayor Dunne had continued to ignore the implications of the court ruling, but not Thompson.[31]

When questioned further about his motives for the Sunday closings, Thompson finally admitted that he had heard the rumors of his possible indictment for failure to uphold the state law on Sunday saloon closings, but insisted that that was not why he acted. The mayor's aides suggested that the move was political, an attempt to win over the reform forces that had previously criticized him and his administration, and a move which might ultimately lead to the presidency.[32]

On the first dry Sunday in Chicago since the days of Mayor Medill and the reformist efforts of the Committee of Seventy, the city appeared relatively quiet. Of the 7152 dram shops in Chicago, only 28 violations of the blue law were reported. Scores of saloonkeepers, though, bemoaned the Sunday closing. For many of them, Sunday was their biggest day.

Alderman "Hinky Dink" Kenna warned that the closings would leave thousands of people without comfort stations on Sundays. "The city has one comfort station," [at Schoenhofen Park], Kenna observed. "Sunday is the only day in the week on which many people can visit friends. If they live at a distance, street cars are used for transportation." Transfer points were usually located on corners as were many of the saloons. Kenna estimated that at least 100,000 people used saloons daily during their commute for purposes other than drinking. "Some of them make use of the place as a comfort station and don't spend a nickel."[33]

Habeas Corpus Anderson

Twenty-two saloon owners tried to get a temporary court injunction against Thompson's order, using the services of William G. "Habeas Corpus" Anderson. Anderson had gained local fame years earlier by defending Captain George Streeter, a defiant squatter who had claimed a parcel of land on the shores of Lake Michigan, formed from the rubble of the Great Fire. In an argument that spoke of the realities of city saloons and their relationship with Chicago's ethnically-dominated citizenry, the African-American lawyer eloquently pointed out to the court the diversity of customs that many of Chicago's foreign-born citizens embraced and the importance to them of the neighborhood saloon.

"Take the stockyards district for instance. There are hundreds of thousands of persons of foreign birth in that district, taxpayers and voters who have customs peculiar to their nationality such as the holding of weddings on Sunday in the rear of the saloons. I dare say there are 500,000 persons in Chicago who believe in that custom," Anderson argued. Without libations, many of these celebrations would be without their customary toast to the celebrants. The court, however, refused his moving appeal for an injunction against the Sunday closing law.[34]

Caught in the middle of Thompson's closing order and its effect on Chicago's many ethnic groups was City Clerk John Siman. City law required that permit applications for festivities running from Saturday night through 3 a.m. on Sundays be submitted at least two weeks before the event took place. City Collector Charles Forsberg had recently approved over 100 applications for such permits for upcoming events, signed by the heads of local Polish, Bohemian, German and Italian social clubs. With Thompson's order, Siman expected trouble. "The enforcement of the Sunday closing will certainly stir up a rumpus in my office. These applications have been approved," admitted Siman. "But since their approval, the mayor has directed that the Sunday closing law be enforced beginning at 12 o'clock midnight next Saturday."

Collector Forsberg was also feeling the heat. A manager of the North Side Turner Hall demanded to speak with the City Collector to personally plead his case. "We have sold hundreds of tickets for a dance next Sunday," he lamented. "The people who bought those tickets expect that we will run a bar. If we cannot have a bar permit between midnight Saturday and midnight Sunday, closed tight for twenty-four hours, then there will be nothing for us to do but close up."[35]

The Brewers React

Throughout the initial uproar of the Sunday closings, surprisingly little was heard from the ranks of the Chicago brewing community. After Thompson had ordered the closings, deputy commissioner of public works Billy Burkhardt, told reporters of a conversation he had had with Tom Chamales, owner of the Green Mill restaurant and bar, about the closings. Chamales had casually remarked that "It would be a big boost for the sale of bottle beer." Some brewers had also appreciated that fact. Within days after the closing order, Milwaukee's Blatz began aggressively advertising in some local papers, promising same day delivery of bottled beer from their Chicago branch. With a telephone call, one could order a case or two of Private Stock, the ads noting that "... it will be appreciated SUNDAY by your family and friends." Local breweries soon followed the out-of-town brewery's lead. Would-be entrepreneurs made ready with their own Sunday delivery services from local breweries in case the breweries were unable to ensure prompt deliveries. It was another sales blow for the saloons but a windfall for brewers as a sense of urgency gripped customers. Picking up a case of beer for the weekend started to become an unbreakable Chicago habit.[36]

The Wet Parade

Anton Cermak and his United Societies finally responded to Thompson's actions on November 7, 1915, with a parade of 50,000 to 70,000 marchers, viewed by over 750,000, some of them wearing lapel buttons declaring "Personal Liberty!" With thousands of participants carrying banners and placards declaring "Why pick on Sunday, the workingman's holiday?" and "Don't take the Sun out of Sunday," reporters noted that this wet parade was at least five times larger than the dry parade organized by Thompson's forces after the mayor's return from California.

The huge pro-drink crowd had a definite ethnic flavor to it, described as ". . . one of the most remarkable demonstrations of Chicago's 'melting pot' product in the city's whole history." German Turner societies, Luxemburger societies, Schwabian Vereins, Saxonian Vereins, Austrian-Hungarian societies, the Deutsche Wacht, the German Mutual Aid society, the Deutscher Unterstuetzunge Bund, the Rheinische Verein, United Swiss societies, the Militaere und Deutscher Krieger Vereins, the Twenty-second Ward Liberty League, the Business Men's Liberty League, the Romanian societies and the Twenty-fourth Ward Personal Liberty League led contingents of the parade. The North Side Division elicited the most approval from the enthusiastic crowds. As the German-American organization passed by the Michigan Avenue reviewing stand, the crowd started to chant "The Goose step! The Goose step!" The members of the reviewing stand, including representatives of the United Societies' executive committee and various wet advocates of the Chicago City Council, leapt merrily to their feet as the contingent obligingly snapped to the distinctive Germanic style of march. Soon, the idea of uniformed German paramilitary organizations goose-stepping down Michigan Avenue would be abhorrent to the average Chicagoan who knew about the sinking of the "Lusitania." But in this time of protest and beery celebration, the *Chicago Tribune* breathlessly described the goose-stepping demonstration as ". . . a spectacle, it was one of the biggest things ever seen in Chicago's streets."

Beer drinking Chicagoans of all nationalities had forcefully demonstrated that they wanted their Sunday beer, but the city saloons remained closed on the Sabbath. Cook County towns just outside the city of Chicago reported land office business in their local saloons following the wet parade as participants made for the less restrictive Sunday environment of wide-open towns like Cicero and Burnham. The issue of Sunday closings would slowly fade away as police continued to enforce the blue law.[37]

Concessions from the Brewers

Responding to the persistent efforts of prohibitionists to close Chicago's saloons, the brewing community made a conciliatory gesture that seemed to indicate a now enlightened sense of awareness by the brewers for the need to implement saloon reform. The Chicago Brewers' Association belatedly announced in mid-1917 that Chicago brewers were elevating the standards surrounding the retail sale of their products, a move that former Mayor Carter H. Harrison had proposed to a delegation of local brewery leaders two decades earlier. William Legner, head of the association, noted that the brewers' goal was "... to place the licensed places where their product is sold on such a basis of respectable conduct that the community will have no cause to complain of their existence ..." As the revenue from local beer sales increasingly came from bottled beer and direct brewery sales, the brewers could afford to assume such a magnanimous stance at the expense of the battered saloon industry. Economically and politically, saloons now were simply more trouble than they were worth to Chicago's brewers. [38]

But the efforts of the Anti-Saloon League and other dry elements wouldn't stop with Sunday closings. With every victory, prohibitionists demanded more. The entrance of the United States in 1917 into the hostilities in Europe and the growing resentment towards German-Americans had fostered a persistent question of the brewing community's loyalty to the United States. In Washington, where congressmen were succumbing to the political intimidation and lobbying efforts of the League, there was talk of a food control bill, perhaps limiting or stopping the use of grain for the production of alcoholic beverages during wartime conditions.

The issues of local option, Sunday closings and saloon reform were beginning to take a back seat to the more frightful possibility of the end of the drink trade, not only in Chicago, but in the entire United States.

Notes

1. Thomas R. Pegram. *Battling Demon Rum. The Struggle for a Dry America. 1800–1933.* (Chicago, IL: Ivan R. Dee, 1998) pp. 113–121.

2. *American Brewers' Review*, March, 1903.

3. *Report of The Special Investigating Committee of The City Council*, Chicago, March 7, 1904.

4. *American Brewers' Review*, January, 1906.

5. *American Brewers' Review*, August, 1907.

6. Perry R. Duis. *The Saloon. Public Drinking in Chicago and Boston, 1880–1920.* (Urbana, IL: University of Illinois Press, 1983) pp. 181–183; Finley Peter Dunne. *Dissertations by Mr. Dooley.* (New York, NY: Harper & Brothers Publishers, 1906) "The Bar," p. 312; Martin Dooley, the Sage of Archey Road, began appearing in the *Chicago Post* in 1893. The columns proved wildly popular, both in Chicago and in national newspapers. A number of books contain Dooley columns on peace, war, and life.

7. *The Western Brewer*, November, 1905.

8. *American Brewers' Review*, December, 1905.

9. *Chicago Record-Herald*, Feb. 3–28, 1906; *Chicago Tribune*, May 6, 1906.

10. Duis, *op. cit.*, p.259; *American Brewers' Review*, September, 1906.

11. Duis., *op. cit.*, p. 260.

12. *American Brewers' Review*, February, 1906; Pegram, *op. cit.*, p. 97.

13. *The Western Brewer*, May, 1907.

14. *American Brewers' Review*, June, 1907.

15. Finis Farr. *Chicago A Personal History of America's Most American City.* (New Rochelle, NY: Arlington House, 1973) p. 308.

16. *The Western Brewer*, December, 1907.

17. *Chicago Tribune*, September 27, 1908.

18. *List of Licensed Saloons in the City of Chicago.* Chicago, July 1, 1908; *Chicago, Illinois Crime Statistics* 1860–1920. Illinois State Archives

19. *The Western Brewer*, February and April, 1910.

20. *The Western Brewer*, March, 1910.

21. *Ibid.*, March 1910.

22. H. C. Stunts to William H. Taft, October 21, 1911. Taft Papers, Library of Congress.

23. A. J. Wilson to William H. Taft, October 21, 1911. Taft Papers, Library of Congress.

24. Duis, *op. cit.* p. 292.

25. *The Western Brewer*, May, 1910.

26. Duis, *op. cit.*, p. 298.

27. Donald Bull, Manfred Friedrich and Robert Gottschalk. *American Breweries.* (Trumbull, CT: Bullworks, 1984) pp. 57–68.

28. *Chicago Tribune*, October 5, 1915; *Chicago Daily News*, October 5, 1915.

29. *Chicago Tribune*, October 5, 1915.

30. *Ibid.*, October 5, 1915.

31. *Chicago Daily News*, October 5, 1915.

32. *Chicago Tribune*, October 6, 1915; *Chicago Daily News*, October 4, 1915.

33. *Chicago Tribune*, October 5–10, 1915; *Chicago Daily News*, October 6, 9, 11, 1915.

34. *Chicago Tribune*, October 9, 1915; *Chicago Daily News*, October 9, 1915.

35. *Chicago Daily News*, October 6, 1915.

36. *Chicago Tribune*, October 8, 1915; *Chicago Daily News*, October 8, 1915.

37. *Chicago Tribune*, November 8, 1915; *Chicago Daily News*, November 8, 1915.

38. *The Western Brewer*, September, 1917.

Chapter 10

Wartime Prohibition, 1917–1919

"I Swill"

Suggested change in the city of Chicago's motto as Chicagoans enjoyed their last legal drinks on the night of June 30, 1919

Congressional Actions

While the brewers and their allies in Chicago battled against the almost fanatical strength and determination of local prohibitionists, national and international events were occurring that would take the matter of prohibition to Washington and out of the hands of local officials.

By the end of 1916, there were twenty-three dry states with prohibition laws on their books. With the well-financed congressional lobbying efforts of the Anti-Saloon League and the American declaration of war against Germany on April 6, 1917, the campaign for national prohibition became interwoven with President Woodrow Wilson's institution of a wartime food control bill.

In 1917, Wayne Wheeler and the Anti-Saloon League lobbied to attach a provision to Wilson's food bill that would make it illegal to use any food material in the manufacture of alcoholic beverages, except for scientific, medicinal or sacramental purposes. Wet Senators promptly threatened to filibuster against the bill. A compromise was eventually reached that took beer and wine out of the prohibition clause of the food control bill but gave the President the discretion to later limit or stop the manufacture of beer or wine as he saw fit. The compromise bill was passed on August 10, 1917. As mandated by a rider attached to the compromised food bill, the production of distilled alcohol ceased on September 8, although sales of the remaining stock of ardent spirits could legally continue.[1]

Most threatening to the nation's brewers was a Senate resolution for a constitutional prohibition amendment that had passed weeks earlier on August 1. With the passage of the resolution, the necessary time for state legislators to ratify the constitutional

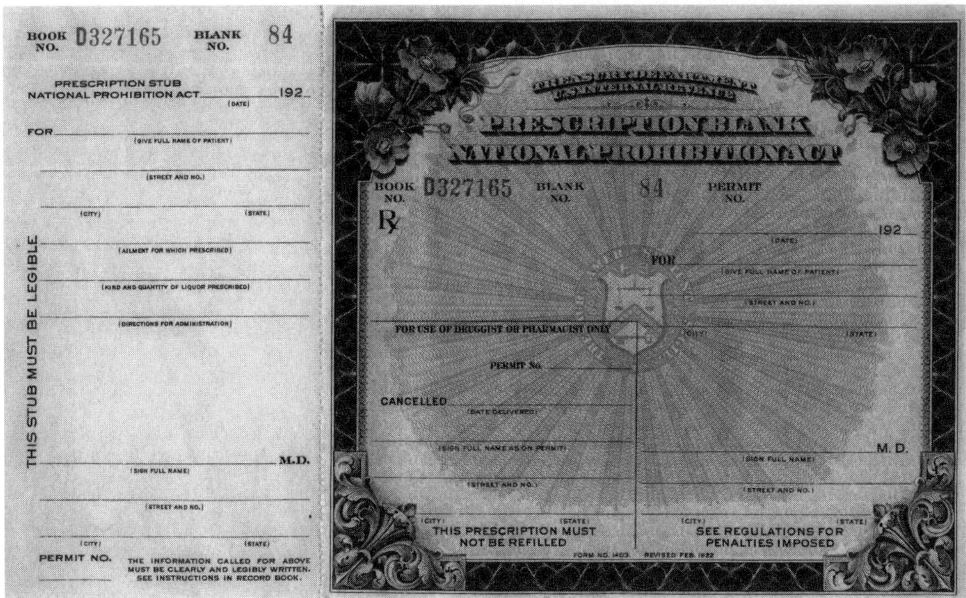
BOOK NO. D327165 BLANK NO. 84

PRESCRIPTION STUB
NATIONAL PROHIBITION ACT ______ 192_
(DATE)

FOR ______
(GIVE FULL NAME OF PATIENT)
(STREET AND NO.)
(CITY) (STATE)
(AILMENT FOR WHICH PRESCRIBED)
(KIND AND QUANTITY OF LIQUOR PRESCRIBED)
(DIRECTIONS FOR ADMINISTRATION)

THIS STUB MUST BE LEGIBLE

______ M.D.
(SIGN FULL NAME)
(STREET AND NO.)
(CITY) (STATE)

PERMIT NO. THE INFORMATION CALLED FOR ABOVE MUST BE CLEARLY AND LEGIBLY WRITTEN. SEE INSTRUCTIONS IN RECORD BOOK.

TREASURY DEPARTMENT
U.S. INTERNAL REVENUE

PRESCRIPTION BLANK
NATIONAL PROHIBITION ACT

BOOK NO. D327165 BLANK NO. 84 PERMIT NO.

℞

______ 192_
(DATE)

FOR ______
(GIVE FULL NAME OF PATIENT)
(STREET AND NO.)
(CITY) (STATE)

FOR USE OF DRUGGIST OR PHARMACIST ONLY
PERMIT No. ______
CANCELLED ______
(DATE DELIVERED)
(SIGN FULL NAME AS ON PERMIT)
(STREET AND NO.)
(CITY) (STATE)
THIS PRESCRIPTION MUST NOT BE REFILLED

______ M. D.
(SIGN FULL NAME)
(STREET AND NO.)
(CITY) (STATE)
SEE REGULATIONS FOR PENALTIES IMPOSED

FORM NO. 1403. REVISED FEB. 1922

Doctors could prescribe alcohol for medicinal or therapeutic purposes during Prohibition, using this government form. From the author's collection.

amendment, which had been originally limited to five years, was compromised to six, avoiding a threatened filibuster but giving the League more time to marshal their forces. If ratified by Congress, the liquor industry would be given one year to close and dispose of its bonded stock. In exchange for this one year grace period, the House of Representatives pushed through the Webb Resolution on December 17th, which further extended the time for ratification of the Constitutional amendment to seven years, allowing considerable time for the Anti-Saloon League to influence the decisions of the legislative representatives from the remaining wet states.[2]

On December 11, 1917, Wilson exercised his authority to further reduce the amount of permissible food materials used for the manufacture of beer by thirty-percent and to limit its legal alcoholic content to a paltry 2¾% by weight.[3]

On November 21, 1918, ten days after the Armistice, Congress passed a prohibition bill as a rider to the Food Stimulation Act. This bill was to take effect the following year but the Federal Food Administration used its authority to order the cessation of brewing nine days after the prohibition bill was passed. Preparing for the cessation of brewing in Chicago, local breweries began to produce all the beer they possibly could before the cutoff date of December 1, 1918. A scarcity of grains and the resultant closing of some plants in order to economize made the challenge of this new post-war measure difficult for the industry to respond to in such a short period of time.

Beginning on December 1, Chicago brewers used the down time after the imposed brewing stoppage to continue to bottle, keg and sell whatever stock was still on hand. There was also a rotated layoff of the 7,500 workers employed by the local industry. In this manner, the local brewers hoped that they would be able to quickly recommence the brewing of beer if given the President's approval. With the brewing moratorium in effect and no hope for a quick resumption of production, Chicago Brewers' Association President William Legner estimated that the country's dwindling supply of beer would run out by May 1, 1919.[4]

The German Brewers and World War I

The German and German-American brewers were not prepared to challenge the dictates of Washington after the declaration of war against Germany. Anti-German hysteria had already gripped Chicago, not only with the nodding approval of the local Anti-Saloon League, but also because of the questionable actions of some German-American organizations. When hostilities in Europe commenced in 1914, the United States Brewers' Association began funneling money to the National German-American Alliance, headquartered in Chicago. But as the U.S. moved from a neutral to a more proactive stance, the USBA continued to maintain their fraternal ties with pro-German organizations. The Alliance used the funds, in part, to send out press releases that were pro-German in tone.

The Anti-Saloon League used the connection between the predominately German-owned breweries and their affiliated saloons as further evidence of the brewers' un-American sentiments. "Pro-Germanism is only the froth from the German beer saloon," declared an Anti-Saloon League superintendent. "Our German Socialist party and the German-American Alliance are the spawn of the saloon. Kaiser kultur was raised on beer. Prohibition is the infallible submarine chaser we must launch by thousands." [5]

As public opinion turned against "hyphenated Americans," including the highly visible German-American brewers, Mayor Thompson, at the time courting the favor of Chicago's German-American voters, caused additional problems for the local German community. His refusal to support the early national Liberty Loan efforts or to assume the role of local draft chairman, infuriated many patriotic Chicagoans and earned him the name of "Kaiser Bill." In an effort to calm down some of the local anti-German bias and prove their loyalty to the U.S., Chicago brewers and members of affiliated trades and businesses later subscribed about $1,400,000 to the Fourth Liberty Loan campaign. Through the efforts of the Manufacturers and Dealers Association of Chicago, brewers distributed several hundred thousand copies of the *Appeal by American Brewers to the American People*, a pamphlet which attempted to repudiate charges that the brewers were pro-German. These efforts proved ineffectual as wartime Chicago developed a siege mentality.[6]

In late 1918, A. Mitchell Palmer, who held the federal position of Custodian of Alien Property, began an investigation of the Schoenhofen Brewery and its owners because of the family's close ties to friends and relatives in Germany. The World War I Office of Alien Property Custodian had been created by an Executive Order on October 12, 1917. The Trading With The Enemy Act of October 6, 1917, had already authorized Palmer to assume control and dispose of enemy-owned property in the United States. Instigated by the Anti-Saloon League's Wayne Wheeler, federal agents seized the corporate and trust files of the brewery. Title to the brewery property was then placed in the control of the federal government in order to prevent the possible use of the company assets by enemy aliens against the United States. German owners of breweries throughout the country suffered similar federal actions. Palmer eventually controlled $506 million of German-owned trusts, including the Schoenhofens. Ironically, Graf Schenk von Stauffenberg, whose failed attempt to kill Hitler at his Wolf's Lair in Eastern Prussia in 1944 would lead to his own death, was purported to have been a descendant of Peter Schoenhofen, founder of the Chicago brewery.[7]

President Wilson finally ruled in December, 1918 that Palmer had no legal right to continue holding the assets of the brewer families. The Schoenhofen Brewery continued to operate during the early years of National Prohibition. It manufactured Green River soda which would continue to be popular through the 1960s. The sprawling brewery complex at 18th and Canalport closed around 1925 following the sale of its name and formulas for its products (including Edelweiss) to National Brewing.

The stigma of the Schoenhofen family's loyalty to Germany would linger through the Second World War. A popular local rumor claimed that the abandoned brewery was used as a clandestine radio site by German spies for the transmission of critical information to Berlin, a claim that was never substantiated.

Ratification of the Eighteenth Amendment

After appeals to the beer drinking public and failed legislative efforts by the brewers to resume brewing, the fate of the drink industry was sealed on January 16, 1919, with the shockingly quick ratification of the Eighteenth Amendment by the constitutionally required thirty-sixth state. One year later, the entire country would fall under National Prohibition. The Illinois Legislature had already followed the twenty-eight other dry states and ratified the National Prohibition Amendment; the Illinois Senate on January 8, with a vote of 30 to 15 and the House by a vote of 84 to 66 on January 14.[8]

But Springfield was not Chicago. Provisions of the wartime prohibition bill, passed in 1918, pushed the last date for the legal retail sale of beer and liquor further back to June 30, 1919. Brewers, distillers and saloonkeepers still held out hope that President Wilson would revoke the wartime prohibition bill and give them until January of 1920 to put their affairs in order, as agreed upon in the Eighteenth Amendment. The Armistice had been signed on November 11, 1918; as far as the brewers were concerned, the wartime prohibition bill was void. Prohibitionists countered that the war could not be considered over until demobilization of the American Expeditionary Forces was complete, a process that could last six months or more.

In Chicago, Deputy City Collector George F. Lohman estimated that the abrupt loss in city revenue from brewery and saloon licensing and permit fees would exceed $8,000,000 per year should the saloons be forced to close. He also took note of the additional loss to real estate owners of useless saloon sites after the closings, speculating that the financial blow to them would be ten times greater than the loss to the city from liquor license fees. It was a loss that would heavily impact local brewers since they owned a significant number of the Chicago saloons.

A local Anti-Saloon League official naïvely suggested that raising taxes to cover the $8,000,000 revenue deficit could easily be avoided by simply reducing expenses in all city departments. A *Chicago Tribune* editorial, however, demanded a quick revision of taxes to make up the huge deficit. Acknowledging the cost of politics in Chicago and a need for municipal belt tightening, the paper also suggested a realistic percentage of the needed money be allocated for the waste of funds that flowed through Mayor Thompson's executive departments.[9]

1919 Referendum

While brewers' and distillers' representatives continued to challenge the wartime prohibition bill and the National Prohibition Amendment in Washington, stocks of beer in Chicago were becoming scarce. By February of 1919, barrel prices had risen to $17, reflecting the dwindling supply.[10]

With prohibition fever sweeping the nation, Anti-Saloon League and Chicago Dry Federation forces successfully managed to include the issue of making Chicago a possible dry territory on the April mayoral ticket, months before National Prohibition would take effect. It had been an uphill battle for dry forces to include such a symbolic issue for city-wide vote, following a ruling by the Illinois Supreme Court that the question had to be included in the April, 1919 election. But the results of the referendum clearly demonstrated the present and future attitude of a majority of Chicagoans. Wets won the issue by a majority of 247,228 votes, 266,529 men and 124,731 women voting against prohibition in Chicago. Had there been a dry victory, local saloons would have been compelled to close their doors on May 1, in compliance with Illinois state law, fostered by local option.

"There will be no let up until fanaticism has been completely overthrown," vowed William Fisher, secretary of the wet Trades Union Liberty League as he reviewed the overwhelming election results. "This is the message Chicago sends to Congress."[12]

CHICAGO WET AND DRY VOTE BY WARDS FOR 1919

WARD	DRY VOTES	WET VOTES	WET MAJORITY
1	1,024	7,792	6,768
2	3,188	12,826	9,638
3	6,087	11,980	5,893
4	873	13,907	2,806
5	2,203	9,637	7,434
6	9,791	12,597	2,806
7	10,693	13,004	2,311
8	3,738	8,329	4,591
9	4,836	7,784	2,948
10	405	7,104	6,699
11	857	8,858	8,001
12	1,105	10,488	9,383
13	10,472	13,730	3,258
14	3,043	10,448	7,405
15	2,486	11,221	8,735
16	509	6,966	6,457
17	568	4,490	3,922
18	2,949	9,496	6,547
19	588	5,247	4,689
20	624	4,685	4,061
21	4,104	9,784	5,680
22	728	6,771	6,043
23	5,131	12,370	7,239
24	2,111	11,811	9,700
25	12,563	16,576	4,013
26	6,826	16,288	9,462
27	8,714	19,865	11,151
28	3,531	10,651	7,120
29	3,026	13,350	10,324
30	2,094	9,033	6,939
31	4,979	12,228	7,249
32	10,145	15,160	5,015
33	9,578	17,011	7,433
34	2,280	17,141	14,679
35	6,943	18,622	11,679
Totals	114,032	391,260	247,228[11]

Congress, however, had its own agenda, something that brewers' attorney Levy Mayer ruefully pointed out. Although the referendum had deflected the local option move to make Chicago a dry territory months before National Prohibition, its results could not stop its inevitability. Passage of the Eighteenth Amendment had been through legislative action, not by a popular mandate. "Members of the legislature and congress . . . have, without a direct vote of the people, undertaken to amend the constitution and say to more than 100,000,000 people that they shall not drink malt, vinous or spirituous beverages of any kind, and that possession of such beverages makes their possessors felons." Mayer then threw down this challenge to the electorate. "I can stand it if the rest of the American people can."[13]

Buoyed by the results of the referendum vote and on the advice of legal counsel, Chicago brewers defiantly restarted the brewing of 2.75 % beer on May 1, following the lead of New York brewers. At this point, low alcohol small beer was better than no beer.[14]

Hoping to influence President Wilson's decision on extending the wartime prohibition bill's effective date of July 1, 1919, the Chicago City Council adopted the following resolution and left no doubt as to its stance on National Prohibition:

> Whereas, In the present day of democracy the majority rules, and the city has by a vote of 300,000 at the last general election declared against a dry Chicago; and
>
> Whereas, If demobilization is not complete before July 1 the country will go dry by presidential decree, which will, when effective, mean a property damage in Chicago of about $15,000,000, a loss of business of $25,000,000 and inability of the administration to meet the pay-roll of the police and firemen; therefore
>
> Be it resolved by the City Council that we petition the United States Senate, Congress and President Wilson to declare the army of the United States demobilized by July 1, 1919.[15]

Hopefully, if Wilson acceded to the City Council's petition and to similar demands from other municipalities which feared that a reliable cash cow was prematurely drying up, it would give local governments six more months to draw additional revenues from the local breweries and their affiliated saloons and give them a little more time to get their financial houses in order. The absoluteness of National Prohibition would still be six months away, not scheduled to take effect until January 16, 1920, but time was running short. Wilson, however, let the wartime prohibition bill and the last date for the retail sale of alcoholic beverages come into law on July 1, 1919. He offered one ray of hope to the drink interests when he stated that when "demobilization is terminated, my power to act without congressional action will be excised." With this ambiguous statement by Wilson hinting at a possible short reprieve, there were predictions that saloons in states that were still wet might be back in operation by the end of August. Local brewer association president William G. Legner was wary, however, of unwarranted enthusiasm concerning the possible reopening of saloons.[16]

Chicago Reacts to the Wartime Prohibition Bill

In Chicago, attitudes towards the up-coming closing date of city saloons proved defiant, not surprising after the results of the April election. Over the back bars of many of the saloons were signs declaring, "THIS SALOON WILL BE OPEN FOR BUSINESS AFTER JULY 1." Rumors abounded that some local brewers were so confident that the ban would be lifted before July 1, that they were not only brewing beer, despite the restrictions, but were once again brewing full strength brew.[17]

When informed that there were strong indications that some Chicago saloons would remain open after July 1, United States District Attorney Charles F. Clyne countered that he would be forced to prosecute any violators. It was pointedly noted that Police Chief Garrity had 5000 policemen at his disposal for enforcement of the closings. As the deadline date approached, however, Garrity was away in New York. Acting as chief in Garrity's absence, First Deputy General Superintendent of Police John M. Alcock startled everyone by declaring that "... after midnight it is a federal question (the enforcement of saloon closings)," and indicated a reluctance to act.[18]

In the seedier areas around Chicago's barrel houses, the crowds of bums and hoboes grew unusually large as saloonkeepers tried to unload their stock. Huge schooners of beer dropped back to a nickel, shots of whiskey from ten to twenty cents, depending on the quality. Authorities predicted a marked increase in the number of drunks who would probably apply for the cure at the healing Bridewell, Washingtonian and Keeley Institutes when the wartime prohibition law took effect.

A last minute price war took place in saloons throughout the city as retailers dumped stock. "Only two days more to shop—do your shopping now!" was a common theme of advertisements placed in many saloon windows as the deadline approached. A majority of dealers were staying open well past the 1 a.m. closing time, hoping to squeeze out the last bit of change from thirsty Chicagoans. Travelling salesmen, their satchels loaded with booze, scurried through the neighborhoods trying to persuade potential customers to buy their products now.[19]

For the would-be home-brewer, small cans of Hopfen und Malz Extrakt were popping up for sale in delis and food stores. By adding water and a packet of yeast to the malted extract, the beer drinker was promised a stimulating malt beverage of at least 5% alcohol in five to seven days.[20]

First Ward Alderman Michael Kenna's Workingmen's Exchange mockingly announced a series of recitations and songs on June 30 to mark the passing of John Barleycorn, including "*The Old Man's Drunk Again*" and "*Father, Dear Father, Come Home With Me Now.*" At the Hamilton Club, a dinner dance was to be held. At midnight the body of the late John Barleycorn would be brought in by pallbearers for a solemn, but tongue-in-cheek, wake. Preparations in hotels, cafes and saloons throughout the city were being made, with proprietors predicting record business. When some establishments still threatened to stay open after midnight on July 1, Alderman Anton J. Cermak of the United Societies warned that those who defied the law would endanger any chance of reopening if President Wilson finally declared the Army demobilized and allowed the bars to reopen.[21]

Goodbye to Beer

On June 30, 1919, Chicagoans celebrated like never before. Whiskey and some of the more exotic mixed drinks seemed to be the drinks of choice. The reason for this was simple: Cermak declared that Chicago saloons had run out of real beer before June 30. "Two days before June 30, the last available barrel of real beer had gone from the breweries. There wasn't a beer jag in town, unless some youngster had a make believe."[22] If Cermak was correct in his sobering assessment, it would have been the second time since the hot summer of 1854 that Chicago had run out of beer. The Green Mill Garden, the Marigold Room, the Sheridan Inn and the Rainbow enjoyed record business. On the South Side, the De Luxe, the Entertainers and the Elite were reported to be open well past midnight. An estimate that over $1,500,000 had been spent on beer and booze caused one observer of Chicago's greatest wassailing occasion to suggest that the city motto be changed from "I Will" to "I Swill."[23]

The Illinois Search and Seizure Act

With a collective hangover affecting tens of thousands, the city slowly awoke the next day to learn that United States Attorney General A. Mitchell Palmer had announced the night before that the manufacture and sale of beer with 2¾% alcohol could continue until the federal courts ruled on whether or not such beer was legally intoxicating. Recent test cases in New York had resulted in a decision to question what amount of alcohol in beer could be legally considered intoxicating. "We will proceed in an orderly fashion to establish whether intoxicating beverages proscribed by the law include those having less than 2¾% percent alcohol," advised Palmer. Until the Supreme Court ruled on a legal definition of intoxicating or until January 16, 1920, 2¾% beer could continue to be sold in those states that did not have dry laws on their books. Impulsively acting on Palmer's ruling, Illinois Attorney General Edward J. Brundage initially issued a statement that the sale of beer and wine with 2¾% alcohol could continue in Illinois until National Prohibition took effect on January 16, 1920. In accordance with these opinions, the Chicago City Council quickly passed an ordinance authorizing the issuance of temporary sixty-day liquor licenses, a move introduced by Alderman Cermak. The licenses now sold for $50 a month instead of the old cost of $83, which would have allowed the sale of hard alcohol.[24]

Later that day, City Corporation Counsel Samuel A. Ettelson conferred with Attorney General Brundage on Palmer's ruling. As a result of their meeting, despite no federal court rulings on the definition of what amount of alcohol in beer was legally considered intoxicating, Policé Chief Garrity was instructed to arrest anyone who attempted to sell any beverage that contained more than one-half of 1% alcohol. Brundage now ruled that "The search and seizure act of the state of Illinois, in force and effect after July 1, 1919, defines intoxicating liquor or liquids as including all distilled spirituous, vinous, fermented, or malt liquors which contain more than one-half of 1 percent by volume of alcohol, and all alcoholic liquids, compounds, and preparations, whether proprietary, patented, or not, which are portable and are capable of or suitable for being used as a beverage." When reporters questioned Brundage on his reversed decision, he claimed that he had been earlier misinformed, stating that:

> I was called on the telephone at my home and informed that the government had modified its provisions of the wartime Prohibition act to permit sale of light beverages containing no more than 2 3/4 percent of alcohol. I said that if this were true, it would be permissible under the Illinois law to sell such beverages here. When the full details of the federal government's action were shown to me I immediately issued the new statement regarding the search and seizure law, which effectually prohibits the sale of anything containing more than one half of one percent of alcohol.

With the enforcement of state law versus a yet established federal opinion, the death knoll for beer in Chicago was sounded at 6:30 p.m., July 1, 1919.[25]

Some saloons and clubs openly defied the closing mandate. It was later reported that fanatical prohibitionist Reverend Arthur Burrage Farwell of the Chicago Law and Order League and his team of vigilant investigators had found violations of the 12 o'clock closing law on June 30. Farwell also disclosed that whiskey was seen purchased at the Dorchester at 67th and Dorchester and at the Tavern, located at 58th and State. The Reverend stayed long enough at these locations to additionally note in his report that women in all stages of undress were seen in both places.

Local Brewers Go on the Offensive

After the closings, the Chicago Brewers' Association passed a resolution to continue to challenge not only the wartime prohibition bill but to also challenge the National Prohibition Act by hastening any test cases through the courts. What they needed was a brewer willing to act as a "victim" for a test case on the legality of manufacturing 2¾% beer. The procedural events leading up to a ruling had already been mapped out by the brewers and their attorneys. Industry leaders anticipated that an expected federal suit would charge a consenting brewer with a violation of the food conservation act and the selling of an intoxicating beverage. After arrest, the association's plan called for the brewer to plead guilty and pay the fine.

On July 14, a suit was filed by District Attorney Clyne against the Stenson Brewing Company. It was charged that the brewery "did use grains and cereals in the manufacture and production of beer for beverage purposes containing as much as one-half of one percent alcoholic content by both weight and volume . . ." and sold the beer on July 2 to Timothy King, a saloonkeeper at 3153 Archer Avenue. Six counts were included in the suit, three for the sale of the beer and three concerning the manufacture of the beer. The Stenson brothers abruptly changed their original strategy of pleading guilty and instead argued that they were innocent of the charges, stating that the November 21, 1918 wartime prohibition bill "relates only to beer which is in fact intoxicating" and that the information used in the charges "fails to allege that the beer made or sold was in fact intoxicating." They also argued that the wartime prohibition bill should be construed as unconstitutional and void since it was a wartime measure and that at the time of the manufacture and sale of their beer "No war affecting the United States was in progress."

Attorney Clyne confirmed that a dozen more suits would soon be filed against the North American Brewing Company, the Hoffman Brewing Company and the Primalt Products Company, the old Independent Brewing Association. The Stenson case was the first suit of its kind in the United States since a criminal statute was brought into question. Levy Mayer, special counsel of the Chicago Brewers' Association, and Attorney Clyne worked together on bringing the test case to the District Court and eventually to the Supreme Court, hoping to force the federal court to arrive at a definitive ruling of what percentage of alcohol was to be considered intoxicating. A demurrer filed on July 21 by attorneys for the brewers once again argued that the wartime prohibition bill was void since it was passed as a war measure, the war was now over, and that the law did not fix the alcoholic content which beer might contain.[26]

All arguments and legal challenges by the brewery industry and their legal representatives were ended with the passage of the Volstead Act on October 27, 1919. The Act clarified prohibition enforcement procedures and mandated a limit of 0.5 percent alcohol of any and all drink as the baseline standard for intoxicating beverages. In doing so, the Volstead Act quashed the final question of legality for National Prohibition.

Early Effects of No Beer in Chicago

Of the forty-three city breweries operating before July 1st, only sixteen had renewed their brewing licenses. It had been expected that most of the remaining twenty-seven breweries would have applied for license extensions to produce 2¾% beer. But now, just days into the end of the drink trade in Chicago, saloonkeepers were serving near beer, pop or numerous other non-alcoholic drinks such as Old Crowe Flavor. Of the 120 bars in the Loop, all but sixteen remained open, waiting hopefully for President Wilson to declare the Army demobilized and allow a return to a whiskey and real beer business. But while the saloonkeepers and brewers waited for a sign from Washington, the early effects of the state-mandated search and seizure law began to cascade throughout the restaurant and hotel industry. Waiters at the downtown hotels and clubs started to bemoan their now sober customers. "I got $1.50 in tips today," complained one frustrated waiter at Vogelsang's Restaurant. "Before July 1, it was a poor day when I didn't clean up $8 to $10 in tips." A Hotel Sherman waiter echoed his comrade's sentiment. "The firewater sure did lubricate a man's pocketbook. How's a man gonna get tips on lemonade?" he asked.

Others realized the futility of it all; whether beer and booze came back briefly next week or next month, National Prohibition was just around the corner. At the famous De Jonghe's, a soda fountain was soon installed. Workers at the Palmer House bar were following suit, converting the business into a soda fountain emporium.[27]

In less than a week after the state search and seizure law had taken affect in Chicago, saloon owners started to complain about poor business. One drink or two of near beer or some non-alcoholic concoction was the limit for regulars who continued to visit their old drinking haunts simply out of habit. But the habit was starting to fade. John Dunne, a saloonkeeper near the Criminal Courts building, gave all his bartenders the day off on the Fourth of July. By noon, manning the bar by himself, he sold one bottle of soda on a day when business customarily boomed. At 12:10 Dunne had enough and closed for the day. Bartenders throughout the city complained that customers didn't loiter like they did before. After the usual rush at lunch and after work, the once busy bars were quickly deserted as near beer and soda pop failed to satisfy the cravings of patrons for something more stimulating. Once thriving saloons lay deserted save for the empty beer kegs piled next to the bar. Slogans on wooden cases still holding bottles drained of their contents and now stacked for disposal beckoned their old customers through dirty saloon windows to enjoy "A Case Of Good Judgment", but to no avail. [28]

Chicagoans had given the state-imposed Search and Seizure Act less than one week before turning in their verdicts; prohibition, in a state or federal form, was not for them. Those who quietly observed the reactions of thirsty Chicagoans with marked interest and heard their grumblings about "no whiskey" and "near beer," watched the frustration and disappointment of desperate saloon owners as their livelihoods slowly collapsed. They realized that the prohibition of beer and strong drink would never satisfy the needs of a population accustomed to serious libations.

One such observer was Johnny Torrio.

Notes

1. Stanley W. Baron. *Brewed in America. A History of Beer and Ale in the United States.* (New York: Arno Press, 1962.) pp. 302–304; *Chicago Tribune*, August 11, 1917.

2. Baron, *Ibid.* p. 304; *Chicago Tribune*, December 18, 1917.

3. Baron, *Ibid.* p. 303.

4. *The Brewers' Journal*, December, 1918; *Chicago Tribune*, November 30, December 1, 1918.

5. As quoted in David Lowe. *Lost Chicago.* (Boston, MA: Houghton Mifflin Company, 1975) p. 201.

6. *The Brewers' Journal*, November, 1918, April, 1919.

7. *Records of the Alien Property Administration*, Schoenhofen Family, National Archives, Trust Files, 2752, 2662, 3436, 49022. For a comment on how this same situation affected the Busch family of St. Louis, see Peter Hernon and Terry Ganey. *Under the Influence, The Unauthorized Story of the Anheuser-Busch Dynasty.* (New York, NY: Simon & Schuster, 1991) p. 94, 102–3; Rudolph Hofmeister. *The Germans of Chicago*. (Champaign, IL: Stipes Publishing, 1976) pp. 71, 74.

8. *Chicago Daily News*, January 9, 14, 1919.

9. *Chicago Daily News*, January, 1919; *Chicago Tribune*, May 1, 1919; *The Brewers' Journal*, December, 1918.

10. *Chicago Daily News*, June, 1919.

11. *The Western Brewer*, Vol. 52, No. 4, April, 1919.

12. *Chicago Tribune*, April 2, 1919.

13. *Chicago Tribune*, April 3, 1919.

14. *The Brewers' Journal*, May, 1919.

15. *The Brewers Journal*, May 28, 1919.

16. *Chicago Tribune*, June 29, 1919.

17. *Chicago Tribune*, April 3, 1919.

18. *Chicago Tribune*, June 30, 1919.

19. *Chicago Daily News*, June 28, 1919

20. *Chicago Daily News*, June 28, 1919.

21. *Chicago Tribune*, June 30, 1919; *Chicago Daily News*, June 30, 1919.

22. *Chicago Tribune*, July 4, 1919.

23. *Chicago Tribune*, July 1, 1919.

24. *Chicago Tribune*, July 1, 1919; *Chicago Daily News*, July 1, 1919.

25. *Chicago Tribune*, July 2, 1919; *Chicago Daily News*, July 1, 1919.

26. *United States of America vs. Stenson Brewing Company*, Number 6721, District Court of the U.S. Northern District of Illinois, Eastern Division; *Chicago Tribune*, July 4, 1919; *The Brewers' Journal*, August, 1919.

27. *Chicago Tribune*, July 4–5, 1919; *Chicago Daily News*, July 7, 1919.

28. *Chicago Tribune*, July 4, 1919; *Chicago Daily News*, July 8, 1919.

Chapter 11

The Torrio Era, 1919–1925

"It is almost impossible to get a
drink of real beer in Chicago now!"

Police Chief Morgan A. Collins as mobster Johnny Torrio's beer-laden trucks rolled through the streets of Chicago

The Milwaukee Invasion

In Chicago, and throughout the United States, the enactment of National Prohibition on January 16, 1920 would soon become a parched reality. Scores of local breweries continued to operate, de-alcoholizing real beer and turning out insipid tasting near beer. Initial sales were encouraging but soon fell flat as Chicagoans began searching for something more stimulating. To add to the frustration of local brewers as their near beer sales stumbled, a steady supply of 2.75% beer, still legal in Wisconsin, was discovered coming across the northern border from Milwaukee breweries into Chicago saloons. Representatives of the Chicago Brewers' Protective Association met with city, state and federal officials to complain about the smuggling and the affect it was having on their near beer sales. As a result of the complaints from the Chicago brewers, a total of nineteen Milwaukee beer trucks were soon seized by federal officials at Zion City, as they surreptitiously attempted to make their way to Chicago. Representatives of the Jos. Schlitz Brewing Company, the Pabst Brewing Company, the Val. Blatz, and Fred. Miller Brewing Companies were ordered to appear before Federal Judge Kenesaw Mountain Landis to explain their beer running activities into the now dry city of Chicago.[1]

Not all of Chicago's breweries were willing to compromise their product and sit back while Milwaukee saturated their market with real beer. In just a few short months of unfavorable test cases and continued beer smuggling, a number of Chicago brewers had had enough of government-mandated prohibition and interference with their traditional means of livelihood. Their futile argument that any form of prohibition was an infringement on their "personal liberties" had fallen on deaf ears. The brewers' only course of action was now obvious, but illegal. The catalyst they needed was someone willing to step forward and protect them from possible arrest and prosecution if they returned to the illegal manufacture of real beer.

Torrio and Joseph Stenson

In the spring of 1919 brewery owner Charles Schaffner sold his Manhattan Brewing Company, located in Bridgeport at 3901 South Emerald Avenue, to Johnny Torrio and brewer Joseph Stenson who were later joined by bootleggers/investors Dion O'Banion, Hymie Weiss and Maxie Eisner as co-owners.[2] Torrio, a pimp and racketeer, had arrived from New York between 1910 and 1912 and soon made a name for himself in Chicago's underworld as he had done earlier in New York. Having interviewed for a position in James "Big Jim" Colisimo's organization, Torrio was offered the role in Chicago as Colisimo's right hand man. "Big Jim" had risen in power through his vice and racketeering activities in and around the infamous Levee District, south of the Loop, under the political protection of First Ward Alderman Michael Kenna.

Torrio became an atypical example of a Chicago gangster. He was a quiet individual who seldom carried a gun or displayed a life of excess, in spite of the huge sums of illegal money he acquired. Although his early career in Chicago was as a pimp for Colisimo's stable of whores, he made it a point never to sleep with them, nor did he smoke or drink. He faithfully arrived home at his Michigan Avenue apartment every night at six o'clock to his wife, Ann. He soon displayed a knack for business savvy, outstanding organizational skills and the delicate art of compromise, traits demanded by any successful business organization. The early Prohibition purchase of the Manhattan Brewery was an example of his intuitiveness and understanding of the frailties of human nature and the profits these weaknesses could bring him.

While some of the local brewers switched to legal enterprises or mothballed their plants, hoping that National Prohibition would one day be repealed, Torrio understood that Chicagoans would want their beer during National Prohibition, illegal or not. But as sophisticated as his organizational skills and understanding of human nature might have been, he still needed someone who understood the practical aspects of the local brewing industry; that man was brewer Joseph Stenson.

In 1919, when the Chicago brewing industry needed a sacrificial lamb to challenge the legality of Illinois Attorney General Brundage's ruling on the wartime prohibition bill, the Stenson Brewing Company had taken up the cause. This willingness by Stenson management to challenge the law had caught Torrio's eye. Shortly before National Prohibition took effect, Torrio had secretly begun working with Joseph Stenson, the youngest of the four brothers who owned the Stenson Brewery, to buy outright, lease or front for the original owners of a growing number of cooperative Chicago breweries. Their plan was simple. Using money from Torrio, Stenson would gain control of the breweries and typically install well-paid flunkies as brewery presidents and plant managers. These Stenson-appointed brewery officers were to take the fall if the breweries were raided, leaving the real principals unmolested. In short time, Torrio with the help of Stenson, owned or controlled through fellow bootleggers Terry Druggan, Frankie Lake and others, the Manhattan, Stege, Pfeiffer, Standard, Gambrinus and Hoffman breweries in Chicago. Torrio's control was reputed to have eventually covered around 65 breweries in and around the Chicago area. In the early years of National Prohibition in Chicago, while Stenson helped build Torrio's brewing empire, he accumulated a sizable fortune for his efforts. In 1924, newspaper estimates of the cost of Joseph Stenson's expertise was $12,000,000 a year, earned from a going price of about $50 to $55 for a syndicate barrel of beer.[3]

Persuading frustrated brewery owners to sell or lease their operations was probably an easy sell for Torrio and Stenson. Many of the city breweries had initially switched, or had made plans to switch, to the production of near beer, soda pop and other products that they didn't understand. With new ventures foisted upon them and the uncertainties of unknown markets, failure, the loss of the business and even the family fortune were distinct possibilities. A list of city breweries with their planned product lines is listed below:

Atlas Beverage Co., a.k.a. Atlas Brewing Co.—Cereal beverages, ginger ale, cider.
Birk Brothers Brewing Company.—Cereal beverages, root beer.
Fortune Bros.—Macaroni and spaghetti.
Primalt Products Co., a.k.a. Independent Brewing Assn.—Cereal beverages, soft drinks, ginger ale, root beer, malt syrups and extracts.
McAvoy Co., a.k.a. McAvoy Brewing Co.—Cereal beverages, distilled alcohol.
Best Brewing Co.—Cereal beverages, root beer, ice.
The Geo. J. Cooke Co.—Cold storage.
Producers Brewing Co.—Cereal beverages, root beer.
Ruehl Brewing Co.—Cereal beverages, ice.
White Eagle Products Co.—Cereal beverages.
The Conrad Seipp Co., a.k.a. Conrad Seipp Brewing Co.—Cereal beverages.
Sieben's Brewery Co. —Closed.
North American Brewing Co.—Cereal beverages.
Stenson Brewing Co.—Cereal beverages, root beer, ice.
United Breweries Co. (Monarch and North Western).—Cereal beverages.[4]

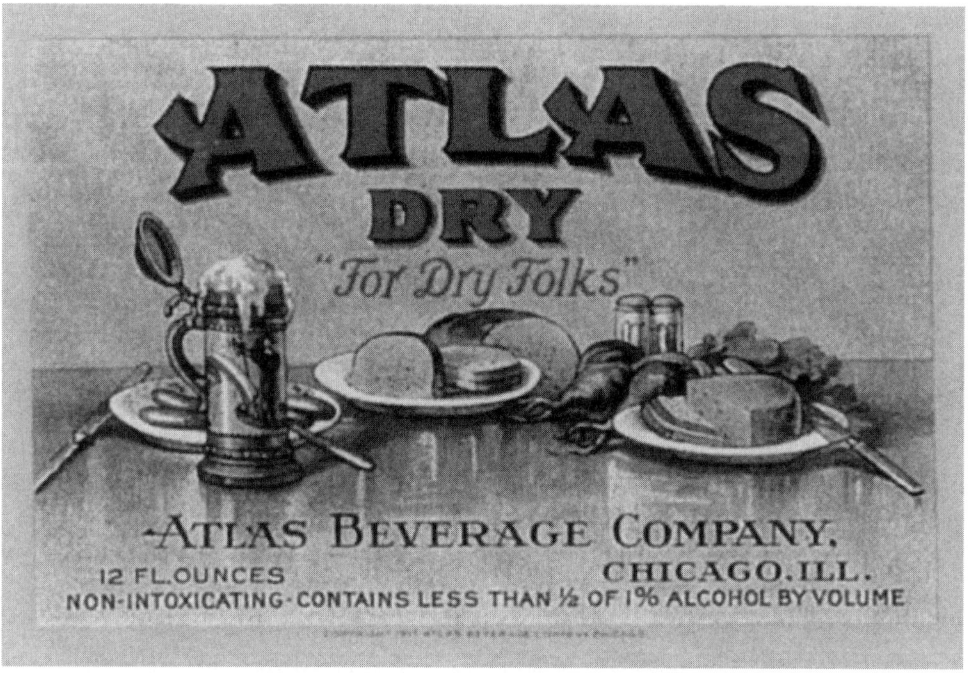

Label for Atlas Dry, a cereal beverage produced during the Prohibition era. Courtesy of Bob Kay.

Within months of starting these new operations, many of the Chicago breweries were forced to take a long, hard look at their bottom lines. Years of grain shortages, brewing moratoriums and reformers' assaults had taken their toll on the local industry. Encouraged by the guaranteed sales of Torrio and other up-and-coming bootleggers, the local brewery owners were now promised more money than they had seen in years. With the guaranteed help and protection of the Torrio cabal, some of them dropped their unprofitable new ventures and quickly reverted to the production of real beer. Their often used rallying cry of "personal rights" merged with the more practical issue of profitability. With a barrel of beer now selling for almost $55, the breweries could easily afford the weekly payoffs to city officials, aldermen, district commanders and the beat cops who patrolled the neighborhoods, and still make a fortune.

National Prohibition or not, it was once again becoming the business of beer as usual in Chicago.

Dever Elected

During the latter part of Mayor Thompson's administration, brewery raids in Chicago had become as uncommon as snow in July. Not only did local saloons continue to operate openly, but thousand of licenses were now being issued by the city for so called "soda parlors." These establishments were licensed to serve non-alcoholic refreshments; but virtually all of them served real beer, produced by the accommodating local breweries. Almost every cop and politician in Chicago knew it, ignored it and profited from it.

Charges of political corruption, a deficit in the city budget and a total lack of control of the Chicago Police Department by Thompson finally led to his ouster in April of 1923. He was replaced by reform candidate William E. Dever. Although the city electorate wanted political and judicial reform, they were convinced that the benign neglect that had allowed the breweries to continue to operate since the early years of Prohibition would go on. After all, these breweries had been illegally providing beer for thirsty Chicagoans for almost four years. During the first few months of Dever's administration, beer continued to flow in Chicago, as it appeared that Dever would maintain the status quo.

Johnny Torrio continued in his quest for a consolidation of all the gangs in the city that were in the expanding bootleg business. The North Side was controlled by Dion O'Banion. Parts of the West Side were run by bootleggers Terry Druggan and Frankie Lake. Torrio held most of the South Side but was having problems with three brothers from the South Side O'Donnell gang.

The O'Connor Shooting

During the early days of Prohibition, Ed "Spike" O'Donnell was serving time in Joliet for a daytime holdup of the Stockyards Trust and Savings Bank. Eventually paroled, "Spike" and his enterprising brothers made up for lost time and hijacked several truckloads of Torrio's beer soon after his release. When Torrio failed to retaliate, they continued their predatory ways and muscled into the South Side territory of Joe Saltis and Frank McErlane, allies of Torrio. Using beatings and intimidation, they quickly built up a clientele among Torrio's former saloon accounts. In many instances, the beatings were unnecessary; most South Side beer drinkers agreed that the O'Donnells provided a better quality beer. Torrio held his street enforcers at bay and retaliated by lowering the price on his beer by $10 a barrel.

The territorial dispute culminated in the shooting of Jerry O'Connor, a beer runner and member of the O'Donnell gang. One of those accused in the shooting was Daniel McFall, a deputy sheriff and known Torrio ally.[5]

Dever's Beer War

Dever used the shooting to implement an attack on the scores of Chicago breweries that had operated for years with impunity. On September 12, Mayor Dever met with the press and announced his plan to shut down Chicago's illegally operating breweries. With Police Chief Morgan A. Collins at his side, Dever declared that every brewery in

Chicago would be placed under police guard and that every shipment of beer leaving the breweries would be seized for analysis of its alcoholic content. With persistent rumors of police officials protecting the illicit beer trade, Dever pledged that "Beer runners and crooked policemen will get the same treatment." He also discounted as false the all too obvious indications that politicians close to him were getting $10 per barrel for beer delivered by beer runners. Collins echoed Dever's comments about the consequences of police corruption. He insisted, though, that with the implementation of their plan, "It is almost impossible to get a drink of real beer in Chicago now." Almost mocking the chief's naïve declarations, local newspapers reported that trucks from the breweries that supplied the O'Donnell gang and from Torrio's Manhattan Brewery were rolling through the streets, continuing to supply their customers.[6]

On the evening of Dever's challenge to the bootleggers and the local beer industry, things began to rapidly change for Chicago's breweries and Torrio's fortunes. During the evening, five trucks of beer were seized as they left from the Manhattan, Keeley and the Conrad Seipp Brewery on the South Side. The next morning, Mayor Dever met with city officials and a representative of the federal government to coordinate a battle plan for the suppression of the illegal beer trade in Chicago. His office announced that no more soft drink licenses would be issued until the applicants had been subject to "the severest scrutiny." Chief Collins began to switch the police guards stationed at the breweries on a daily basis, hoping to stop any chance of beer runners corrupting his beer patrols. He also expanded the patrols to include all highways leading into the city from suburban towns where there were known breweries still operating. It was the first real attempt by local officials since the beginning of National Prohibition to try to stop the flow of beer in Chicago.[7]

The Bootleggers' Counteroffensive

With the initial enthusiasm and success of the beer patrols by Collins' men, the breweries began to develop their own counteroffensive to thwart local officials. Brewers started to send out trucks from the front entrances of the breweries loaded with near beer, holding the attention of the police, while trucks packed with real beer slipped out the back exits unchallenged. After all, insiders pointed out, the money from the illegal beer trade was simply too good *not* to put up a fight. Before Dever announced his beer war, it was estimated that Chicago's breweries had been producing 18,000 barrels of real beer a week. At a minimum of $30 per barrel, often going as high as $55 , the business of beer in Chicago was generating well over $28,000,000 a year in illegal sales. From that figure, insiders claimed that $10 per barrel was earmarked for a slush fund for "fixing."[8]

As the pressure to stop the illegal beer trade continued and listings of saloon closings became a daily feature in the local press, another wave of murders took place as beer runners jockeyed for new accounts to replace those that had been forced to close. Police Chief Collins admitted there would probably be more killings, commenting that his department was up against "a powerful foe." He continued to pressure his force for results, suspending a police captain from the South Side suspected of acting as a Torrio ally, as a warning to other corrupt police officials.

Brewery Raids

On a tip from an informant, police staked out the Pfeiffer Brewery on North Leavitt, a brewery controlled by mobster Terry Druggan and under the protection of Torrio, and seized three trucks loaded with beer plus an additional 2300 barrels of real beer ready for delivery to Chicago's North Side. Druggan's men had planned to break the police blockade surrounding the brewery by rushing the police with the loaded trucks and quickly delivering the beer to their saloon accounts. The plan fell through when police arrested Martin O'Leary, a member of Terry Druggan's Valley Gang, who was to have led the mad dash from the brewery. In an embarrassing counteroffensive by local bootleggers, a member of Torrio's gang brazenly stole a confiscated truckload of beer from in front of a police station on Irving Park while the driver was being grilled inside. "Someone will be out of a job before tomorrow morning," vowed an embarrassed Chief Collins to the press.[9]

Dever's crusade continued with the revocation of the licenses of saloons caught selling real beer or whiskey. In addition, Dever pulled the operating licenses of three hundred and fifty-five soda parlors in just a few short days. Drug stores, coffee shops and even local groceries started to receive the attention of the beer patrols. In one week, five hundred and forty-nine people were charged with violations of the Prohibition Act. The Hoffman Brewing Company was the first brewery casualty of Dever's beer war when it lost its license after the city health commissioner reported that his men had been refused samples of the brewery's products for analysis.[10]

Decent Dever

In an address to four hundred Methodist ministers meeting in Chicago, Mayor Dever admitted that his recent crackdown on prohibition violators was probably political suicide but stated his belief in his actions. "Even if I were interested only in politics, doesn't everything point to an enforcement of this law?" Buoyed by the positive reception from the ministers, Dever vowed that there would be no end to his campaign to dry up Chicago until every business that had been selling alcohol "hung out the calamity sign." The mayor's one-man public relations campaign against bootlegged beer continued with an address to over 10,000 skeptical lager-loving participants on German Day at Municipal Pier. Dever's speech would reflect a common refrain through his mayoralty; he insisted that he was not a prohibitionist but merely an advocate of law and order and the protector of the public's health. "I could never excuse myself as long as 7,000 so-called soft drink places are selling poison," declared the mayor. The theme of poisoned beer prevailed throughout Dever's term with encouragement by the Health Commissioner of Chicago. "The bootleggers' 'real beer' is either adulterated with certain drugs or is beer recently made, known as 'green beer,'" a somber Doctor Herman N. Bundesen declared.[11]

Beer runners continued their resourcefulness in providing beer to thirsty Chicagoans. With road checks of trucks becoming more common on the streets of the city, newspaper reports stated that beer was now being smuggled down the Chicago River concealed under cargoes of fruits and vegetables.[12]

Saloon and Soda Parlor Shutdowns

Police Chief Collins boasted triumphantly that the recent successes of his daily raids would leave Chicago bone dry by early October. He comically observed that a recent tour of the city revealed no signs of liquor, ". . . but I did see the finest collection of padlocks in town, hanging on the front doors of these so-called soft drink parlors." Either shut down by the raids or simply closed because of fear of arrest, the 6000 soda parlor owners who had openly operated in Chicago selling beer were now shocked by their loss of immunity. Everyone knew they sold beer. As long as they kept away from liquor, the police had always left them alone. "There was an unwritten law under which the government sanctioned the sale of beer," complained Anton Cermak.[13] In two months, Dever had revoked the operating licenses of over 1600 businesses for Prohibition-related offenses. In addition, 4031 saloons had been shut down. The crusading mayor seemingly had the upper hand.[14]

Wets Counterattack

Politicians sympathetic to the wet cause or under the influence of local bootleggers started a move in the City Council to place a referendum on the ballot of the upcoming judicial election. Chicagoans were to vote yes or no on the question, "Do you approve of the city administration's present policy in the enforcement of the liquor laws?"

Alderman "Bathhouse" John Coughlin presented a resolution in the City Council requesting that the prohibition laws be amended to permit the sale of beer and light wines. Suspending the normal council procedure of sending proposed resolutions to committee, the City Council of Chicago quickly adopted the following resolution:

> Whereas, Since the enforcement of Article XVIII (the amendment to the Constitution of the United States of America prohibiting the manufacture, sale and transportation of intoxicating liquors for beverage purposes); and
>
> Whereas, The City of Chicago has lost through license revenue the sum of eight million dollars annually; and

> Whereas, During the so-called 'dry period', which has been over four years, the City of Chicago alone has lost a total revenue of over thirty-two millions of dollars; and
>
> Whereas, On account of such tremendous loss to the taxpayers, the burdens of the taxpayers have increased two-fold, and as a consequence thereof taxes on real and personal property have doubled; therefore, be it
>
> Resolved, That we, the City Council of the City of Chicago assembled, hereby petition the Congress of the United States to amend the Act commonly called the Volstead Act, so that the sale, manufacture and transportation of light wines and beers for beverage purposes will be permissible; and, be it further
>
> Resolved, That a copy of this petition be forwarded to Congress and the Senate as a body and to each and every member thereof.[15]

Dever countered these moves by once again going to the people, expressing the legality of his beer war. "I believe in good, wholesome beer at moderate prices for those who like it if it can be sold legally, but as long as it is banned by a law of the nation, ratified by the States, and strengthened by auxiliary legislation of the States, we cannot have it. And if the people of Chicago cannot have good beer, wines and liquors legally, they are not going to have poisonous green beer, deadly hooch or moonshine so long as I can stop it, and I believe I have." With Dever's persuasive argument against the dangers of poisoned beer being so strong, the proposal to place the wet versus dry issue on the judicial ballot soon faded away.[16]

Events Leading to the Sieben Brewery Raid

One of the most famous Prohibition-era brewery raids in Chicago began with a routine inspection on August 29, 1923, of the George Frank Brewery (the old Sieben Brewery) on north Larrabee street, weeks before the start of Dever's beer war. Prohibition agents entered the brewery and were shown about by a member of the Sieben family. The Sieben family had leased the property to George Frank, whose neighborhood brewery was now licensed to produce near beer. As the group neared the racking room, the agents could hear employees frantically knocking off bungs from barrels of beer. Sieben refused to let the agents enter the locked room as the beer drained from the containers, heightening their suspicions that real beer was being bottled. Frank soon arrived and allowed the agents access to the racking room. When they entered, they saw that the floor of the room was wet and covered with foam, indicating to them that an attempt had been made to dispose of the contents of the barrels in the room. In their haste, the employees neglected to empty all the barrels and samples were taken for testing. As a result of the raid and the subsequent lab results, the permit of the Frank Brewery to brew real beer, dealcoholize it and create near beer, was revoked. The criminal case against Frank was later dropped, however, on a technicality.[17] Although in violation of federal law, the brewery defiantly continued to operate.

Dion O'Banion

North Side gangster Dion O'Banion had made quite a name for himself in the early years of Prohibition. O'Banion, described by the local press as a "florist and brewer," was a volatile member of Torrio's fragile coalition of mobsters that ran the city beer rackets in the early twenties. O'Banion's business style was quite different from that of Torrio. Where Torrio would customarily smooth over objections between rival gangs over territorial boundaries and mediate disputes that arose in everyday bootlegging operations, Dion was combative in his approach to rival gangs. The contrast in Torrio's and O'Banion's business demeanors was apparent when two enterprising Chicago policemen held up a Torrio beer truck one night. "You can have the beer," the crooked cops told the drivers after taking $250 from them, "if you come across with $300 more. Go get the money and we'll hold the beer." The men called O'Banion on a line that police headquarters had earlier tapped and explained their predicament. "Three hundred dollars to them bums?" O'Banion screamed over the phone. "Why, say, I can get 'em knocked off for half that much."

Sensing they might be in over their heads, the beer runners gave Torrio a call and reported their conversation with O'Banion. "I just been talking to Johnny," one of the drivers later called back to O'Banion, "and he says to let them cops have the three hundred. He says he don't want no trouble." When word of the incident was later picked up by the local press, the *Chicago Daily News* rightfully commented that "it was the difference in temper that made Torrio all powerful and O'Banion just a superior sort of plug-ugly."[18]

Chafing under Torrio's influence, O'Banion became furious when members of the Genna family began to sell cheap homemade alcohol in his territory. O'Banion demanded that Torrio send the Gennas back to the Taylor Street area where they had initially done business and enjoyed success. Before Torrio could reach a deal with the Gennas, O'Banion's men hijacked a truckload of the Gennas' cheaply-made alcohol in retaliation. Torrio's compromising skills somehow managed to stop the Genna family from striking back at O'Banion and his crew, but the animosity between Torrio and O'Banion festered.[19]

O'Banion's Betrayal

Shortly after the Genna incident, O'Banion met with Torrio and his protégé Al Capone and shocked them by announcing that he was getting out of the bootlegging business and retiring to Colorado. He offered to sell his share of the Sieben Brewery (a.k.a. The Frank Brewery), which the three of them jointly owned, for $500,000. Torrio and Capone jumped at the offer, happy to hear that the troublesome Irishman was leaving town. As a final gesture of goodwill, O'Banion offered to make a final, symbolic shipment of real beer from the illegally operating brewery with his partners, and asked that Torrio and Capone accompany him in the transaction. What Torrio and Capone didn't know was that O'Banion had been tipped to a federal raid on the brewery set for the early morning of May 19, 1924, the same day that they were to meet at the brewery for the final sale. Because Torrio had a prior conviction for violating Prohibition laws, O'Banion hoped that his Machiavellian plot would lead to their arrests, including his own . . . a chance he was willing to take. With Torrio facing a second federal conviction for bootlegging, a possible fine of up to $10,000 and a jail term of three years, there could be time enough for O'Banion to wrest away control of all Chicago operations from Torrio and the up-and-coming Capone.[20]

The Raid

On the early morning of May 19, 1924, the raid was conducted on the brewery with Torrio and O'Banion present, but Capone never showed up. After arresting a number of armed lookouts outside the brewery, the police and federal agents entered the property and discovered five trucks loaded with 150 barrels of real beer. Inside the brewery, agents found wet mash and a number of barrels of beer in the racking room. Outside, O'Banion was seen by one of the raiding party as he threw a book underneath the loading dock. Scribbled inside the seized book were recent delivery dates of beer from the brewery with the names of Chicago police officers and a prohibition agent who had been taking bribes for protection of the illegally operating brewery.

Throughout the raid, O'Banion seemed quite amused with the whole affair, joking to one of the raiding party, "You ought to get a raise!" At the Federal Building, O'Banion slipped out of the police bullpen behind two detectives and almost managed to escape, getting as far as the marshal's office before he was seized and escorted back. Unfazed by his recapture, he slipped a janitor $20 and had him buy breakfast for himself and his fellow prisoners.

But Torrio knew something was wrong. He had expected to be brought to the district police station, not the Federal Building. When it came time to make bail, Torrio peeled off $7500 from a wad of bills he carried but left O'Banion to wait until his bail bondsman showed up with the required $5000 for his release.[21]

The seizure of real beer from the Sieben Brewery and its crippling effect on Torrio's organization was reflected in the price per barrel of beer which immediately went from about $50 per barrel to $100 after the raid. O'Banion's captured book, which detailed payments to police officials and a crooked prohibition agent, caused a further tightening of security around those legally operating breweries that were still licensed to make near beer. Chief Collins ordered that three police guards now be stationed at each of the breweries, not only to monitor possible criminal activity at the brewing sites, but more importantly, to watch each other.[22]

Needle Beer

Five legally operating breweries, the National, Ruehl Brothers, Monarch, Atlas and Primalt breweries, were now busy in Chicago making near beer.[23] The high priced real stuff started giving way to the stronger needle beer, which was near beer injected with alcohol through the bung-hole of the barrel. Near beer, labeled with a legal federal revenue stamp, left the breweries unmolested by police squads. Cooperating beer joints carried a bootlegged supply of alcohol on site for final processing. Many of the owners of Chicago's 10,000 speakeasies favored needle beer over real beer simply because of the price; near beer was selling for the low price of $35 a barrel.[24] Another, more flavorful method of adding alcohol used a mixture of ginger ale and alcohol to replace an equal amount of near beer which was drawn from the barrel. With this method, the beer took on a sweeter profile, a taste difference that some brewers took into account upon the repeal of Prohibition.[25]

Torrio's Revenge

Months after the Sieben raid, O'Banion continued his bootlegging operations on the North Side. His actions indicated no preparation for a Colorado retirement as he had confided to Torrio and Capone in early May. If Torrio had any lingering doubts as to whether O'Banion had set him up for a second federal conviction, they were now gone.

On November 10, 1924, three men entered the flower shop that O'Banion owned on North State Street. As O'Banion greeted the men, they fired six shots into him, the last shot to his head. It was the final act of revenge for Torrio who had abandoned his compromising demeanor and finally allowed one of the Genna brothers and two accomplices to end the life of the double-crossing O'Banion.[26]

Assassination Attempt on Torrio

O'Banion's influence, however, would reach from beyond the grave. Still under indictment for the Sieben raid, Torrio and his wife returned from a day of shopping downtown. As Torrio followed his wife into their apartment building, gangsters Hymie "Earl the Pollack" Weiss and "Bugs" Moran, friends of the departed O'Banion, pulled up in a blue Cadillac and jumped out of the car. Thinking that the chauffeur still sitting in the car was Torrio, they opened fire, wounding him. Realizing their mistake, they spotted Torrio nearby and fired wildly, hitting him in the chest and neck. One of the assassins stood over Torrio as he writhed in pain on the street and fired one shot into his arm, another to his groin. Moran finally reached down to put a final bullet into Torrio's head and squeezed the trigger but the chamber was empty. Both men panicked and fled, leaving Torrio critically injured, but not dead.

At Jackson Park Hospital, Al Capone slept on a cot in his mentor's room, offering protection in case another assassination attempt might take place. Capone was lucky to be there himself. Less than two weeks before Torrio's shooting, Capone had narrowly escaped an attempt on his life at 55th and State by Weiss, Moran and Schemer Drucci.[27]

Torrio Relinquishes Control to Capone

While mulling over his own mortality as he lay in the hospital, Torrio must have realized that his fragile coalition of pimps, racketeers, bootleggers and murderers had fallen apart. In less than one month, Johnny Torrio left the hospital to recuperate at home. On February 9, 1925, he showed up in federal court to answer to the charges from the Sieben Brewery raid. Still weak and wearing bandages from his wounds, he pleaded guilty and was sentenced to a fine of $5000 and a prison term of nine months in the Lake County Jail in Waukegan, Illinois. While still in prison, Torrio sent for Capone. Sure that he was still a marked man and that a third federal conviction would probably mean life imprisonment, Torrio told Capone that he was handing over the remnants of the organization to him and his brothers, beginning a new, more dangerous era in Chicago.

After serving his jail sentence, Torrio spent a few years overseas and eventually returned to New York where he led a quiet life as a bootlegger. After Repeal, he secretly held an interest in a liquor distributorship in New York. His genteel solitude was broken in late 1938 when the Internal Revenue Service began investigating his ownership of the firm. Fearing that Torrio would flee the country, federal agents arrested him on charges of evading almost $87,000 in taxes when he attempted to pick up a passport at a local post office. An older Torrio, with much of the fight knocked out of him, threw himself on the mercy of the federal court and received a two and a half year prison term at Leavenworth. He lived out the rest of his life in White Plains, New York.[28]

Notes

1. *The Brewers' Journal*, October, 1919.

2. *Chicago Daily News*, September 11, 1923.

3. *Chicago Daily News*, November 17, 1924; *Chicago Tribune*, November 18, 1924; John H. Lyle. *The Dry and Lawless Years.* (Englewood Cliffs, NJ: Prentice-Hall, Inc., 1960) p. 84; John Landesco. *Organized Crime in Chicago* (Chicago and London: The University of Chicago Press, 1929) p. 97.

4. *Western Brewer*, September, 1919, October, 1919.

5. Herbert Asbury. *Gem Of the Prairie.* (DeKalb, IL: Northern Illinois University Press, 1986) pp. 326–327; *Chicago Daily News*, September 11, 1923; Landesco, *op. cit.*, p. 87.

6. *Chicago Daily News*, September 12–13, 1923.

7. *Chicago Daily News*, September 13, 1923.

8. *Chicago Daily News*, September 15, 1923.

9. *Chicago Daily News*, September 21, 28, 1923.

10. *Chicago Daily News*, September 29, 1923.

11. *Chicago Tribune*, October 8, 1923.

12. *Chicago Tribune*, October 3, 1923.

13. *Chicago Tribune*, October 8, 1923; *Chicago Tribune*, September 23, 1923.

14. *Chicago Journal*, November 3, 1923; *Chicago Herald and Examiner*, September 23, 26, 29, 1923; *Chicago Daily News*, November 8, 1923.

15. City of Chicago Council Proceedings, December 12, 1923.

16. *New York Times*, November 18, 1923.

17. Testimony of Prohibition Agents John Showalter and Andrew Hermanson, May 20, 1924. United States of America, Northern District of Illinois, Eastern Division, State of Illinois, County of Cook; *Chicago Herald Examiner*, May 20,1924.

18. *Chicago Daily News*, November 19, 1924; Kenneth Allsop. *The Bootleggers and their Era.* (Garden City, NY: Doubleday & Co., Inc.. 1961) p. 71.

19. Herbert Asbury. *op. cit.*, pp. 345–347.

20. Herbert Asbury, *Ibid.*, pp. 348–349, *Chicago Herald Examiner*, May 20, 1924.

21. *Chicago Herald Examiner*, May 19, 1924.

22. *Chicago Herald Examiner*, May 22, 1924.

23. *Chicago Tribune*, November 18, 1924.

24. *Chicago Daily News*, November 17, 1924.

25. Mezz Mezzrow and Bernard Wolfe. *Really the Blues.* (Garden City, NY: Doubleday, 1972) pp. 52–53; Peter Hernon and Terry Ganey. *Under the Influence. The Unauthorized Story of the Anheuser-Busch Dynasty.* (New York: Simon & Schuster, 1991) p. 155.

26. Laurence Bergreen. *Capone The Man And The Era.* (New York. Simon & Schuster, 1994) pp. 134–135.

27. *Ibid.*, pp. 141, 143–145.

28. *Ibid.*, pp. 146–147, 564–566.

Chapter 12

The Capone Era, 1926–1931

"There's plenty of beer business for everybody.
Why kill each other over it?"
Al Capone, peacemaker.

Capone's Wildcat Breweries

Capone now completely controlled what was left of Torrio's crumbling empire. Although the output of near beer from the federally licensed breweries continued to provide a base for needle beer, output could not keep up with demand. In addition to the problems of meeting supply, the federal government had finally started to pick up the enforcement pace of the National Prohibition laws, working with local police officials when necessary. With police attention regularly paid to the former illegally operating breweries, now shut down as a result of Mayor Dever's campaign, Capone was forced to start a number of clandestinely-located wildcat breweries throughout the city and suburbs to supplement the insatiable Chicago demand for beer. These makeshift breweries, usually tucked away in deserted industrial areas, produced real beer but often experienced trouble in securing the raw materials needed for the brewing process.

Unexpected help for Capone's supply dilemma came from brewing giant August A. Busch who somehow discovered that Capone had recently directed some of his men to steal golden gates, devices used to tap barrels, from his St. Louis brewery. Busch sent his young son Gussie to talk to Capone in Miami where the mobster was relaxing on an extended vacation. During the meeting, the two ultimately reached a deal that provided Capone's breweries not only with over 250,000 of the tapping devices, but also with yeast, sugar and malt extract for their makeshift brewing operations. Malt extract was a critical ingredient for these small, unsophisticated brewing operations. Bypassing the lengthy operation of mashing the bulky malted barley to extract the sugars needed for fermentation, a process that could take hours, the bootleggers and their brewers could now dilute the syrupy malt extract with boiling water, add hops, and in a short time, have the wort chilled down and ready for the addition of yeast. In a week or two, they would have real beer available for their customers.

Momentarily forgetting with whom he was dealing during their discussions, young ambassador Gussie asked for Capone's signature to seal the deal. Capone shrugged off the naïve demand and Busch wisely backed down. At a cost of $2 per golden gate plus additional income from unknown amounts of brewing supplies, Capone made a small fortune for the Anheuser-Busch Brewing Company during the lean years of Prohibition. As a young man Gussie would often tell friends of the golden gate episode and his meeting with Capone, but as he grew older (and wiser), he avoided the subject. The story was corroborated by Gussie's daughter Lotsie in her family history.[1]

Capone's Peace Conference

While these makeshift arrangements for the production of real beer took some of the pressure off Capone's recently acquired organization, the deadly problems of dealing with O'Banion's old gang continued to plague Capone. "Hymie" Weiss had recently spurned Capone's attempt to form a business alliance, a successfully proven technique that Capone had learned from his mentor, Torrio. Capone had reasonably offered Weiss all the beer concessions in Chicago north of Madison Street, keeping the rest of Chicago for himself. Weiss, however, would only agree to Capone's peace overture if Al agreed to turn over the two remaining murderers of Dion O'Banion. Capone refused and realized he had to have Weiss killed before Weiss killed him. On October 5, 1926, assassins took care of Weiss just across the street from O'Banion's old flower shop.

With Weiss out of the way, Capone arranged a city-wide peace conference with the remaining rival gang leaders on October 20th. It was a highly publicized meeting that took place at the downtown Sherman House. At the mobster summit, Capone made his pitch for unity, offering to share the lucrative beer market with his former adversaries. "There's plenty of beer business for everybody," he reportedly said. "Why kill each other over it?" As a result of the conference and a pact made there with his rivals, Capone acquired all of the territory south of Madison Street as far as Chicago Heights and the territory west of Chicago, including Cicero.[2]

Securing New Accounts

Capone's beer drummers methodically went to work in their agreed upon business territory, securing every and all accounts. Their approach to securing new and even wayward accounts was straightforward and absolute, with intimidation and physical violence having become effective motivators. If initial attempts to persuade a saloon owner to take on their bootlegged beer proved fruitless, a well-placed pipe bomb would usually close the deal. The next morning the owner would show up and the whole front of his place would be blown out. Soon after, Capone's drummers would show up again and say, "Gee, if you'd had Ace Beer [Capone's beer] I don't think that would've happened to ya." Unable to file an insurance claim and having taken a financial loss, the hapless owner now had one last choice if he wanted to continue in the saloon business. "So he goes back to the Capone group to get the money for repairs and from then on he only does what they tell him." It was Al Capone's version of the tied-house concept.[3]

But some saloon owners resisted these drastic measures. One former Pilsen resident recalls how a neighborhood saloonkeeper defiantly handled the aftermath of a pipe bombing.

> When beer drummers came around telling the owner he was going to buy beer from them, he said no. He was a tough Bohemian. That night they threw a pipe bomb at the front of his saloon. It blew out the windows and damaged part of the bar. The next morning he boarded up the front of the saloon but let everyone in the neighborhood know that he was going to open up later that day for business.
>
> Down in the basement of the saloon was a small brewery. That's where he got his beer, but he was no different than most of the families on the block. Almost everybody made their own beer; he just made more of it.
>
> When he finally opened up, there was a line of customers waiting to get into the side door of the saloon. I was a kid then but I can still remember how funny it looked to me, you know, the old timers all lined up and waiting patiently for their beer.[4]

The End of the Dever Administration

Local politics, as usual, were the center stage of attention in late 1926 in Chicago. "Decent" Dever was how critics now referred to the crusading mayor. His campaign to dry out Chicago through brewery raids and wholesale closings of saloons and soda parlors had even begun to target Ma and Pa corner groceries. As a result of the fanatical tempo of the closings and Dever's unwavering adherence to an unpopular law, he began to unintentionally alienate a sizable portion of Chicago's ethnic electorate and flame the violence between rival bootleg gangs as they continued to fight over territory.

While his beer war outwardly showed results, organized crime continued to flourish. Corruption still permeated local government, in spite of the personal integrity of both Mayor Dever and Police Chief Collins. National Prohibition with all its confusing moral baggage was slowly bringing Dever's administration down.[5]

Hoping to pacify some of his more vocal opponents, Dever once again brought his dry campaign to the people, continuing his familiar argument that he was really a wet, forced to enforce an unpopular law. Chicago, though, was ripe for a change. National Prohibition was a dismal failure in Chicago. Its blanketing of "personal liberty" still projected the perception of nativism to the thousands of Germans, Irish, Italians, Poles and other ethnics who controlled the vote. The Chicagoans who had voted Dever into office were now ready to abandon him.

After considerable soul searching, Dever began to realize that Prohibition did not and could not work, since strict enforcement of a law which the majority of law abiding citizens found offensive, was not possible. But it was too late for Dever to change course. The well-meaning mayor had lost touch with the very people who had put him into office.

Big Bill, Part II

After the typical primary dance of local candidates, William Hale Thompson's name once again oozed to the top as Republican choice for Mayor of Chicago in 1927. With promises to reopen every speakeasy in Chicago that Dever had closed and after declaring himself "wetter than the middle of the Atlantic Ocean," Thompson's campaign pledges caught the attention of not only the disenfranchised electorate but also of "Schemer" Drucci and Jack Zuta of the "Bugs" Moran gang, who readily contributed $50,000 to Thompson's campaign. Not one to be outdone by a rival gang, Capone secretly contributed a $260,000 pay-off to Big Bill's campaign. The *Chicago Tribune* later reported that the money was "ladled out to Thompson workers from a bathtub in the Hotel Sherman, filled with packages of $5 bills." In return for the payoff, an agreement was reached with Thompson forces that Capone would be granted immunity to operate whorehouses and gambling dens and retain control of all beer and booze joints south of Madison Street. It was his old territory, but now the heat would be off. It was the real beginning of the Roaring Twenties in Chicago.[6]

A few weeks before the mayoral election, the United States Circuit Court of Appeals upheld the decision of Federal Judge Adam C. Cliffe that the mere smelling of liquor in a restaurant or cabaret was grounds to close the business. As a result of the decision, called "smell raids," incredibly, some of the more famous nightclubs in Chicago closed, including the Moulin Rouge, the Friars' Club and Al Tearney's Town Club. Prohibition Agents who conducted the raids admitted that they had not actually attempted to purchase any liquor at the clubs nor had they even seen any alcohol served; they simply claimed they smelled it. Dever's campaign to rid the city of alcohol was now bordering on questions of constitutionality and just plain lunacy.

Thompson's Win

Thompson easily won the mayoral election with a total of 515,716 votes to Dever's 432,678 and was sworn in on April 13, 1927. Later analysis of ethnic voting patterns showed a dramatic drop in support for Dever and the Democratic Party in the 1927 election from the winning results they had enjoyed in 1923. The heavy handedness of his beer war, the feeling by much of Dever's ethnic constituency that National Prohibition had an underlying nativist tone to it and the later assertion that Dever was secretly dumped by the local Democratic Party chieftains, including wet advocate Anton

Cermak, all contributed to the inevitability of his political demise. For those appalled at the strength of Thompson's victory, it was suggested that the real mystery was not how Thompson had won, but how Dever had found so many people to vote for him.[7]

For Chicagoans, it was a full and complete repudiation of National Prohibition. In disgust, Dever had Thompson sworn in before his term actually ended, allowing himself time to slip out of town and avoid Thompson's scheduled public inauguration. It was the first time in the history of Chicago that an outgoing mayor had ever skipped his successor's swearing in ceremony.[8]

Eliot Ness

Soon after Dever's defeat, Capone swung into action, reaping the benefits of his political contribution to Thompson. Later findings by the Chicago Crime Commission showed that Capone had quickly taken over the lucrative beer territories of the Saltis and O'Donnell gangs after the election, increasing the size of his crime empire.[9]

In 1928, with a staff of 300 agents, the Chicago unit of the Prohibition Bureau was joined by a young agent named Eliot Ness. Hired by U.S. Attorney George E. Q. Johnson, Ness' first forays into the bootlegging operations of the Capone organization took place in nearby Chicago Heights. On the strength of his success in busting a number of the suburban gambling and bootleg operations in "The Heights," Ness was ordered to move his efforts to Cicero and Chicago. An analysis of Chicago Prohibition Bureau records revealed to Ness that prisoners had never been captured inside a Capone brewery. These breweries were wildcat breweries, usually operating in warehouses in secluded industrial areas. Past experiences indicated that the raided breweries were normally occupied for only forty minutes in a twenty-four hour period. In order to locate new clandestine brewing sites and their workers, Ness sent two-man teams to trace the movement of empty beer barrels hauled by trucks from the thousands of speakeasies in Chicago as they headed back to the wildcat breweries.

Brewery Raids

From the back of "Big Jim" Colisimo's former restaurant, two agents anxiously watched as workers loaded empty beer barrels onto a truck. After stopping at a number of other South Side joints, the fully laden truck made its way back to an old factory at 38th and Shields, just a foul ball away from Comiskey Park. After a few days of observation, it was determined by Prohibition Agents that the site was merely used to clean empty barrels. It was not a brewery. Disappointed, Ness and his men continued the strategy of following trucks loaded with empty barrels, but with no results.

A few days later, the agents got lucky. Ness' men found an operating brewery in the Singer Storage Company at 2271 South Lumber Street by tracing the route of the cleaned barrels back to the secret brewery. They were confident that this new target was a brewery and not another barrel cleaning operation by the way the trucks were weighted down as they left the site. Equipped with sawed-off shotguns, crowbars and axes, the agents watched as a number of trucks entered the premises. Armed with an ax, Ness rushed the entrance and frantically hacked away at the wooden double doors of the suspected brewery as another agent attempted to jimmy it open with a crowbar. Behind the wooden door, however, stood a second, steel door. Having lost the element of surprise, Ness desperately fired two shots through the lock. The door finally opened revealing nineteen 1500 gallon vats, two new trucks and 140 barrels of real beer; but no one was in sight. It was later estimated that the plant was capable of producing 100 barrels of beer a day. There was no one to arrest, but for Ness and his men, it was a triumphant beginning.

Frustrated by the clumsiness of the raid, Ness drew up a design for a heavy duty steel bumper attached to a ten-ton truck for ramming any door, reinforced or otherwise. The target this time was a brewery at 1632 South Cicero Avenue. Once again watching activities at the suspected brewery, they determined that it was, indeed, another wildcat brewery. As the battering ram of the truck crashed through the doors, Ness was initially disappointed to find that the warehouse was empty. But after their eyes had adjusted to the darkness of the warehouse, Ness and his men realized that the apparent emptiness of the brewery was really another false wall, painted black for deception. Ness ordered the driver of the truck to ram it. This time they found another brewery with seven 320 gallon fermentation vats and five men on site including Steve Svoboda, a master brewer for Capone's organization.

Thompson Campaigns against Federal Intervention

In early 1928, the stepped-up presence of prohibition agents in Chicago was beginning to show its affect on the corrupt administration of Mayor Thompson and his City Hall cronies. Around the time of George E. Q. Johnson's appointment as U. S. Attorney in Chicago, a squad of federal agents had raided a saloon on the South Side of the city, shooting a municipal court bailiff in the back during the struggle. The bailiff, William Beatty, claimed that he thought the federal agents, waving weapons when they entered, were holdup men and that he had merely attempted to flee from harm's way. Myron C. Caffey, the agent who had shot Beatty, later testified that Beatty had pulled a gun on him during the raid. As a result of Agent Caffey's testimony, Beatty was indicted by a federal grand jury for resisting a federal officer.

Thompson's Chief of Police, Michael Hughes, demanded that Agent Caffey be turned over to his authority to answer charges of shooting Beatty. When George E. Golding, head of the federal squad involved in the raid refused, Chief Hughes took out a warrant for the arrest of Caffey and assembled a squad of Chicago police, ready to storm the Federal Building and seize Caffey. The assault on the Federal Building, however, did not take place. Federal Judge H. Wilkerson ruled that Caffey would be turned over to the police after the April primary, defusing the awkward and embarrassing struggle between Thompson's police and federal officials.

Thompson spent the next few weeks preaching of his attempts to save the local citizenry from the dangers of federal intervention in Chicago law enforcement, and incredibly claimed, "We took out a warrant and we'll throw every damn dry agent in jail." But federal agents ignored Thompson's bluster and continued their drive to solve the Prohibition problems that the city had woefully failed to do.[10]

The Untouchables Continue Their Raids

One of Ness' biggest brewery busts was his raid on The Old Reliable Trucking Company at 3136 South Wabash. The agents destroyed 40,324 gallons of unbarreled beer and 115 barrels of racked beer. Brewer Svoboda was once again caught in the raid along with four accomplices. This time, Ness and his men cagily left most of the equipment in place, setting a trap for anyone who might return to claim it. The next day, four men, including Bert Delaney, another Capone brewer, dutifully returned for the equipment and were captured.

Soon after the success of the Wabash raid, Ness and his men seized a smaller brewery at 1712 North Kilbourn, operated by mobster George "Red" Barker, and one more Capone brewery at 2024 South State. The Barker brewery raid was the result of a telephone tip that would cause a wave of paranoia to ripple throughout the illicit brewing trade. One telephone call to the feds could wipe out another rival gang's brewery; it was much easier and less costly than sending out a bunch of goons to shut it down.

Probably the most publicized brewery raid was the result of a tap on the phone of Ralph Capone. In a tapped phone conversation agents heard a reference about reopening a spot on South Wabash Avenue. They alerted federal agents to watch a previously raided and closed Capone brewery at 2108 South Wabash. On June 12, 1930, federal prohibition agents, led by Special Agent Alexander Jamie, seized the brewery. Fifty thousand gallons of beer, 150,000 gallons of mash, two trucks and six men were seized in the raid. However, the *Chicago Tribune* never mentions Ness in their article about the raid the following morning, crediting Agent Jamie for the raid. Ness' account of the raid in his book reads quite differently. Alexander Jamie was Ness' brother-in-law and had recommended Ness for the position of prohibition agent in 1928. In describing the Wabash Street raid in his book, *The Untouchables*, Ness takes total credit for the raid, never mentioning Jamie.[11]

Agent Ness Beats His Drum

Apparently, Ness' heroics made better press in New York than in Chicago. In often gushing prose, a 1931 article in the *New York Times* described Agent Ness, his youth, integrity and intelligence. But Chicago newsmen viewed Ness quite differently. Tony Berardi, a *Chicago Tribune* photographer, recalled that "Ness was considered (by Chicago newsmen) not quite a phony but strictly small time."[12] Ness seems to have had a habit of tooting his own horn; years later, he claimed to have raided twenty-five breweries and seized forty-five delivery trucks, but a report by Ness to U. S. Attorney George E. Q. Johnson indicates otherwise:

> . . . six breweries with total equipment valued at $140,000 were seized . . . total income based upon the wholesale (price) of beer manufactured would have totaled $9,154,200 annually. Five large beer distributing plants were seized in addition to the breweries. The total amount of beer seized . . . was approximately 200,000 gallons having a wholesale value to the Capone organization of $343,750. Twenty-five trucks and two cars were seized, the value of which totaled approximately $30,950 . . .[13]

In his autobiography, Ness described an unusual parade he claimed to have organized to infuriate Capone, though no evidence corroborates this event. Assembling trucks which he and his men had seized from Capone's breweries, a collection of pick-ups, ten-ton vans and glass-lined tank trucks for transporting beer, he and his men brazenly drove them by Capone's headquarters at the Lexington Hotel on Michigan Avenue. Before they got underway, Ness wrote, he had telephoned Capone and told him to look out the front windows of the hotel at exactly eleven o'clock that morning. Right on time, the rag tag collection of the mobster's seized trucks slowly drove by the hotel. From the windows of the Lexington, heads bobbed and arms pointed as the show on South Michigan passed by. The next morning, Ness continued, a snitch met Ness and told him of Capone's reaction to the parade. "I'll kill 'im! I'll kill 'im with my own bare hands!" the enraged hoodlum screamed as he busted a couple of chairs over a table.[14]

Capone Indicted

On June 5, 1931, the United States government finally indicted Capone on charges of tax evasion. A week later, Capone was once again indicted, this time for National Prohibition violations. It was the culmination of all the efforts by Ness, his men and other federal agents who had worked to bring Capone and his empire down. The indictment listed Alphonse Capone with all his known aliases (Al Brown, A. Costa, Albert Costa, Frank Rose, John Brown, Snorky Capone, Frank Hart and Louis Hart) and charged him with 5000 offenses against the United States. Over five hundred offenses dealt with the manufacturing of beer with more than one-half of one percent of alcohol without first obtaining a permit from the Commissioner of Internal Revenue, the Commissioner of Prohibition, the Commissioner of Industrial Alcohol and the Director of Prohibition and the other 4000 offenses were for transporting the illegally-brewed beer. By linking

Capone's name to the purchase of a number of trucks seized during the brewery raids by Ness and others, the government had conclusive evidence that Capone was guilty of Prohibition violations.[15]

However, the violations described in the tax evasion indictment were the ones used by George E. Q. Johnson to eventually convict and sentence Capone. Although the work of Ness and his agents caused considerable damage to Capone's bootlegging operations, the dry crusade was little more than a distraction used to tie up Capone's organization while the federal government delved further into Capone's murky tax situation. But even with Capone's arrest and later imprisonment, beer continued to flow in Chicago.

Thompson Defeated

A few months before Capone's arrest, the results of the mayoral election of 1931 once again forced William Hale Thompson and his cronies out of City Hall, replacing him with wet advocate Anton Cermak. Chicago had been chosen as the site of the 1933 World's Fair, to be called *A Century of Progress Exposition*. With the election of wet advocate Cermak and the potential of millions of cash-laden tourists coming to Chicago to visit the World's Fair, both the new city administration and the remnants of Capone's organization prepared for the prosperity that 1933 might offer.

Notes

1. Peter Hernon & Terry Ganey. *Under the Influence. The Unauthorized Story of the Anheuser-Busch Dynasty.* (New York, NY: Simon & Schuster, 1991) pp. 131–132.

2. Kenneth Allsop. *The Bootleggers and Their Era*, (Garden City, N.Y: Doubleday & Co., 1961) p. 125.

3. Laurence Bergreen. *Capone. The Man and the Era.* (New York, NY: Simon & Schuster, 1994) p. 181.

4. Interview with Ed Chensky, March 4, 1998, Riverside, Illinois.

5. John Kobler. *Capone: The Life and World of Al Capone*, (New York, NY: Putnam & Sons, 1971) pg. 111; John H. Lyle. *The Dry and Lawless Years.* (Englewood Cliffs, NJ: Prentice-Hall, Inc. 1960) pg. 16; Edward D. Sullivan. *Rattling the Cup on Chicago Crime.* (New York, NY: The Vanguard Press, 1929) pg. 149. Kobler reports that Collins was offered $10,000 per month. Lyle claims the bribe was $1000 per day. Sullivan reports that Dever was offered $100,000 for his cooperation during the Beer Wars.

6. Kenneth Allsop. *op. cit.*, pg. 211; *Chicago Tribune*, February 17, 1931.

7 John R. Schmidt. *The Mayor Who Cleaned Up Chicago. A Political Biography of William E. Dever.* (DeKalb, IL: Northern Illinois University Press, 1989) pp. 163–166, 169.

8. *Chicago Herald and Examiner*, April 13, 1927; *Chicago Post*, April 7, 1927.

9. *Chicago Tribune*, February 17, 1931.

10. Allsop, *op. cit.* pg. 209.

11. Eliot Ness. *The Untouchables.* (New York, NY: Pocket Books, Inc., 1966). Most of the account of Ness and his raids is taken from chapters 6 through 19; *Chicago Tribune*, June 13, 1930; *New York Times*, June 18, 1931.

12. Laurence Bergreen. *op. cit.* pg. 433.

13. Eliot Ness to George E. Q. Johnson, March 26, 1932, as quoted in Bergreen, *op. cit.* p. 411.

1.4 Eliot Ness, *op. cit.* pp. 200–209.

15. *Indictment of Capone*, June Term, 1931, District Court of the United States of America for the Northern District of Illinois, Eastern Division.

Chapter 13

New Beer's Eve, April 7, 1933

"I recommend . . . the passage of legislation . . . to legalize the manufacture and sale of beer."

President Franklin D. Roosevelt

The Beginning Of The End

By 1932, National Prohibition was dying. Its dry policy and enforcement had caused a generation of Americans to be raised with a casual disregard for the law. Probably no issue had done so much to divide the country since the Civil War. After some political maneuvering, Democratic presidential candidate Franklin D. Roosevelt, had finally declared himself to be an advocate for Repeal. Incumbent President Herbert Hoover, however, continued to state his belief in National Prohibition.

The economic logic of Repeal was eloquently expressed by August A. Busch of the Anheuser-Busch Brewery in St. Louis. In 1931, Busch issued a pamphlet titled *An Open Letter to the American People*, sent a copy to every U.S. Senator and Congressman and took out ads in leading national magazines explaining his position on legalizing the production and sale of beer. With the country facing problems of the Great Depression, Busch proclaimed that the legalization of beer would put over one million people back to work, including farmers, railroad employees and even coal miners. In addition, the St. Louis brewer argued that the government would save the $50 million a year it was now wasting through its efforts to enforce Prohibition. Taxation of beer would also help the federal government recoup the estimated $500 million in revenues it had lost since the beginning of Prohibition.

Attending a meeting in February of 1933 of the National Malt Products Manufacturing Association at the Hotel Sherman in Chicago, and knowing that the tide had turned, Busch declared himself "100 per cent for beer" and boasted that his St. Louis brewery was ready to restart the production of beer as soon as the law would permit.

The Siebel Institute of Technology in Chicago was so sure of the relegalization of beer that the faculty announced the resumption of their regular five month training course for brewers in January of 1933. The sweet smell of malt was in the air.[1]

Support in Washington for the reintroduction of 3.2% beer began with an opinion by Representative Beck of Pennsylvania that Congress already had the power to legalize beer and that the Supreme Court would more than likely uphold any favorable congressional action. After some political foot dragging, President-elect Roosevelt finally added his opinion to the debate, saying that he favored the 3.2% beer bill that now was pending in the Senate. The Senate continued negotiations on a bill to legalize beer and made no change to a proposal to tax a barrel of beer at the rate of $5, effectively acknowledging the eventual reinstitution of the legal brewing industry. On February 15, 1933, the Senate took the debate even further when it voted 58 to 23 to begin formal consideration of a resolution proposing repeal of the Eighteenth Amendment. Later that same day, the Senate passed its approval of the Blaine resolution, proposing repeal of the Eighteenth Amendment. The issue was then passed on to the House of Representatives. When Speaker of the House Garner heard of the quickness of the Senate's actions, he commented surprisingly, "The vote was better than most of us anticipated. We will pass the amendment here Monday—I should say, consider it." With a slip of the Speaker's tongue, there was little doubt on what the outcome of the vote in the House would be.[2]

The same day, the Illinois State Senate also voted its approval of repeal of the Illinois dry laws and the state Search and Seizure Act which had been invoked by State Attorney General Edward Brundage back in July of 1919. Brundage's narrow interpretation of the law had shut down the sale of beer and booze in Chicago six months before National Prohibition actually took effect.[3]

3.2% Beer

On February 20, 1933, Congress passed the repeal of the National Prohibition Amendment and submitted its final approval to the states for ratification. In Springfield, Governor Horner presided at a meeting of state senators and representatives and agreed to a June 5 election for a state convention to decide if Illinois delegates would vote for repeal of the Eighteenth Amendment. With the anticipated results of the state convention being in favor of Repeal, the resumption of the manufacturing, transportation and sale of beer in Illinois was imminent. Horner confirmed this when he indicated his readiness to sign the necessary bills invoking revocation of the Search and Seizure Act and the state prohibition laws as soon as they came to his desk.

On March 13, President Roosevelt used the bully pulpit of his office to formally recommend a looser interpretation of the Volstead Act to Congress. "I recommend to the Congress the passage of legislation for the immediate modification of the Volstead Act, in order to legalize the manufacture and sale of beer . . ." Upon hearing Roosevelt's recommendation, Governor Horner signed the bill repealing the two State of Illinois dry enforcement laws, now leaving the enforcement of National Prohibition to the federal government.

Finally, on March 21, 1933, the United States House of Representatives completed action on the Cullen-Harrison bill, permitting the resumption of the manufacture and sale of 3.2% beer and light wines in those states that were now legally considered wet. The next morning, President Roosevelt was scheduled to sign the bill, but a bureaucratic mix-up postponed his signing until March 23.

In the meantime, Roosevelt talked of a possible amnesty for violators imprisoned for the manufacturing and sale of beer up to an alcoholic content of 3.2% by weight. In Illinois, there were 3,380 incarcerated federal Prohibition offenders. Roosevelt's sentiments were perhaps more economic in scope than benevolent. The release of Illinois Prohibition violators, along with the release of similar offenders throughout the United States, would save the federal government millions of badly needed dollars. The President's amnesty proposal was held by Congress for consideration. With a fifteen day wait required after Roosevelt's signature, 3.2% beer would again be available on April 7 in nineteen states that had removed their dry laws. Wet advocates cheerfully anticipated that an additional fifteen states would soon join these wet states.

One day after Roosevelt signed the Cullen-Harrison bill, the Justice Department quietly announced that it was dropping its National Prohibition exhibit at Chicago's World's Fair. No reason was given; for Chicagoans, no reason was needed.[4]

New Retail Outlets for Beer

As Chicago prepared for the resumption of legal brewing, local issues of home rule, licensing, taxation and dispensing arose, especially after the wording of the congressional beer bill declared 3.2% beer as non-intoxicating, a legal technicality needed to nullify the alcoholic restrictions of the Volstead Act. With this ruling by Congress, concurred in by Illinois Attorney General Otto Kerner, Chicago's saloons would no longer hold domain over the retail sale of beer as they had done before Prohibition. As a non-intoxicant, beer could now be available in such places as grocery stores and drug stores, even Ma and Pa corner grocery stores. In a meeting of city officials, lawyers advised acting Mayor Corr and key city aldermen that simply the repeal of the Illinois prohibition law did not revive the old liquor laws. As a result, the sale of this 3.2%, non-intoxicating beer, now having fallen into the same category as soda water or ginger ale, would be unregulated in off-premise sites unless the Chicago City Council and Springfield acted quickly to correct this unexpected legal quirk.[5]

The City Gets Ready for 3.2% Beer

Unfazed by the political logistics of the resumption of beer, local old time beer establishments made ready. At the Berghoff on West Adams, eighty-year old Herman J.

Herman J. Berghoff tends the barrels for his famous saloon. Courtesy of the Berghoff Restaurant.

Berghoff proudly displayed Beer Retail License Number 1, issued by the City Collector's Office permitting the serving of beer at his famous bar. Installed in 1897, the Berghoff's wood inlaid bar from Amsterdam, which still serves as the focal point of this Chicago landmark, was made ready for business. In pre-Prohibition days, Berghoff estimated that he sold as high as forty-two barrels of beer a day. Anticipated demand for the golden nectar seemed just as positive. At the Righeimer bar on North Clark, Acting Mayor Corr and a host of local politicos rededicated the establishment's famous 100 foot bar. Corr had been thrust into this position after Mayor Cermak had been shot by a crazed assassin while meeting with President Roosevelt in Miami, Florida. Sadly, the man who represented the local wet interests for so long, died just weeks before he could see the return of beer to the city and nation.

Clerks at the City Collector's office worked overtime to take care of the rush of new applications for beer licenses. Unexplainably, the City Council had already passed the required ordinance providing for the $150 licensing fee for saloonkeepers in December, 1932, four months before legal beer would flow again in Chicago. Seven hundred and forty-one saloonkeepers had actually paid the fee for the first half of the year even though they were in violation of state and federal dry laws. The Chicago City Council tried unsuccessfully to pull off a similar revenue-enhancing stunt in 1929. At the time, there was a movement afoot in the council to license the 5000 bartenders who regularly poured illegal drink for thirsty Chicagoans. With a $10 annual fee, it would have meant an additional $50,000 income to the financially desperate city. Referred to committee for further study, the idea was abruptly dropped from the council agenda when someone mentioned that National Prohibition was still in effect. It would be hard to license bartenders when, in theory, there were no bars. By April 7, more than 2600 bars were legally licensed to sell beer, a dramatic drop from the over 7000 licensed bars of pre-Prohibition days.

City breweries hired several hundred workers with promises of an additional hiring of one thousand more men and women by April 7, as the bottling of beer in Chicago began on March 25. At the Schoenhofen Company, workers on two eight-hour shifts began a daily regimen of filling 14,000 cases of beer a day. The politically-connected Atlas Brewing Company, granted the first license to resume the brewing of real beer in the Northern District, including neighboring Milwaukee, began plans to bottle 20 to 25 thousand cases a day. Realizing that they'd probably never fill all their outstanding orders by April 7, even with a planned hiring of 200 to 300 more employees, Atlas President Charles Vopicka ordered outdoor posters to be printed for distribution throughout the city during the early morning hours of New Beer's Eve. Under a picture of a smiling Uncle Sam hoisting a beer, the posters asked for the indulgence of any customers who had not yet received their promised beer delivery. At the Prima Company, management estimated that they would soon begin the bottling of over 3,000,000 bottles of beer a day. The brewery had recently been expanded to a 500,000 barrel capacity in anticipation of Repeal. Employees of the United States Brewing Company on North Elston decorated the exterior of the plant with flags and bunting. A picture of Franklin Roosevelt hung above the entrance of the brewery, celebrating the man who represented Repeal. Coopers readied thousands of new wooden barrels for delivery to breweries. Fifteen hundred beer delivery trucks were prepped for the big night, supplemented by moving vans, milk wagons and coal trucks. Federal inspectors started to make the rounds of Chicago's seven licensed breweries, measuring the aging tanks, which were also used for the computation of federal tax due. A final industry estimate, made days before the resumption of beer in Chicago, figured that approximately 15,000 men and women had found work in breweries and related industries in Chicago. A heady sense of festivity was settling over Chicago.[6]

There was, however, a sobering note to all the gaiety at the breweries. District police captains quietly placed guards at all the breweries to discourage any possible attempts at hijacking when the trucks finally rolled out for deliveries.[7]

When does the Party Begin?

In an amusing misunderstanding prior to the big event, E. C. Yellowley, head of the Prohibition Department in Chicago, ruled that the local delivery of beer could begin at

11:01 p.m. on April 6, which would correspond to 12:01 a.m., April 7 in Washington, E. C. Yellowley's interpretation of the commencement time was clarified by United States Attorney General Cummings who ruled that legal beer deliveries could begin at 12:01 a.m. in each respective time zone.

Illinois House Representative Fred A. Britten thought he had a better idea as to when beer deliveries should begin in Chicago. In a telephone conversation with the Attorney General, Britten suggested that the commencement time for the serving of legal beer would better serve Chicago interests if it began as early as 10:00 p.m., April 6th. When Cummings reminded the Illinois representative that federal law distinctly stated that beer deliveries could only begin at 12:01 a.m., April 7th, Britten, in an amazing display of political chutzpah, suggested a solution to that little time problem. "Chicago will set all the clocks ahead two hours at 10:00 p.m.," he explained to the skeptical Attorney General. "The City Council will pass the ordinance," he assured Cummings. To emphasize the seriousness of his request and the careful planning he was ready to carry through to get fresh beer to thirsty Chicagoans, Britten added this assurance to his request. "The trucks will leave the breweries at 10 with all streets cleared and motorcycle squads as escorts." The U. S. Attorney General could not be persuaded to allow Britten to implement his bizarre plan.[8]

12:01 a.m.?

As New Beer's Eve moved closer to reality in Chicago, the Chicago Hotel Association started to put pressure on the brewers and the local hotels, urging the hotel owners and managers not to take delivery of beer until 7 o'clock Friday morning, hours after beer could legally be sold in the city. John Burke, president of the association and manager of the Congress Hotel expressed his concerns that a wild night of revelry in Chicago might endanger future repeal of the Eighteenth Amendment, which still needed to be ratified by a two-thirds vote of all the states. "We feel that we should be careful not to kill the goose that laid the golden egg," he emphasized, and added that the anticipated celebration ". . . might give a black eye to things at the very beginning," a very real concern.[9]

Hilmar Ernst, president of the Prima Company and the Illinois Brewers' Association, brushed off Burke's criticism. The problem, if there was one, he noted, was a problem for the hotel men, not the brewers. "Even if the hotels want to begin selling at 9 or 10 in the morning, we'll have to start delivering at midnight to get them supplied. Our brewery alone now has orders calling for the immediate delivery of between 200,000 and 300,000 cases and there will be a lot more by the 7th." Ernst failed to mention that local breweries had also collected over $2,000,000 in deposits and guaranteed delivery. The I.B.A. president pointed out that the hotels were placing the biggest orders. Worried that delaying the sale of beer until the morning would cut hotel owners out of the

Chicago newspapers counted down the days until New Beer's Eve (April 7, 1933), as this cartoon from the Chicago Daily News *shows.*

huge volume of beer sales that was anticipated, Burke and his concerns were pushed aside by hotel owners and managers. Even a *Chicago Tribune* suggestion in favor of later day deliveries was ignored by the brewers. "The public demands it (beer) at once," sighed Anton Laadt, general manager of the Atlas Brewing Company.[10]

WGN radio, anticipating the wild night ahead and its historic significance, scheduled special programming throughout Thursday evening and Friday morning, broadcast from the Atlas Brewing Company at 21st and Blue Island. Radio personality Quinn Ryan was scheduled to give an on-site description of the beer manufacturing process straight through to the loading of the beer onto the waiting trucks ready for delivery. The brewery was preparing for delivery of 2,000 barrels and 100,000 cases of beer to retailers on the first night. Additional off-site radio pickups from the Palmer House and the Blackhawk Restaurant would allow at home celebrants to join in Chicago's New Beer's Eve festivities. CBS Radio Network arranged a radio hookup to broadcast the festivities in the Midwest's most important brewing centers of Chicago, Milwaukee and St. Louis.[11]

A Warning from the City

Because of the quick reinstitution of 3.2% beer and the time-consuming efforts needed to debate, write and implement new legislation, the City of Chicago and the State of Illinois discovered that they currently had no legislation on their books to regulate the sale of the soon-to-be-legal beer. The City Council urged Chicagoans to behave themselves during the celebration and warned hoteliers and would-be beer retailers that the Council's course of action on the eventual regulation of beer would be determined by how well the retailers conducted themselves in the first few weeks of beer sales. In some Loop hotels, cards and table tents were prepared for placement in their dining rooms, informing patrons that hotel management was forbidden by federal statute to provide ice, glasses or ginger ale while the customers awaited the serving of beer at 12:01 a.m. It was a little white lie, but hotels feared that celebrants, using hotel provided set-ups, might mix them with bootleg liquor, causing their establishments to be shut down by snooping police or federal agents. Particular attention was to be paid by Chicago police to the more famous Prohibition-era night spots. Clubs like the Frolics, the Chez Paree, Follies Bergere, Vanity Fair and the Green Mill along with the College Inn and the Terrace Garden were warned to be on their best behavior.[12]

Throughout the mix of confusion and anticipation, there seemed to be a sense of serenity coupled with the festivity of the upcoming big event. No one really anticipated any trouble. "Why shouldn't there be a little celebration?" a night club manager was quoted as saying. "Doesn't the country need to add a little gaiety to its gloom, and is there a better time than right after the legal restriction is first lifted to see whether 3.2 beer can be trusted to add to it?" State's Attorney Courtney added to the beery mellowness of the moment saying that he expected no trouble. Jacob Ruppert, New York brewer and President of the United States Brewers' Association wasn't so sure and recommended that Chicago's breweries delay their shipments until the late morning. The local brewers cried that they would be swamped by back orders if they waited until morning and continued with their plans for a 12:01 a.m. delivery time.[13]

Beer and Food

Absent from the local papers for years, ads for the Berghoff Brewing Company of Ft. Wayne, Indiana, reappeared in the *Chicago Tribune*. In a backhanded reference to Milwaukee's Jos. Schlitz Brewing Company, the Berghoff advertised its beer as "The Beer that made itself Famous." Ads for Schoenhofen's "Good Old Edelweiss" and Pabst Blue Ribbon Beer as "The Old Favorite," were seen once more in the Chicago papers. In a matter of days, beer was transformed, changing from an Old World German concoction, an intoxicating product of the "brewery interests" as it was sinisterly portrayed in years past, into a refreshing family staple that Mom could now add to her weekly grocery list.

". . . Profitable beer merchandising will take into account the successful adaptation of food sales strategy . . ." advised *Modern Brewery Age*, an industry trade publication. Local stores took heed. As if overnight, beer joined hands with food and, as a result of this marriage of retail convenience, finally became *the* drink of moderation. The Great Atlantic & Pacific Tea Company (A&P) heralded the arrival of real beer in their local stores. To accompany the customer's supply of beer for the weekend, the A&P ads listed Grandmother's Rye Bread, liver sausage, butter pretzels, kippered herring and Spanish salted peanuts. It was everything a Chicago family needed to ". . . make it a gala weekend—right in your own home." Hillman's reminded the shopper that they, too, would be carrying beer, "And Don't Forget the Accessories!" which included Limburger cheese

The Schoenhofen brewery emphasized taste and tradition, "since '52" in this post Prohibition advertisement for its Edelweiss beer.

and frankfurters. Loblaw-Jewel proclaimed that they had "BEER at its best!" The Mandel Brothers department store on State Street rushed to open a new shop called The Tavern, equipped to sell beer steins, six favorite brands of beer and all the foods that go with them. The store's Men's Grill Room quickly converted half of its space into a German beer garden. The Walgreen drug store chain announced that it had also made arrangements with local breweries for a limited supply of bottled beer to be placed on shelves for sale at their outlets. On April 7, the featured daily luncheon special at their soda fountain counter was a roast beef sandwich and a bottle of beer for a quarter. Sales later that day were reported as "phenomenal."

On the North Side, a new pretzel company opened to meet expected demand. Pretzels were becoming big business in the city. One snack food plant manager described the industry's reaction to legal beer. "We . . . are ready to turn out pretzels by the billion." Even the local press got in on the food and beer relationship. Mary Meade's food column in the *Chicago Tribune* suggested making a Rye Bread Torte with dark bread left over from "your beer party," and discussed how pretzels were now back in style. Chicago families were getting ready for beer and a new classification of food, beer snacks.[14]

New Beer's Eve

At 12:01 a.m ., Friday morning, April 7, 1933, the drinking light was turned on in Chicago and legal, "democratic beer" was reintroduced to the public. With cheers for President Roosevelt ringing through the air, Prohibition agents, city police, and Brink's bank guards allowed the brewery trucks to leave the plants and make their deliveries. Things got off to an embarrassing start near the Atlas Brewing Company. Acting Mayor

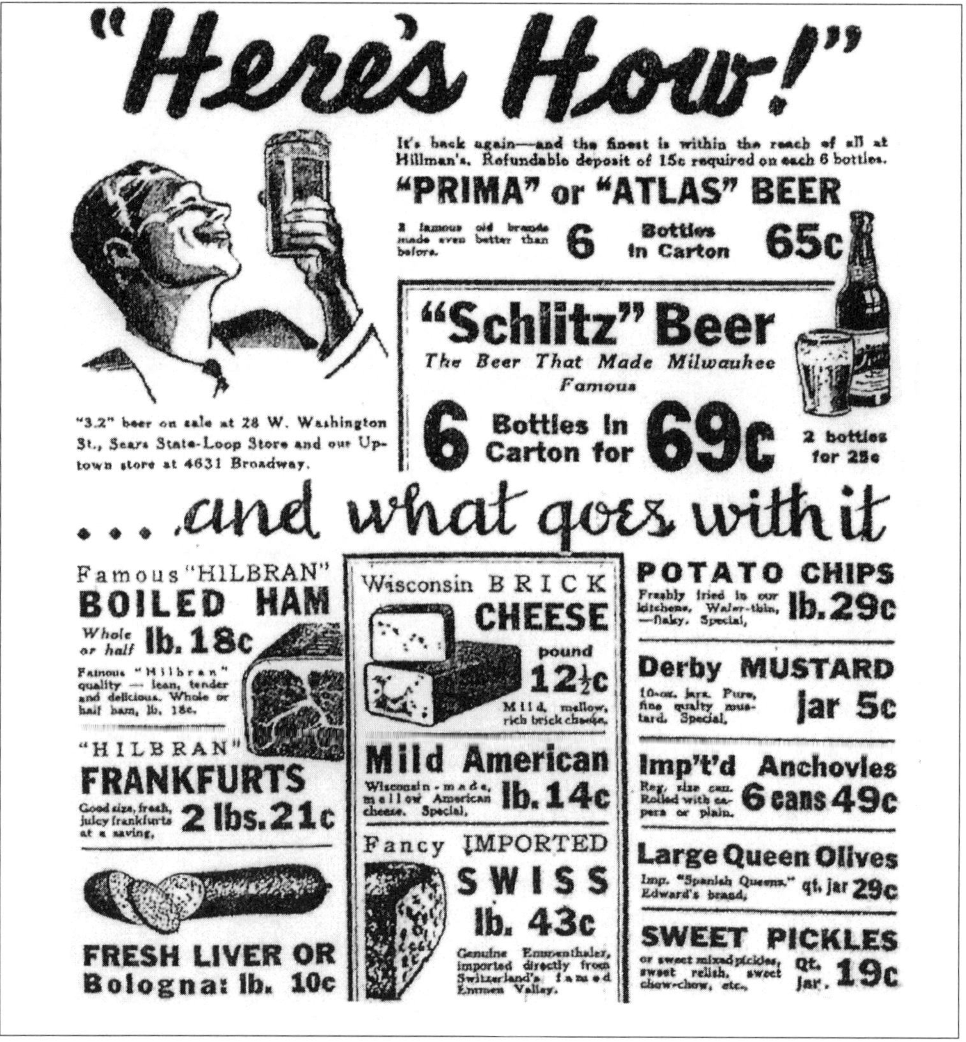

After Repeal shoppers could buy 3.2 beer "and what goes with it" at Hillman's and other local markets as this advertisement from the Chicago Daily News *indicates.*

Frank Corr, Atlas President Charles Vopicka, Coroner Frank Walsh and a host of other Democratic Party hacks and functionaries had gathered at the Iroquois Club at 11 p.m. where the guests had been assured that legal beer would be served an hour before the official deadline. They were forced, however, to wait with the rest of Chicago's eager beer drinkers until beer was finally delivered to the Iroquois and tapped for serving at 12:15 a.m. To their delight, and to the delight of thousands in the city, the beer was conveniently delivered cold from the brewery, saving the valuable time the pre-Prohibition retailer usually needed to ice it down. After a beer or two, acting Mayor Corr stepped before the WGN Radio microphone and hailed beer as a hope for prosperity. Atlas Brewing Company President Charles Vopicka next came forward and proudly announced that the first case of bottled beer from his brewery was on its way by airplane to President Roosevelt in Washington, D. C.[15]

Delays were worse at the Schoenhofen Company. Soon after midnight, trucks and cars were stretched in a mile long line as crews loaded the beer as quickly as possible. At the Prima Company, management had scrambled to hire an additional 300 extra trucks for city and county deliveries, and had chartered an entire train to deliver some beer into Milwaukee and Minnesota that weekend. Escorted by motorcycle policemen, the delivery truck caravan slowly moved from the front gates of the Prima Company and through the celebrating crowd as it cautiously headed eastward towards Halsted Street. All the city breweries had requested police escorts since they continued to fear hijacking during the early morning hours.

Milwaukee brewers were also ready for the Chicago market. At the Brevoort Hotel, forty cases of Miller High Life beer arrived at 1:30 a.m. after being flown in from the Cream City. The Premier Pabst Corporation, consisting of the Pabst Brewing Company and the Premier Malting Company of Peoria, had a fleet of 100 trucks being readied at their docks in Milwaukee for eventual delivery of their beer to Chicago.[16]

Three of Chicago's licensed breweries were left in the lurch, unable to take full advantage of New Beer's Eve. The Bosworth Products Company was in the process of a $75,000 plant renovation and company reorganization; it would soon be known as the Atlantic Brewing Company. The Frank McDermott Brewing Company had a comparatively small inventory of its Senate Extra Pale on hand and shipped 15,000 cases and 800 barrels on the first night. Two thousand Bridgeport residents patiently waited outside the brewery hoping to make case purchases. The Monarch Brewing Company showed similar small numbers of inventory available.[17]

In The Loop

Downtown, things were festive but controlled. On North Clark, crowds from Manny Goodman's spilled into the street as other beer lovers fought their way inside. In the alley behind the Bismarck Hotel, a throng of one thousand made it difficult for a beer delivery truck to make its first drop off of twenty barrels. When the truck finally backed into the loading dock, attendants quickly grabbed six barrels and rolled them into the hotel for the thirsty celebrants. At the Brevoort Hotel, revelers still crowded the famous round bar at 5 a.m. State Street, on the other hand, was comparatively quiet. Malachy N. Harney, Prohibition Administrator, thought he knew why. "Experienced beer drinkers will wait until tonight (Friday) or Saturday night to try the new product. They know that beer just freshly delivered is 'angry' from the bouncing it gets. They'll wait until it has had a day or two to cool and settle before sampling."

Agent Harney was obviously an out-of-towner who didn't understand thirsty Chicagoans.

One of the most noticeable features of the Loop crowd was the large number of young females who were joining in the celebration. Operators of the Hotel Sherman, the Brevoort Hotel and other "MEN ONLY" watering holes had prepared themselves for this intrusion. "What can we do about it?" bemoaned James Galbaugh of the Brevoort. "If the ladies insist on coming in—and I suppose they will—we can't put them out." Waving beer bottles or hoisting heavy steins, their appearances in bars and clubs were a far cry from the restrictive traditions of the pre-Prohibition era. At that time, women were seldom seen in saloons. If so, they were always accompanied by their husbands and routinely hustled in through the family entrance. An unescorted women in a drinking establishment was normally considered a working girl, whether she was or not, trying to drum up some needed business.

National Prohibition and 20,000 speakeasies had, in many ways, liberated Chicago's women. The next day, an older lady, accompanied by her daughter, was overheard describing her feelings towards women and public drinking. As the two generations of women sat at a drug store counter, the younger girl brazenly ordered a beer and goaded her mother to order one, but the older woman refused. "I can't get used to women drinking in public. In my day, a lady averted her eyes if she had to pass a saloon." Her next comment was revealing. "I remember how I longed to look inside those swinging doors," she admitted. And now, in the midst of New Beer's Eve, women in Chicago were not only looking in, they were pushing their way to the bar, ordering beer alongside the men. But at the Berghoff Restaurant, the bar would remain an all-male enclave that night and would be until 1969 when the National Organization for Women finally forced the integration of the sexes at the bar. Herman Berghoff's vow that "ladies will not be seated at the bar" held firm for another thirty-six years.[18]

At the Speakeasies

Despite pressure from mob beer drummers, many of the speakeasies curtailed further ordering of bootlegged draft beer, and as a result, ran out by April 5. Those speaks that still held a small draft supply continued to sell at the inflated price of 25 cents a stein even though the barrel price had dropped significantly. At 12:01 a.m., however, the stein price quickly dropped to 10 to 15 cents, the competition of the lower priced legal beer having its affect. Canadian bottled beer was also plentiful and dropped in price from $1 per bottle to 50 cents as owners hurried to unload their illegal inventory.

With the return of legal beer, some speakeasy owners began to cautiously remove the iron bars from their doors and windows; they openly displayed bottles of whiskey and gin on the back bar to anyone who now freely entered their premises. Even with its open availability, most owners reported little call for the harder stuff. Anticipating late deliveries of legal beer as the breweries serviced the licensed, legitimate establishments first, most speakeasy owners placed duplicate orders with three and four breweries, hoping to get at least one beer shipment in before the last of the wildcat and needled brew ran out. But as one delivery quickly followed another, a number of the speakeasies actually had more beer on hand than they could use. The situation would rectify itself by the next day.[19]

Back at the Breweries

The principal areas of confusion and celebration were around the breweries themselves. In the streets adjacent to the breweries, cars were lined up, waiting to get to the loading docks for cases, half barrels or even the unwieldy 31 gallon barrels of beer. Some local breweries reported that delivery trucks were still waiting in line to be loaded with beer as late as 5 o'clock in the morning. Police later confirmed that they spent most of their time just trying to untangle the traffic jams around the breweries which began around 9 p.m., with few other problems throughout the rest of the city.[20]

Supplies Start Running Short

In the early morning of April 7, as the sun broke over Lake Michigan, Chicago was still en fête. The local breweries were now operating on a 24 hour basis, exhausting workers who were putting in double and triple shifts, trying to keep up with mounting orders. Between two and five o'clock in the afternoon, frantic requests for beer tied up local phone lines, making it impossible to reach any of the breweries with additional orders.

In Mandel's new Tavern Room, a lack of sufficient waitresses caused a minor ruckus when they couldn't keep up with the initial round of orders. Store detectives were quickly called in to maintain order. The Tavern Room manager wisely placed the first round on the house and pulled store personnel from other departments to handle the demanding crowd. Those satisfied beer drinkers who eventually wandered outside were treated to the sight of six one-ton champion Clydesdales from Anheuser-Busch (A-B) pulling a bright red beer wagon through the Loop. A-B owner August Busch had big plans for Chicago.

Joe Durbin, editor of *Brewery Age*, had earlier estimated that there would be enough beer on hand for the initial celebration to provide every Chicagoan with 35 steins of beer. But unrelenting demand for legal beer soon outstripped supply. The shelves at A & P, National Tea, and Kroger-Consumer stores were stripped of beer before noon. Ecstatic store representatives added that sales of "beer snacks," were the biggest of any day in the history of their chain grocery stores, with the greatest demand being for rye bread, pretzels, cheese and sausage. Hillman's and other grocery stores reported similar sales. A local cheese wholesaler later noted that city-wide demand for Swiss, Brie and American cheese had been record breaking.

At the Bismarck Hotel, 20 barrels of fresh beer were emptied between 12:30 a.m. and 2 a.m. Perhaps overreacting to the initial rush, Bismarck Hotel officials announced later that morning that 50 barrels of beer would now be part of their normal inventory. The Berghoff took stock of that night's business to find that they had rolled out an unbelievable 81 barrels of beer since 12:01 a.m.[21]

Where Did all the Beer Come From?

Even with the overwhelming demand, prices for beer remained stable. An eight ounce glass was selling for ten cents, a twelve ounce stein for ten to fifteen cents. Cases ran between $2.30 to $2.90. But by the end of the second day of sales, questions arose about the quality of the legal brew. After years of drinking needle beer with an alcoholic strength of around 7%, some neighborhood beer connoisseurs complained that the new beer didn't quite have the taste or jolt of illegal brew, an opinion with which city officials agreed. Reports from chemists working for Dr. Herman N. Bundesen, president of the Chicago Board of Health, revealed that veteran Prohibition-era beer drinkers were probably correct in their criticisms. Even comparative analysis of recently-seized home brew indicated that homebrewers were making stronger beer.

Doctor Robert Wahl, head of the Wahl Institute, explained that his laboratory was in the process of checking the new beer for taste, effervescence and clarity. Because of the higher alcoholic content normally found in darker beers such as a Kulmbacher or Muenchener, Wahl advised that Americans be content with the pale or Pilsner-type beers. He noted that research was being conducted at the Institute to develop a dark, flavorful beer that would be under the legal alcoholic content of 3.2% by weight, 4% by volume. In developing such a beer, Wahl mentioned how important it was for the beer to have what the Germans call "suffigkeit." "A beer has 'suffigkeit,'" explained Wahl, "when you can drink it all afternoon and still not have enough." Less filling, tastes great?

Wahl later reported that his tests had indicated that the new beer was indeed disappointing. Out of ten beers analyzed in his laboratory, only three were deemed to be of good quality.[22]

His assessment of the new beer was immediately challenged by local braumeisters. Brewers William Faude of Schoenhofen and Charles Ellman of Atlas proclaimed their beer better than pre-Prohibition beer. "Prohibition taught us how to make beer," Ellman argued. "When you are selling a beverage for its taste only, and not for a kick, you must strive for perfection. It's hard to make a drink out of nothing, but the brewers did it!"

Looking back at the fact that most of the near beer that left the Chicago breweries was eventually needled with alcohol, Ellman's argument fell short of local reality.

Federal chemist John W. Fonner, in making his analysis, found that none of the beers he tested exceeded the legal limit for alcoholic content; on the contrary, most were well under it. Fonner speculated that some of the brewers might have been overly cautious in brewing the new beer, since some of it tested at a low of 2.48%. Fred D. L. Squires, research secretary for the American Business Men's Prohibition Foundation, agreed with Fonner's analysis of the new beer. "We had forty investigators out (testing) with ebullimeters," said Squires. His findings concluded that the new beer was ". . . a mere froth, running as low as 2.6 percent alcohol by weight."

A more probable cause as to why the tested beer failed to meet the maximum legal alcoholic content was the fact that the beer now available had been brewed under the old Prohibition formula for near beer. This opinion made more sense. Why brew a full-bodied beer with choice ingredients only to have it dealcoholized? This would explain why the brewers had hundreds of thousands of cases of beer ready for sale in such a short period of time. After all, old-time local brewers had been stating for decades that their beer required two months for lagering purposes. Despite the loud protests of local brewers, Chicagoans were getting a weakened version of the kind of beer they had drunk before Prohibition. City brewers continued to insist that their beer was up to government standards but weekend arrests for drunkenness suggested otherwise. Police records showed only 63 persons were charged with drunkenness on Saturday night in Chicago. This was about one-third of the normal arrest figures during a typical Prohibition-era weekend.[23]

Economic Success

August A. Busch's prediction of a greatly increased cash flow to the coffers of the federal government proved true. For the first day of nationwide beer sales, it was estimated that the federal tax for beer would bring in $7,500,000 to the United States Treasury. The federal government, anxious to grab its share of this new source of revenue had placed a $1000 annual federal license fee on each brewery and a five dollar excise tax on every barrel of beer that left the breweries for delivery.

In just forty-eight hours, $25,000,000 had been pumped into various beer-related trades from the bottling manufacturers to the sawdust wholesalers whose product lay strewn on the floors of saloons. In Chicago, early estimates placed the retail sale of beer at close to $4,000,000. Even the non-beer related State Street department stores enjoyed a sales boom as store owners recorded the greatest spending spree since the stock market collapse and the beginning of the Depression. Downtown hotels were forced to turn away potential guests as rooms were booked as quickly as they became available.

Nonetheless, revelers from out-of-town and the far reaches of the city continued to migrate to the Loop for the beer drinkathon.

Chicago and Springfield, still arguing about who would handle licensing of the brewing industry in Illinois and Chicago, looked at these tax and revenue numbers and decided that they, too, wanted their fair share of this new cash cow. In the meantime, both brewers and retailers enjoyed the local tax and license lull, harvesting a profit far in excess of what would eventually be realized when the city and the state started to take their share.[24]

Notes

1. St. Louis Globe-Democrat, July 20, 1931; Modern Brewery Age, January, 1933; Chicago American, February 9, 1933.

2. Chicago American, February 16, 1933.

3. Chicago Herald and Examiner, January 8, 12, 14, 16, and 24, 1933; Chicago American, February 15, 1933.

4. Chicago Tribune, February 21 and 24. March 2, 22, 24 and 25, 1933; Chicago Herald and Examiner, March 13 and 25, 1933; Chicago Daily News, April 6, 1933.

5. Chicago Tribune, March 19 and 22, 1933; Chicago Herald and Examiner, March 19 and 24, 1933.

6. Chicago Tribune, March 17, 24 and 30, 1933; Chicago Daily News, April 6, 1933; The Chicago Herald and Examiner, March 14, 16 and 23, 1933; The Brewer and Maltster and Beverageur, March, 1933; *Western Brewer*, April, 1933, George Murray. The Legacy of Al Capone. (New York, NY: G.P. Putnam's Sons, 1975) p. 238.

7. Chicago Herald and Examiner, April 4, 1933.

8. Chicago Tribune, March 28, 1933.

9. Chicago Tribune, April 2, 1933; Chicago Herald and Examiner, April 2, 1933.

10. Chicago Tribune, April 2–3, 5, 1933; Chicago Herald and Examiner, April 2–3, 1933.

11. Chicago Tribune, April 2, 1933; Peter Hernon and Terry Ganey. Under the Influence. The Unauthorized Story of the Anheuser-Busch Dynasty. (New York, NY: Simon & Schuster, 1991), p. 153.

12. Chicago Tribune, April 5, 1933; Chicago Daily News, April 6, 1933.

13. Chicago Tribune, April 6, 1933.

14. Chicago Tribune, March 22 and 30, April 6–8, 1933; Modern Brewery Age, April 15, 1933; Chicago Herald and Examiner, March 20, 1933.

15. Chicago Tribune, March 30, April 6, 1933.

16. Chicago Tribune, April 7, 1933; Chicago Daily News, April 7, 1933; Chicago Herald and Examiner, April 4, 1933; Brewery Age, April, 1933.

17. Chicago Tribune, April 7, 1933; Chicago Herald and Examiner; April 7, 1933; Brewery Age, April, 1933.

18. Chicago Tribune, April 7–8, 1933; Chicago Herald and Examiner, March 28, 1933; Nation's Restaurant News, February, 1996, p. 31; American Breweriana Journal, July–August, 1996, p. 7.

19. Chicago Herald and Examiner, April 7, 1933.

20. *Ibid.*, April 7, 8, 1933; *Chicago Daily News*, April 7, 1933.
21 *Chicago Tribune*, March 23 and April 8, 1933; *Chicago Herald and Examiner*, April 7, 1933.
22. *Chicago Tribune*, January 2; April 9 and 11, 1933.
23. *Chicago Tribune*, April 8, 10–11, 1933; *Chicago Herald and Examiner*, March 15, 25–27, 1933.
24. *Chicago Tribune*, April 8–9, 1933; *Chicago Herald and Examiner*; March 27, April 8, 1933.

Chapter 14

The Morning After, 1933

"Only a dictator for the breweries
can meet the problem."

Eliot Ness, describing the problem of former bootleggers entering the Chicago beer trade

The Mob and the Legal Breweries

Simply thinking about legal 3.2% beer was affecting the Chicago bootleggers and their operations. Speakeasy owners were cutting back orders of needle beer and wild-cat brew, hoping to be left with little or no syndicate beer by April 7. Chicago boot-leggers, reacting to this new threat of competition, tried to compensate for the fall off in orders by bringing down the price of their beer to a record low of $25 a barrel. To further entice saloonkeepers to continue to order their beer, syndicate prices started to tumble on bonded Canadian whiskey from $95 to $65 a case. The price of alcohol used for gin blending fell from $27.50 to $17 for a five gallon tin. Even with bootleggers giving these deep discounts to local speakeasies in order to keep sales steady, owners and managers of Chicago's thousands of watering holes continued to squeeze out whatever profit they could from the illegal brew, refusing to pass the price cuts on to their customers. A glass of bootleg beer was still going for fifteen cents a glass and twenty-five cents for a stein, which were normal prices when beer was selling for $55 a barrel.[1]

The money-losing situation of syndicate beer makers started to take a more desper-ate turn, bringing back the mob intimidation tactics of earlier years. Days before legal beer became available in the city, the business manager for the Brewery Drivers' Union and the secretary of the Brewers' and Maltsters' Union complained to State's Attorney Courtney that hoodlums were not only trying to take over their organizations but were even trying to organize their own unions. In spite of a report that Al Capone, now at the federal penitentiary in Atlanta, had ordered his mob to "... lay off the beer and stick to the red and white" (whiskey and alcohol), local mobsters were making their moves into the legitimate beer trade. The *Chicago Tribune* reported that bootlegger "Red" Bolten was making plans to continue brewing wildcat beer and force it upon West Side retailers. Quite the beer connoisseur, Bolten claimed that the legitimate brewers could not exceed his brew in taste and quality. The paper went on to say that Capone's old gang still controlled an unnamed Chicago brewery (the Manhattan Brewing Company, first acquired by Johnny Torrio back in 1919). The *Chicago Herald and Examiner* claimed that Joe Fusco, described as the "present chief of the Capone outfit," had brought in an old-time brewer as a figurehead operator for some of the breweries they still controlled. Fusco had worked for Capone since 1923, first as a bootleg beer truck driver, then graduating to a trusted mob lieutenant position handling beer accounts. With all the reports, rumors and innuendoes surrounding old bootleggers and the reestablishment of the legitimate brewing industry, one thing was certain . . . the Chicago bootleggers' syndicate would not leave the profitable brewing industry without a fight.

As days passed, Courtney received additional information that hoodlum beer drummers were posing as brewery agents throughout the city and forcing sales of beer on terrified retailers. For bootleggers convicted of Prohibition violations and unable to secure a federal brewing permit, the distribution of legal beer seemed to hold lucrative possibilities. Approaching representatives of legal breweries, hoodlum beer drummers tried to convince the owners that they could secure retail accounts for their legal brew. These accounts would chiefly consist of their old bootleg beer accounts. A Milwaukee brewery was reported to have been courted by Chicago hoods with a list of saloons that would buy the brewery's beer if a deal for exclusive distribution rights could be made between the Milwaukee concern and the mobsters. A manager for the Chicago branch of Anheuser-Busch recounted that he also had been approached with a distribution offer by syndicate beer reps.

Federal Agent Eliot Ness, still working in the Chicago Prohibition Unit, held the opinion that if a brewery made an agreement with agents of a bootleg syndicate, the hoodlums might come back to the brewer at a later date and threaten to turn over his retailers to a rival brewery. In this manner the syndicate could demand an even larger cut of the brewer's profits. If any participating brewer did complain to authorities, the mobsters would probably hide behind their political connections. With competition expected to be strong after April 7, the temptation for the legitimate brewers to join forces with the old bootlegger gangs would be there. After all, Chicago brewers and bootleggers had profitably tippled from the same barrel of greed and corruption for the last thirteen years.[2]

Protecting the Legal Breweries

Courtney acted at once to keep the legal brewing industry free of hoodlum influence. Days before New Beer's Eve, the State's Attorney called together all the licensed

Chicago brewers to discuss a plan of action. "We will drive the gangsters out if they attempt to enter this new legitimate industry," he assured the brewers but warned them that he would pull their licenses if he thought there was any indication that the mobsters had somehow muscled into their businesses. But the hoodlum beer syndicates were not taking "no" for an answer. In the next few days, retailers reported bomb threats and other strong arm tactics by hoods as the pressures from ex-bootleggers continued.

E. C. Yellowley, who was in charge of federal brewery permits in the city, said that his office was scrutinizing every application for a brewing permit to weed out anyone with a bootlegging or criminal background. In addition to the permit request, Yellowley warned that applicants would have to submit to character and financial scrutiny from his investigators, a subjective procedure. "We'll investigate them from top to bottom," he declared. Several applications had already been rejected by his office because of obvious hoodlum control. But Agent Ness and others pointed out that hoodlums might bypass the application process for a federal brewing permit and install men of good reputation to act as fronts for their mob controlled breweries, a tactic that was extensively used during Prohibition. Yellowley agreed with Ness' statement, admitting that there was no effective way to ensure that licensed breweries were not indirectly under the control of mob elements. He noted that federal regulations did not require his department to look into the stock ownership of a brewery, a legal way to gain brewery control. This legal technicality would soon be exploited by the mob.

Three days later, the *Chicago Tribune* reported that Yellowley had issued a permanent brewing permit for the Gambrinus Brewery to a nephew of Judge Joseph Sabath and Congressman A. J. Sabath. The Congressman had been a leading proponent of Roosevelt's plan to grant amnesty to Prohibition violators charged with making beer at or below the 3.2% alcohol level, a plan that was later dismissed as being impractical. Prohibition Administrator Malachy Harney, who investigated the application for the permit, admitted that Terry Druggan of the old Druggan and Lake bootlegging syndicate still had a possible claim on the brewery building. His current incarceration in Leavenworth for tax evasion, however, left his existing ownership of the title clouded. Nonetheless, the permit was issued by Yellowley's office. Rumors also circulated that bootlegger Joe Saltis had tried to buy a Chicago brewery with $100,000 cash and $200,000 in notes, purportedly financed with the cooperation of saloonkeepers from his old beer territory. "Only a dictator for the breweries can meet the problem," declared Ness as similar reports filtered in to his office.[3]

As the legal day for beer drew closer, State's Attorney Courtney and Agent Yellowley disclosed that Leonard Boltz, a reputed bootlegger, had secured corporate charters from the Illinois Secretary of State for twelve brewing companies that had allowed their articles of incorporation to dissolve. With his new company charters, Boltz was incorporating new firms under the names of Schoenhofen Brewing Company, Seipps Brewing

Company, Miller Brewing Company and nine other names, similar in name to defunct or existing breweries. Using this legal subterfuge, authorities were worried that Boltz and his gang might convince retailers that they were dealing with legitimate breweries.[4]

Less than twenty-four hours after the sale of legal beer resumed in Chicago, a bomb placed near the bottling department rocked the Prima Company at 325 Blackhawk Street. Although no one was injured by the blast, the explosion blew an iron door off its hinges and towards an empty stainless steel tank used to temporarily store alcohol during the dealcoholization of beer. Damage to the plant was estimated at $1500. Brewery officials claimed that the bombing was probably the work of a disgruntled customer who had requested a small order of beer for immediate delivery at 12:01 a.m. but had been forced to wait while the larger orders were filled first, a highly unlikely scenario. "We have had no threats nor any trouble with hoodlums or others," a Prima spokesman said. In spite of the claims of the brewery owners, police brought in Jerry Donovan, an official of the newly organized beer drivers union for questioning about the bombing.

A day later, Chicago police fought off an attempted hijacking of a truck containing 250 cases of legal beer. After a car chase and moving gun battle, the hijackers escaped but the beer was recovered. It was starting to seem just like the old Capone days in Chicago.[5]

Joe Fusco

For Joe Fusco, the resumption of 3.2% beer meant even more business opportunities than during Prohibition. Fusco, who had taken over the day-to-day beer operations for Capone, was now working for Frank Nitti in the same capacity. In 1931, the Chicago Crime Commission had listed Fusco as Public Enemy Number 1, further disclosing that he was "the beer boss of the Capone Syndicate." Even before acquiring this dubious distinction, Fusco was already well known to the Chicago Police Department.

On the night of July 13, 1931, a well-intentioned Police Sergeant, John T. Coughlin, had seized a truckload of Capone beer. Coughlin parked the truck in the back alley behind the police headquarters and assembled a police guard to watch over it. Fusco was incensed by the seizure, especially since he knew that the Capone gang was current on its regular weekly payoffs to the downtown police. With a federal court order for his arrest on a prior beer sales indictment still unserved, Fusco nonetheless stormed into police headquarters and demanded the return of the truck. Federal agents, newspaper beat reporters and photographers gathered nearby as the situation started to become an embarrassment to the police.

"How would it look if we let you walk out of here and drive away with that truckload of beer?" a perplexed officer asked the mobster.

"You should have thought of that before you drove it into the alley," Fusco growled back. Dennis Cooney, Capone vice chief for the First Ward, was summoned to the station to mediate the situation. Cooney first threatened to make all cops in the district live on their small salaries for the next month if they didn't release the truck, something most of them hadn't done for years. In a face saving compromise, Fusco was refused the return of the truck and asked to leave. Later during the night, the truck was accommodatingly *stolen* and driven back to his warehouse. While all this negotiating was going on, nobody bothered to bring up Joe Fusco's federal beer indictment.[6]

With the resumption of legal brewing operations in Chicago, Fusco now controlled the territory from 35th Street on the South Side, to 61st. As Frank Nitti's beer baron, he also held control over other Capone-sanctioned operatives. In and around the Loop, Harry Cusack and "Hymie" Levine controlled the retail outlets. From 12th Street to 29th ruled Sammy Cusack, brother of Harry. Jack Heinan ruled the territory from 29th to 35th Streets and Danny Stanton held watch from 61st Street to the south city limits.

When necessary, threats and intimidation were used against those saloonkeepers who tried to remain independent of the mob beer drummers. A show of force was seldom required, however. The syndicate was offering one week's worth of credit if a saloonkeeper took on their beer. The legitimate breweries were demanding immediate payment upon delivery. For many saloonkeepers, their choice of distributor was an easy one.[7]

Legal Beer Shortage

Only a few short days after New Beer's Eve in Chicago, most of the legal beer was gone. Officials at Atlas Brewing Company reported that they still had 50,000 barrels of green beer on hand in the aging tanks and were seventy-two hours behind on orders. They vowed, however, that "Not a bottle of green beer will leave this plant." At the Prima Company, employees couldn't keep up with orders in the bottling department. "The place is like a madhouse," said an employee, ". . . but (we) are doing our level best." Irving Solomon, plant manager at the Schoenhofen Brewing Company, claimed to have back orders of 200,000 cases and 200 railroad cars of beer. Even Anheuser-Busch, Inc. acknowledged a beer shortage at their depot in Chicago.

By the end of April, Blatz Brewing Company of Milwaukee felt obliged to take out a quarter-page ad in the *Chicago Tribune* saluting President Roosevelt and pledging to him and all their customers that ". . . no beer is to be released until it is *Fully-Aged*," trying to quell mounting complaints that beer was being sold before completing the lagering period.

As beer shortages continued to be reported throughout the city, hopped and unhopped malt extract ads started to run again in the papers, suddenly resurrecting the dying home brew trade. Ever since the announcement that beer would be legally available in Chicago on April 7, the malt shops had been frantically selling off their highly discounted inventories as interest in home brewing waned. With the slowdown in beer production and the unavailability of fully-aged beer, malt shops were busy again.[8]

Licensing of the Brewing Industry

By early April, neither the City of Chicago nor Springfield had reached agreement on beer licensing requirements. Newly elected Mayor Kelly held the opinion that if the state were to license retail outlets wanting to sell beer, the fee should be low enough for independent retailers such as neighborhood grocery stores and drug stores to afford. Beer, he reasoned, was simply a sideline for these businesses and would only be purchased for home consumption. To place an oppressive beer license fee on them might force them to drop beer as part of their normal store inventory and place the exclusive sale of beer back into the waiting arms of saloonkeepers, something that most city officials said they were trying to avoid.

Along with Kelly's observations was a strong recommendation to the City Council to force breweries in and out of Chicago to print the alcoholic strength and bottling date on the label of their products, Kelly's idea of Budweiser's contemporary "born on" date. In addition, the mayor wanted bottle manufacturers to produce bottles with raised lettering on them and breweries to burn their brand name onto the wooden barrels before they left the plant. By adding these steps to the manufacturing process, Kelly hoped to end any chance of Chicagoans purchasing green beer and, more importantly, eliminate the real possibility that bootleggers might attempt to bottle their own wildcat beer for distribution.[9]

Days before the Chicago City Council acted on Mayor Kelly's recommendations, the Springfield legislature reached agreement on state licensing requirements for the sale of beer. The bill imposed a state tax of two cents per gallon on beer, a $50 state license fee on all beer retailers and limited the amount of local license fees to $200, except in Chicago which could determine its own fee, a concession to home rule advocates. In addition, beer could not be sold "on-premise" unless food was sold or offered for sale.

On April 26, the City Council passed two amendments to the city beer licensing ordinance. The first ruling decreed that all retail beer outlets, rather than just saloons, would be liable for taxation. This $150 license fee, which had already been imposed on on-premise sites would now be required of all carry-out locations. The fee would be pro-rated to July 1, when the new licensing period would begin.

Edward J. Kaindl, Chicago City Collector, seemed happy with the new arrangement. He had recently reported to the subcommittee on licensing fees that Chicago had already received $570,000 in retailers' fees since beer had become legal. If the $150 fee was retained for the rest of 1933, he projected that $900,000 more would flow into city coffers.

The second amendment compelled brewers to have their company names blown in glass bottles and labels printed with the alcoholic content and dates of manufacture and bottling. It passed unanimously, 47 to 0. Brewers were given just ten days to comply.[10]

The Brewers React

The bottling and labeling requirements immediately came under fire from brewers. "The amendment is unnecessary and ridiculous," said H.F. Ernst, owner of the Prima Brewery. Ernst claimed that the amendment would mean the disposal of bottles already in inventory and would place a further burden on overworked bottle manufacturers who were trying to keep up with demand. Countering this argument, Kelly replied that the brewers could etch existing bottles with the company and brand name using an acid procedure.

Ernst went on to challenge the need of the amendment. "The consumer is assured right now that any bottle carrying the label of a given brewer contains the beer of that brewer. Federal inspectors see to that." As for the possibility of a brewer bottling green beer, Ernst felt the offenders, if there were any, should definitely be punished, but not the entire local brewing industry. Depot managers for some of the out-of-state breweries threatened to pull out of the Chicago market if the ordinance were upheld in court, a bit of puffery in such a lucrative retail market.[11]

The euphoric fizz of early April was starting to go flat for Chicago brewers. On top of threats from bootleggers trying to muscle in on their businesses, the brewers saw federal, state and local taxation as destroying any chance for a reasonable profit. A $1000 federal licensing fee, a $5 per barrel federal revenue stamp, a $50 state license and a two-cent per gallon tax, coupled with a 3% retail state tax and Chicago's well-intentioned but restrictive bottling requirements, swept away almost all hope that Chicagoans might ever again enjoy a nostalgic, pre-Prohibition priced, nickel glass of beer. Things couldn't have appeared worse for the newly resurrected brewing industry when Democratic Representative Benjamin E. Adamowski of Chicago jumped up on the House floor in Springfield and questioned why the brewers were "... charging $17 a barrel for beer they can afford to sell for $8."[12]

Goodbye, Nickel Beer!

For a group of politicians that stood to reap so much from the anticipated benefits of the brewing industry, in terms of increased local employment and additional revenue for federal, state and city treasuries, some local legislators appeared ready to kill this new golden calf; and a golden calf it was. From April 7 until June 1, the Chicago district reaped approximate earnings of $1,667,229 from federal beer stamp taxes, reported Gregory T. Van Meter, Collector of Internal Revenue. Chicago had received a total of $570,000 from retail beer license fees, brewers' licenses and wholesalers' licenses. Projections placed the federal share of yearly earnings from Chicago's brewing industry at around $10,000,000.[13]

Instigated by Representative Adamowski's demands to have the brewers explain their pricing structure, a House legislative committee began hearings at Chicago's

City Hall. On the first day of testimony, not one of the seventeen subpoenaed local brewers appeared with their company records, as ordered by the committee. Things seemed to be going from bad to worse for the brewers when the legislators began to chastise John P. Hart of Aurora, counsel for the Illinois Brewers Association who had also been requested to appear. Hart had angered the committee members by publicly claiming that legislators were trying to make political hay by holding the inquiry, a charge that probably had merit. "Most of them," Hart had earlier commented to the press, "are from the poorer districts, where five cent beer might be made a hot political issue."

Because of the swiftness of legalization and the heavy demand for product, the brewers were brewing and bottling beer as quickly as possible. The variables of new taxes, expansion of the plants and costs of production were making it difficult for them to come up with reliable cost figures. Any preliminary numbers would have to be based on what it had cost to make near beer, giving an inaccurate production cost analysis of real beer. Hart refused to be intimidated by the rebuke from the committee for his comments and affirmed his earlier statement.

As Representative Albert Mancin began shouting at Hart for his failure to answer Mancin's questions to his satisfaction, Senator Frank "Bull" McDermott, owner of a small Bridgeport brewery strode into the proceedings and was requested to take the stand. A portion of the questioning went as follows:

MANCIN: "How long have you been in business, Senator? You own a brewery, don't you?"

McDERMOTT: "I've owned one for 16 years."

MANCIN: (smiling) "I suppose you've lost a lot of money?"

McDERMOTT: "Half the legislature knows I've lost money. The mayor (former Mayor Dever who shut down the breweries in 1923) of this city certainly knew it. The brewing business is an up and down business. I've taken it on the chin for years."

MANCIN: "What do you charge for a barrel of beer?"

McDERMOTT: "Thirteen dollars."

MANCIN: "Well, you're making money now, aren't you?"

McDERMOTT: "Sure I am. But so were your friends making money when they were charging $55 a barrel." (the old speakeasy price)

MANCIN: (his face turning red) "So were your friends making money at that price?"

McDERMOTT: (calmly) "I don't doubt it."[14]

Mancin next turned his anger on John G. Weisbach, attorney for the local brewers. "Do you realize the breweries are in contempt?" Weisbach agreed with Mancin but pointed out the difficulty in making an accurate assessment of current costs. "By___, we'll get it or you'll stop manufacturing beer!" Mancin threatened.

With the conclusion of the threats and verbal jousting, Representative Gary Noonan diplomatically announced that representatives of Prima, the United States, Atlas, Monarch and Schoenhofen breweries had agreed to allow independent auditors to inspect their company books and would pay any fees incurred. The feisty McDermott agreed to follow the lead of the other breweries and also open up his books for inspection. Everyone seemed to be pleased with the compromise.[15]

Not to be outdone by state representatives, a Chicago City Council subcommittee, drafting a new city regulatory ordinance for beer sales, also questioned Senator McDermott in a meeting in late June. McDermott had appeared to protest the committee's proposed $1000 retail licensing fee plus an additional fee of $25 for every brewery, distributor and jobber delivery truck. The new city licensing period was to begin on July 1. McDermott initially tried to appeal to the committee's sense of fair play. With a straight face, the Senator claimed that Chicago brewers had made no money in the last fourteen years, a claim that any local politician knew was not entirely true. Alderman Mathias "Paddy" Bauler, who no one in Chicago ever accused of being a saint, jumped on McDermott's weak argument of poverty. McDermott, however, was ready for Bauler and assumed the same adversarial approach he had taken at the House inquiry.

BAULER: "You're charging $17 a barrel for beer, aren't you?"
McDERMOTT: "Say, you got $55 a barrel, so you needn't holler."
BAULER: "Don't say that unless you can prove it."
McDERMOTT: "You even got $60 a barrel."

McDermott defiantly walked out of the room after rattling Alderman Bauler. George H. Kiefer of the United States Brewing Company then jumped into the fray and protested the proposed $1000 licensing fee for retailers. T. J. Doyle, a representative of the Atlas Brewing Company explained to the committee that, under the new proposal, anyone who was a distributor and jobber would have to pay a double fee.[16]

Some members of the City Council soon realized the dilemma a $1000 beer licensing fee would have on the small, independent retailer. Mayor Kelly acknowledged the real possibility that the unaffordability of a high licensing fee might mean a return to the old tied-house saloon and its prior monopoly on retail beer sales and hinted at a compromise. On July 11, the City Council voted to increase the beer license to $300, rather than $1000, for all retail on and off-site premises but knocked down a provision to merge beer retail licenses with other licenses for food dispensing and amusement. Separate licenses would now be required for restaurants serving beer, cabarets with food, beer and entertainment sites and even saloons, which were now required by state regulations to sell food with drink.

When he heard of the City Council's actions, George Patris, the President of the Restauranteurs of Illinois, took note of the new licensing fees and somberly declared the nickel glass of beer dead in Chicago.[17]

Illinois Readies Its Vote for Repeal

As required by Congress, Illinois was busying itself in late April of 1933 in preparation for a state election and convention to act on the 21st Amendment, hopefully to repeal the disastrous 18th Amendment. After Congress had refused the state's request for a special cash grant to fund state elections for Repeal, Illinois decided to incorporate a June judicial election with the Repeal election, combining the expenses of two separate elections. Downstate Democrats, however, worried that incorporating the judicial election and the vote for Repeal might bring about a backlash from local dry advocates and hurt the chances of some of their Democratic judges running for reelection. As a result of this political concern, the Illinois State Senate, led by these wary Democratic forces, unbelievably voted to postpone the election for Repeal until April of 1934.

Republicans had a field day with the Senate vote, expressing disbelief that the same party that had been swept into the Oval Office on a platform of repeal, the party of "democratic beer," was now voting to delay the state ratification of Repeal. "Evidently," sneered Martin R. Carlson of Moline, "you Democrats don't care to repeal the 18th Amendment."[18]

Colonel Ira L. Reeves of Chicago, Commander of the anti-Prohibition organization called the Crusaders, and a pro-Repeal lobbyist, thought he saw a darker explanation for the actions of the Democrats. "Naturally they (the brewers) want to prolong their present monopoly as long as possible, and apparently they are lining up the downstate dry legislators to accomplish that purpose." Reeves went on to suggest that brewers had made a pact with Prohibitionists. Reeves singled out the boisterous State Senator Frank McDermott with his brewery in Bridgeport. How could McDermott go back to his Stockyards constituency and tell them he voted to defer Repeal until next year, Reeves wanted to know?

The logic of Reeves' argument seemed solid. Other Repeal advocates affirmed his contention. Since before Prohibition, brewers and distillers had maintained an adversarial relationship. Their divisiveness was one blatant reason that later prohibitionist efforts had been so successful. Commenting on the charge that brewers wanted to continue a monopoly on the drink trade, Captain W. W. Bayley, Chicago Chief of the Association Against the 18th Amendment said, ". . . it would not be surprising to have proof show up that such is the situation now." It was too much for editors of the trade magazine, *The Brewer and Maltster and Beverageur*, who demanded an apology from Reeves. "It is unthinkable that they (the brewers) would ally themselves with the bootleggers and gangsters and the fanatics of the Anti-Saloon League."[19]

Days later, with pressure from all sides and a chance to rethink their positions, the Democrats capitulated. The Illinois Senate voted to restore June 5, 1933, as the day for the election of delegates to the State Repeal Convention. Additional pressures from Governor Henry Horner and various lobbyist groups, including the Women's Organization for National Prohibition Reform, had persuaded the Senate to wisely reverse their ill advised prior decision. The Illinois House of Representatives concurred with the Senate's actions.[20]

Illinois' Repeal Election

On April 28, 1933, at 1:43 a.m., Governor Horner signed the House bill ordering the Illinois Prohibition Repeal Convention to assemble on July 10. The sudden haste in passing the bill was to allow the longest amount of time possible to secure the 35,000 signatures needed to place the names of delegates on nominating petitions. In a show of unity, Democratic and Republican Party leaders agreed to equally split the slate of fifty delegates, but only after a unification proposal by Democratic leaders.

With the required nominating petitions finally signed, Chicago precinct workers started to flood their wards with sample ballots. Mayor Kelly asked the people of Chicago to support the vote for Repeal. "I urge that all citizens of our great city support the President and his administration in his efforts to bring back prosperity and eliminate the evils which Prohibition has cast into our midst. This can best be done by voting for the Repeal candidates." Perhaps as a further inducement to the electorate to get out and vote, Kelly overruled an earlier opinion by Leon Hornstein, first assistant to Chicago Corporation Counsel William H. Sexton, that the sale of beer on election day would be illegal. Hornstein claimed that the state legislature had forgotten to repeal the pre-Prohibition election law requiring saloons to be closed during elections. Kelly disagreed, Sexton demurred and the saloons of Chicago were allowed to stay open on Election Day.[21]

Election Day

On the morning of June 5, expectations were high for the repeal of the 18th Amendment. With chances for thunderstorms forecast through Monday, a voter turnout for a Chicago judicial election would normally have been predicted to be low. Historically, this pattern of a small voter turnout was, and still is, typical for such an election. But, this was no simple judicial election. With reports coming in from ward headquarters throughout the city, the Cook County Democratic Organization was predicting an unprecedented turnout of 710,000 votes. Nonetheless, ward heelers continued to heavily canvass the city during the day. As a further enticement to get constituents out to vote, local Democratic leaders pragmatically stressed the household economics of Repeal. As part of their door to door strategy, it was pointed out by Democratic party officials and ward heelers that unless the 18th Amendment was repealed, $6 to $10 out of every $100 earned would revert back to the Federal Government in new taxes. Repeal meant beer, booze and no new taxes . . . one hell of a "read my lips" argument that any tax paying voter could understand.

Democratic Party leader Patrick A. Nash wasted no words in his final communiqué to Chicago voters before the polls opened. "Support President Roosevelt. Repeal the 18th Amendment. Elect judicial leaders. Vote the Repeal ticket straight. Vote the Democratic judicial ticket straight." Republican County Chairman William H. Weber was not quite as direct or forceful in his party's approval of Repeal. "Vote the Republican judicial ticket straight and destroy the receivership ring," taking a final shot at the Democrats. Although the parties shared an equal amount of delegates for the Repeal of the 18th Amendment, Weber's statement conservatively avoided the paramount issue of Repeal. The national Republican's Party endorsement and enforcement of Prohibition and the local organization's lukewarm embrace of Repeal were noted by beer drinking Chicagoans. From post-Prohibition on, the Democratic Party, the party of "democratic beer" and Repeal, has held sway in Chicago.[22]

Election Results

The tally of votes was no surprise. Not only was the vote for Repeal in Chicago overwhelming, it was a vote of approximately 11 to 1 in favor of it. In Committeeman Moe Rosenberg's 24th Ward on the West Side of the city, reports showed that Repealists had voted yes at an astounding ratio of 76 to 1. Not surprisingly, a Republican precinct captain complained that in one precinct of Rosenberg's ward, 200 votes had been stuffed into a ballot box when that many voters had not even registered in the precinct. Rosenberg, recently indicted by a federal grand jury for income tax evasion, scoffed at the report. In Bridgeport, voters followed the dictates of native son County Treasurer Joe McDonough and voted 40 to 1 for Repeal.[23]

The next day, the editorial page of the *Chicago Tribune* declared National Prohibition officially dead in Illinois and expressed hope that the remaining dry states would soon follow Illinois' lead. "A law which made the drinking of a glass of beer a crime was unenforceable..," said the paper. As evidence of the state citizenry's overwhelming rebuff of Prohibition, a total of 883,000 voters turned out to vote for approval of the 21st Amendment to the Constitution, more than 560,000 votes for Repeal coming from Chicago. All that was left was the state convention.[24]

The Repeal Convention

On July 10, Governor Horner opened the convention and officially signaled the beginning of the end of National Prohibition in Illinois. "The eighteenth amendment is doomed. Let us pray that with it will go the political cowardice that made it possible." At noon, Democratic state leader Patrick A. Nash presented the resolution to ratify Repeal of the 18th Amendment at the state repeal convention. In just fifty-four minutes, the fifty bipartisan delegates went through the necessary procedural motions and unanimously voted to ratify the 21st Amendment, nullifying the 18th. The Prairie Schooner, Illinois, now became the tenth state to moor at the wet dock of Repeal.[25]

Notes

1. *Chicago Tribune*, March 19–21and April 11, 1933; *Chicago Herald and Examiner*, March 25, 1933.

2. *Chicago Tribune*, March 29 and April 11, 1933; *Chicago Herald and Examiner*, March 20, 31, 1933.

3. *Chicago Daily News*, April 6, 1933; *Brewery Age*, April, 1933; *Chicago Tribune*, March 3, April 3, 11, 1933; *Chicago Herald and Examiner*, April 4, 1933.

4. *Chicago Herald and Examiner*, April 3–4, 6, 1933.

5. *Ibid.*, April 8–9, 1933.

6. George Murray. *The Legacy of Al Capone*. (New York, NY: G. P. Putnam's Sons, 1975) pp. 201–202.

7. *Chicago Herald and Examiner*, April 10, 1933.

8. *Chicago Tribune*, April 11, 30 and May 5, 1933; *Chicago Herald and Examiner*, March 20, April 14, 1933.

9. *Chicago Tribune*, April 25, 27–28, 1933.

10. *Ibid.*, April 20, 27, June 16, 1933; *Brewery Age*, April, 1933, *Journal of the Proceedings of the City Council of the City of Chicago 1933–1934*, Amendment to Article VIII, Chapter 62 of the revised city code, Section 1, 3143–H, p. 92.

11. *Chicago Tribune*, April 28, 1933; *Chicago Herald and Examiner*, March 26, 1933; *Chicago Daily News*, April 29, 1933.

12. *Chicago Tribune*, April 20, 1933.

13. *Chicago Tribune*, June 10, 19, 1933.

14. *Chicago Tribune*, June 6, 1933.

15. *Chicago Tribune*, June 5–6, 20, 1933; *Chicago Daily News*, June 5, 1933; John Landesco. *Organized Crime In Chicago*. (Chicago IL: University Of Chicago Press, 1929) pp. 240–241 states that McDermott had been indicted for violations of the Volstead Act but the particulars of his arrest were never recorded in the Chicago Police Department's Identification Bureau, a typical action during Prohibition. This absence of arrest information usually occurred if the case was dismissed or reduced to a small fine.

16. *Chicago Tribune*, June 6, 1933.

17. *Chicago Tribune*, July 12, 1933.

18. *Chicago Tribune*, April 20, 1933.

19. *Chicago Tribune*, April 22, 1933; *The Brewer and Maltster and Beverageur*, March, 1933.

20. *Chicago Tribune*, April 26, 1933.

21. *Chicago Tribune*, April 26, and June 2, 5, 1933; *Chicago Daily News*, April 29 and June 3, 1933.

22. *Chicago Tribune*, June 5, 1933.

23. *Chicago Tribune*, June 6, 1933; *Chicago Daily News*, June 5, 1933.

24. *Chicago Tribune*, June 7–8, 1933.

25. *Chicago Tribune*, July 10–11, 1933; *Chicago Daily News*, July 11, 1933.

Chapter 15

The Pre-War Years, 1933–1940

"How would your old lady look in black?"
Frank Nitti, beer distributor

Early Problems

By late September of 1933, twenty-three breweries were up and running in Chicago. Logistically, it appeared to have been an easy rebirth for the local industry, especially for those breweries that had operated under federal permit, producing near beer during National Prohibition. For the breweries that had been idle during all, or part, of Prohibition, the capital outlay for rehabbing the equipment and the plants was formidable. In spite of considerable rehab and expansion expenses, the strong initial demand for beer created a time of unrestrained prosperity for many of the local breweries. But for the smaller, undercapitalized breweries, the next few years would become a challenge as the euphoria of high demand for their products leveled off.[1]

Problems started to arise as soon as the cooler months of 1933 rolled in, coinciding with local overproduction. In a rush to keep sales high in the face of the coming relegalization of the liquor industry and the planned openings of more breweries in the area, some brewers began releasing green beer into the local market to keep pace with strong demand. But as demand inevitably tapered and sales started to level off, breweries that had inadvertently overproduced now found themselves with the opposite problem of too much aged beer on hand, some actually going sour in the storage tanks. Prices started to tumble further since inventories were high. With distributors demanding barrels of beer for as low as $10 and the brewers desperate to unload their excess product, earnings were low and profits absent. Even the return of warm weather the next spring failed to bring relief to some undercapitalized brewers. For the financially sound and well managed breweries, the average net profit per barrel was now estimated at around $1. The industry average was much less, some breweries showing as little as twenty-five cents net profit per barrel.[2]

The Shipping Brewers

Chicago brewers, most without the deep pockets of the national shipping brewers, could only watch as St. Louis and Milwaukee out advertised them in the local press. The bigger, more financially sound Chicago breweries such as Schoenhofen-Edelweiss and the United States Brewing Company, recognizing the need to develop local brand loyalty and, most importantly, stronger demand, began using the services of local ad agencies to help them accomplish this goal. Though a new and seemingly effective method in selling product, the use of ad agencies nonetheless added a new drain on the operating expenses of the larger, more secure local breweries.[3]

Salesmen from out-of-town breweries also reinstituted the turn of the century practice of giving inducements to taverns in the forms of free signage and bar fixtures. Some

After 1933 Chicago bars had to provide chairs or stools. The patrons at Skilniks, a South Side tavern, were obviously grateful. Courtesy of Barbara Gallagher.

offered up to two free barrels of beer if bar owners would take on their product. Reports of salesmen once again reverting to the use of spendings to secure new accounts were becoming increasingly common. The trade publications sought to address these problems, pointing out that these practices ran not only counter to Illinois Department of Finance Regulations, but also to the recently instituted Code of Fair Competition for the Alcoholic Beverage Industry. This brewing code was intended to foster the concept of industry self-regulation, dealing with the issues of pricing, labeling and wholesale practices and, in a strong sense, leveling the playing field for the small and mid-sized breweries.[4]

Brand Loyalty

Justifying these predatory marketing practices, one brewery executive from a large shipping brewery saw the local brewers, and not the shippers, as having the sales advantage. "If he (the small brewer) can build up a local pride in his product and a local appreciation of the economic value of the business to his locality, we can never sell our products in a more substantial way than he can." But the problems of developing and nurturing brand loyalty were formidable. For almost fourteen years, Chicagoans had been drinking needle and wildcat brew. There had been no favorite brands or full-page ads extolling the virtues of locally brewed "Torrio's Nut Brown Ale" or "Capone's Best Lager Beer." To the Prohibition-era Chicagoan, beer was simply beer.

Blatz of Milwaukee recognized this lack of brand loyalty by the beer drinking consumer and started a newspaper campaign in the late summer of 1933 with half-page ads in Chicago papers for their premium-priced Old Heidelberg beer. Blatz ads featured recommendations from the managers of Chicago's Bismarck and Windemer hotels, and testimonials from Chicago personalities extolling the virtues of their products. Blatz's Old Heidelberg Inn, the largest restaurant at the 1933 World's Fair, with a seating capacity of 4000, became the headquarters for thirsty Chicagoans and visiting out-of-town guests as they enjoyed the sights and sounds of the fairgrounds. WGN radio broadcast six days a week from the Inn, offering the swing sounds of Ernie Kratziner's Orchestra and WGN's Herr Louie, interspersed with plenty of commercials for Old Heidelberg. Local brewers were becoming increasingly worried by the tactics of out-of-town competition as sales declined. Circling the wagons, nineteen Chicago area brewers organized the Chicago District Brewers Association, formed to present a united front opposing the mercenary practices of the out-of-town breweries.[5]

Mob Influences Continue

The "Century Of Progress" Fair had been a boon for the Chicago economy and the local mob. Most of the saloons which enveloped the approaches to the fair from Roosevelt Road to 23rd Street were being supplied by syndicate-controlled breweries. Those saloon owners who refused mob overtures or defiantly switched beer brands often found their businesses on the receiving end of a pipe bomb. On the fairgrounds, the syndicate also had a big piece of the hot dog and hamburger, popcorn and soda concessions. Mobster Charlie Fischetti probably wasn't exaggerating when he said, "We got the whole place sewed up."

But the Fair would one day come to an end. Plans had to be made for the future. Frank Nitti, now heading up Capone's gang, saw the takeover of the bartender and restaurant unions as the key to the future success of the mob-owned and controlled local breweries. At a Capone syndicate meeting in the fall of 1933, Nitti laid down his plans for the continued success of the organization. "The bartenders' union is our biggest lever. After we get national control we will have every bartender in the country pushing our brands of beer and liquor."

Union Takeovers

Nitti's plan for domination began with the local bartenders' union. At the time, George B. McLane, a former speakeasy owner and union thug, was running Local 278, the Chicago Bartenders and Beverage Dispensers Union (AFL). In the spring of 1935, McLane received a telephone call from a Nitti emissary requesting his presence at the La Salle Hotel. When he arrived, Nitti bypassed any social niceties and demanded point blank that McLane install one of his men as a union officer. When the union boss refused, Nitti threatened him. "You put our man in or you will get shot in the head," challenged Nitti.

Weeks later, McLane was again summoned by Nitti to the Capri Restaurant, located on North Clark, just across the street from City Hall and the County Building. At this second meeting were mob chieftains Joe Fusco, Charles Fischetti, Louis Campagna, Paul Ricca and Nitti. Nitti once again demanded that McLane put a syndicate man on the union board as an officer. When McLane told Nitti that the union executive board would not accept such a move, Nitti said, "Give me the names of any board members who oppose. We'll take care of them." Almost as an afterthought, the mobster asked McLane, "How would your old lady look in black?"

Still refusing to follow Nitti's order to relinquish control of the union, McLane was once again summoned before Nitti in July of 1935. After a final death threat to him and the members of his union board, the union executive board reluctantly agreed to install Louis Romano, one of Al Capone's bodyguards during Prohibition. One of Romano's first acts was to see that all the syndicate-controlled taverns joined McLane's union.

Lou Greenberg

The next meeting of McLane and Nitti was facilitated by Alex "Lou" Greenberg. Greenberg had acted as business manager of the Manhattan Brewery since the early years of National Prohibition when Johnny Torrio had taken over the brewery. Torrio turned over the brewery to Hymie Weiss and Dion O'Banion, and Greenberg took control of the brewery after the deaths of both gangsters. Although Arthur C. Lueder, Republican candidate for mayor in 1923 and former Chicago Postmaster was the company president in early 1933, Greenberg still controlled the brewery.

In 1933, when Lueder had accepted the position of company president of the brewery, he was asked by reporters what he knew about of the past owners of the Manhattan Brewery. Lueder deadpanned that he understood that gangsters had formerly owned the brewery but that "they were all dead." When Lueder ran successfully for the office of State Auditor in 1940, his loyalty as president of the South Side brewery was rewarded with a $20,000 campaign contribution from Greenberg.[6]

When McLane and Nitti met, with Greenberg present, Nitti instructed McLane that all the city bartenders were to push Manhattan Brewery products including Manhattan and Great Lakes draft beer, Badger and Cream Top bottled beer. On the spirits ticket were Gold Seal Liquor and Capitol Wine and Liquor Company products, owned by Joe Fusco, and Fort Dearborn whiskey, the syndicate's own house brand. McLane questioned the effectiveness of this forceful tactic, especially since the national brands such as Budweiser, Miller High Life and Schlitz were making such a strong drive for control of the Chicago market. "Tell those bartenders that if they don't push our stuff they will get their legs broken," threatened Nitti, deflecting McLane's objections.

Throughout the meeting, Greenberg remained silent but his presence and influence were overwhelming. His years of experience in the brewing, restaurant and finance businesses helped guide the local crime syndicate to invest their unreported profits from bootlegging, vice, gambling and extortion into the legitimate, tax reportable assets of hotels, restaurants, laundries and unions.

The hapless McLane was eventually pushed out as president of the Bartenders' Local 278 when Romano took over control of the union in 1935. To complete Nitti's plan of local union control, Romano organized and led a food and beverage joint council consisting of fifteen union locals, most relating to bartenders, waiters, hotel clerks, cooks and other similar trades. McLane later testified that the joint council collected a tax of ten cents per member a month from the 30,000 members of the fifteen unions.

With the Chicagoland unions under his control, Nitti made ready for the takeover of the AFL bartenders' international, a move that later failed.[7]

Repeal

At 4:31 p.m., December 5, 1933, Repeal took effect in Chicago with the ratification by Utah of the Twenty-first Amendment. The Noble Experiment had lasted 13 years, 10 months, 19 days, 17 hours, and 32½ minutes. President Roosevelt officially proclaimed an end to National Prohibition and urged all Americans to confine their purchases of alcoholic beverages to licensed dealers. The President also issued a special plea to state officials not to allow the return of the saloon. A check of the City Collector's Office, however, indicated that close to 7000 liquor dealers were now ready to serve the 3,500,000 residents of Chicago, averaging one saloon for every 500 Chicagoans. It was about the same number of saloons that had operated in Chicago before the onset of National Prohibition. Two distinctions, however, now separated the pre-Prohibition saloon from the watering hole after Repeal. In late November of 1933, the Chicago City Council banned the use of the word "saloon" in any establishment sign or ad. In an attempt to civilize the new tavern environment, standing at the bar was now prohibited, leading to the use of stools at the bar. The pre-Prohibition practice of brewers paying for liquor licenses and distributing free signage was also addressed in the new city liquor license application. Now a tavern owner could not accept signage worth more than $100. Credit or money advances from breweries beyond that normally occurring in a retail operation were not permitted, either.[8]

Strong Beer Returns

There was some initial confusion as to whether liquor could actually be legally sold until the restriction of the 3.2% beer law could be modified. Attorney General Otto Kerner clarified this concern by stating that "The 3.2 statute was purely a licensing device to provide revenue for the state, and has nothing to do with the sale of liquor or other beverages of more than 3.2 percent after Repeal. It was more or less an emergency measure to meet the needs which arose when beer was legalized." With that opinion by Kerner, the local breweries announced that ales, stouts and porters as strong as 4 and 5 percent would be placed on sale, though 3.2% beer would still be available.

Beer doctor Max Henius questioned the attempt by some brewers to increase the alcoholic content of beers to place them in direct competition with distilled spirits. In an address to the U. S. Brewers Association in 1934, Henius asked, "Why, then, undermine the position (that beer is a drink of moderation) by exploiting the higher alcohol content of the heavier beers?" Beer expert Robert Wahl saw the production of higher strength beer as an unfortunate result of market demand, noting that as far as some opportunistic brewers were concerned ". . . the public is going to get what it wants."[9]

But the brewing industry was worried by the reintroduction of ardent spirits. As a result, Repeal was not looked upon by the industry as favorably as one might think. An entire generation of drinking Chicagoans had grown up with bathtub gin and "Halsted Street Scotch." In many instances, the more portable, stronger and readily available booze had been mixed with soda pop or other sweet confections to smooth out the rough taste of the alcohol. Cocktails had changed the tastes of many. With the resumption of the brewing industry in April of 1933, brewers held a legally monopolized drink market for almost eight months that would soon fade away. During that short time, beer formulas were being adjusted, many beers made lighter and sweeter in an attempt to win over those drinkers who favored the sweeter drinks of Prohibition, especially the new exploitable market of women. As a result of this change in taste, most beer now contained rice and corn to lighten the body of the beer, almost three and one half pounds of sugar per barrel and just a "kiss of the hops." Beer became a light, bubbly drink, quite different in taste from the richer pre-Prohibition brew.

Repeal dropped the exclusiveness that the brewers temporarily held with the drinking public, once again pitting distillers against brewers. To some brewers, stronger beer with an alcoholic kick and sweeter, lighter tasting beers were just additional weapons in the battle with distillers for new customers. While Chicagoans had to settle for limited quantities of whiskey, domestic and imported wines and liquors during the early days of Repeal, local brewers flooded the market with stronger beers and sweeter reformulated brews.[10]

Packaged Beer

Tainted by the stigma of pre-Prohibition corruption and newspaper reports of mob involvement in Chicago taverns, underage drinking and solicitation, bottled beer offered the more sedate beer drinker an alternative to draft beer and the associated evils of the tavern, thus weakening draft sales. The brewing industry's emphasis on the enjoyment of beer in the home and at social events also helped foster a widening shift in beer consumption from draft to packaged beer.

In 1935, the American Can Company introduced the so-called "Keglined" can. This non-returnable container offered a number of advantages over breakable deposit bottles. The cost of a canning line, however, was more than many of the smaller breweries could afford. A conical shaped can offered an alternative for those breweries with bottling lines; the coned cans could be run through the same lines. In addition to the new flat and coned cans, stubby shaped, non-returnable bottles called "steinies" were introduced. For those brewers who had settled on the traditional production of draft beer after Repeal, the continuing shift to drinking at home and the introduction of new containers now made the purchase of a bottling or canning line imperative.

The Birk Brothers Brewing Company and the Hoerber Brewing Company were some of the first local breweries to abandon all draft production and switch to bottles and draft. The Best Brewing Company was chosen by the American Can Company to test an experimental canning line. After feeling the effects of the aggressive advertising campaigns of Anheuser-Busch and other invading nationals, Best Brewery president Jerome Hasterlik dropped his dwindling tavern accounts. Pleased with the performance of the experimental canning line, he quickly seized upon the idea of providing canned beer to A & P, Kroger and National food stores and the house brand, Hillman's Export Beer, to local Hillman's stores. The operation became so successful that the brewery would eventually provide private label beer to the Katz drug store chain in Missouri and the

California-based Safeway Foods. Lou Greenberg's Manhattan Brewery, with its vast reserves of mob money, was also one of the first Chicago breweries to put in a canning line. By 1938, the brewery laid claim to being second in canned beer production in the United States, surpassed only by the Pabst Brewing Company of Milwaukee.[11]

Post-Repeal Fatalities

Without the benefit of the unreported, untaxed income of Prohibition-era sales and once guaranteed accounts from mob beer drummers, the Gambrinus Company, Incorporated and the Frank McDermott Brewing Company passed into Chicago brewery history. Bankruptcy, later followed by a federal indictment of bootlegger Terry Druggan and

Although beer in bottles or cans was growing steadily more popular, Gambrinus advertised its beer on tap in the Chicago Daily News. This brewery closed first in 1935 and again in 1938.

four brewery officials, sealed the fate of the Gambrinus. A grand jury alleged that Druggan's interest in the brewery had been concealed when an application for a federal license had been made. The Kiley Brewing Company of Marion, Indiana, took over the location of the defunct Gambrinus Brewery and incorporated the Patrick Henry Brewing Company. The new owners appeared to have had big plans for turning the location into a regional production and distribution point, even introducing a richer tasting, all-malt beer to compete with European imports. By 1939, however, they ceased brewery operations in Chicago.[12]

McDermott and his brother reorganized their failing brewery in early 1937, renaming the South Side plant the Beverly Brewing Company. Their reorganization efforts, however, were to no avail and the brewery closed in late 1937.[13]

The problems of the Prima Company were symptomatic of many of the weaker Chicago breweries after Repeal. During the last five years of Prohibition, the brewery reported earning more than $200,000 a year. As with the other Chicago breweries that manufactured legal near beer during the dry era, there was no real competition. Even the most mismanaged brewery made money during this period. Whether poorly made or of the finest quality, virtually all of the near beer produced locally went to the guaranteed accounts of the city speakeasies as needle beer.

During the first year of Repeal, the Prima earned $340,000, not unexpected after the initial strong demand by thirsty Chicagoans. After the heyday of 1933, however, the brewery started claiming a steady loss of income, culminating with a disastrous loss of $155,953.43 during the first nine months of 1936 and a petition by management to reorganize with the U.S. District Court. As a result the brewery was forced to borrow $200,000 each from Harris Trust & Savings Bank and the First National Bank and Trust Company. The brewery later petitioned the Federal Court that the ousting of the Ernst family which had controlled the brewery after Repeal, and the replacement of the brewing family by a bank appointed manager (at the insistence of the Harris and the First National banks), had caused an additional loss of nearly $600,000.[14] After a court ruling in favor of the Ernst family, an appeal by the Harris and First National banks reversed the ruling in favor of the banks. The Supreme Court reaffirmed the ruling, noting that the brewery had been losing money long before the banks had become involved in the plant operations.

In February, 1938, a federal judge ordered the acceptance of a meager bid of $145,000 by the management of the South Side Westminster Brewery for the assets of the Prima Company, including its trade names. A few months later, the Westminster Brewing Company filed an amendment to its charter and changed its name to the Prima Brewing Company. It appears unlikely, however, that the small brewery on South Union Avenue, located just a block away from the Manhattan Brewing Company, had the means to make a successful bid for the assets of the Prima Company. Later canning arrangements between the newly-named Prima Company and the Manhattan seem to

The financially troubled Atlas Brewery, in the 1950s. Courtesy of Ernie Oest.

indicate more than a simple show of cooperation. More than likely, the assets of Prima were bought by the mob controlled management of the Manhattan Brewing Company, indicating that the Westminster Brewing Company was probably also owned or controlled by the management of the Manhattan.[15]

A suit alleging mismanagement and neglect filed by the widow of Otto Kubin, former president of the Atlas Brewing Company who died in 1929, revealed the financial woes of another famous Chicago brewery. Spurred on by the filing of a bankruptcy petition by the brewery, Kubin's wife charged that the Chicago Title and Trust Company failed to sell the Kubin estate's holdings of company stock at a time when it would have brought a profitable return to the heirs of the estate, although the Company knew that the existing brewery equipment was old and needed rehabilitation, and that expansion of the plant would have been costly. The suit further noted that the price of Atlas stock was $28 per share during the giddy heydays of 1933. At the time of the widow's suit in early 1938, Atlas stock was selling for only fifty to seventy cents a share, a loss to the estate in excess of $1,000,000.[16]

In late 1940, the trade journal, *Modern Brewery*, reported that "interests associated with the Manhattan Brewing Company" had gained control of a sizable portion of the outstanding stock of the financially crippled Atlas Brewery. It would be safe to conclude that the new masters of Frank Nitti's organization now controlled at least four Chicago breweries.[17]

Notes

1. Donald Bull, Manfred Friedrich and Robert Gottschalk. *American Breweries.* (Trumbull, CT: Bullworks, 1984) pp. 58–67; *Modern Brewery*, September 15, 1933.

2. *Brewery Age*, November, 1933, December, 1934.

3. *Ibid.*, December, 1934; *Modern Brewery*, April, August, 1933.

4. Stanley Baron. *Brewed in America. A History of Beer and Ale in the United States.* (New York, NY: Arno Press, 1962) pp. 325–326.

5. *Brewery Age*, July, November, 1933; *Modern Brewery*, November, 1933; *Chicago Tribune*, September 6, 14, 1933.

6. *Chicago Herald and Examiner*, July 23, 1933; Ovid Demaris. *Captive City.* (New York, NY: Lyle Stuart, Inc. 1969) p. 224.

7. The account of Nitti's activities is based on George Murray. *The Legacy of Al Capone.* (New York, NY: G. P. Putnam's Sons, 1975) pp. 181–194.

8. *Chicago Herald and Examiner*, December 1, 1933; *A Handbook of Facts and Figures*, New York, NY, 1937, United Brewers Industrial Foundation; *Journal of the Proceedings of the City Council, 1933–1934*, Article VIII A, 3143-N, 3143-R, p. 1126; *Application for City Retailer's License Alcoholic Liquor*, Form C Z 502-Corporate Form.

9. *Chicago Tribune*, December 12, 1933.

10. *A Handbook of Facts and Figures*, 1937.

11. Baron, *op. cit.* pp. 327–328; *Brewery Age*, March, 1937; *The Breweriana Collector*, Journal of the National Association Breweriana Advertising, Vol. 74, Summer, 1991, p. 10; Phil Pospychala and Joe McFarland. *The Great Chicago Beer Cans.* (Libertyville, IL: Silver Fox Productions, 1979), p. 23.

12. *Brewery Age*, May 1938; *Chicago Tribune*, August 10, 1939; Bull, *op. cit.*, p. 61.

13. *Brewery Age*, April, 1937, May, 1937, June, 1937.

14. *Ibid.* April, 1937.

15. *Brewery Age*, February, 1938, April, 1938; Pospychala and McFarland, *op. cit.* pp. 64, 73.

16. *Brewery Age*, March, 1938.

17. *Modern Brewery Age*, October, 1940.

Chapter 16

The War Years and Beyond, 1941–1968

"Lack of fair play, commercial bribery . . .
and the dumping of beer on local markets
at less than cost . . ."

John E. O'Neill of the Small Brewers Committee describing problems faced by the small brewer in the post-war era

Local Advertising

In the months after the U.S. entrance into World War II, the use of local print and radio media by Chicago's breweries became unprecedented. Extensive use of tavern window displays, newspaper ads, billboards and local radio broadcasts brought home the idea that Chicagoans should be enjoying locally brewed beer. Atlas Brewing Company was one of the first breweries to tie in the consumption of their products with the survivalist theme of local brand loyalty starting with their "Be a Chicago Booster, Consume Chicago Beers" campaign. Its hometown appeal to Chicagoland beer drinkers was soon joined by a similar advertising strategy from the Monarch Brewing Company. Ads for Monarch Beer in local papers regularly ended by begging customers to "Be loyal to your own community" in an effort to deflect the growing popularity in Chicago of the national brands. Birk Bros. Brewing Company placed the logo of their Trophy Beer on one side of their cardboard beer coasters and the message "Drink Illinois Made Beer, Create Employment Here" on the other side.

Some Chicago breweries focused their sales campaigns on the more elite taste of a small segment of niche beer drinkers, emphasizing the super-premium quality of their products and developing an advertising theme like those used for some of today's higher priced super premium beers . . . beer snobbery. The Schoenhofen-Edelweiss Company used this elitist marketing approach, flooding community papers with an extensive ad campaign enticing beer drinkers to buy a discriminating, but higher-priced Edelweiss Beer, "A Case of Good Judgment."

A World War II advertisement for Manhattan Brewing Company's Canadian Ace beer has a neck label urging "Buy War Bonds." Courtesy of Phil Pospychala.

The Atlantic Brewing Company used a demographically diverse newspaper campaign to undercut the average price of beer throughout Chicagoland, offering a normally priced fifty-two cent package of one quart of beer, one 12 ounce throw away steinie and one export bottle of their Tavern Ale for only twenty-five cents. Initial consumer reaction was so strong that the brewery was forced to withdraw the ads in the *Chicago Tribune*, the *Cicero Life* and the *Chicago Defender* after only three days. As a result of the huge demand for this limited 1,000,000 bottle promotion package, the brewery successfully increased its distribution almost one hundred percent in Chicago liquor stores and added hundreds of grocery, drug store and tavern accounts to its local distribution network.

Discounting of product, however, would become a problem for Chicago beers as profit margins narrowed in the next few years. Early post-Prohibition beer marketing campaigns in Chicago offering discounted prices seemed to prove the most effective in stimulating sales. It was a sales tactic that would later backfire. Given a choice between spending money for advertising or applying the less costly method of price reductions, most local breweries took the discounted product approach. In time, the local beers often became trade footballs, bouncing from one price level to another, unable to compete against the prestige of the higher priced national brands. It's a beer pricing truism that exists even today: significantly lower the price of your product and customers will reject any future attempt to bring the price back up to its higher former level.[1]

Early Affects of the War

The Japanese attack on Pearl Harbor and our treaty obligations to our allies in Europe made the war a two-sided front, and with it came the need for conservation of food stuffs and raw materials at home. Nervous brewers nationwide kept a wary eye on Washington, willing to accept grain restrictions and any other reasonable sacrifices that might be asked of the industry, but ready to quickly challenge any potential attempts by prohibitionists to implement a moratorium on brewing operations. The painful lessons of grain rationing during World War I and its backdoor use by drys to institute National Prohibition had not been forgotten by brewers.

A defense tax increase of $1.00 per barrel of beer now totaled at $6 on the federal level, was quietly accepted by the industry but added a further strain on dwindling profits. A trade study in 1940 of cost and profit breakdowns for small (under 100,000 barrels), medium (100,000 to 300,000 barrels) and large breweries (over 300,000) proved once again that quantity production reduced costs. The study, exclusive of taxes, calculated the cost of production for the small breweries at $9.65 per barrel, $7.61 for the medium sized breweries and $7.18 for the large breweries. Adding the new $6 barrel tax to these cost figures dramatically demonstrated the problem of economic survival faced by local smaller-sized breweries.[2]

Brewers' fears of the creeping influence of prohibitionist ideas and a possible return to the restrictive years of the First World War and beyond were highlighted locally when the Chicago City Council voted to prohibit women from standing at bars, forcing them to sit at tables. Challenged by Mayor Kelly, the Council later rescinded the ordinance, allowing women to once again take their place at the bar, but only with a male escort.[3]

The Peter Fox Brewing Company

A popular Chicago brewery that seemed to defy all the problems and ensuing challenges that the local industry as a whole experienced after the relegalization of beer in Chicago was the Peter Fox Brewing Company. After acquiring the old Hoffmann Brothers Brewery on west Monroe Avenue, reportedly "... from Al Capone ..." and issuing $500,000 in common stock, the seven Fox brothers began brewing operations in July of 1933. Originally involved in a wholesale meat operation on Fulton Avenue, they entered the brewing business with a financial advantage that would be the envy of any start-up operation . . . no debt or preferred stock. Within a year, they began to pay dividends on outstanding shares of common stock and contemplated further acquisitions.[4]

In early 1942, the Chicago-based brewery bought the Kiley Brewing Company in Marion, Indiana, a brewery that had entered the Chicago market in the mid-1930s but pulled out around 1939. The Indiana brewery, now known as Fox De Luxe Brewing Company of Indiana, was the third part of the brewery empire which would be owned and operated by the enterprising Fox brothers. Shortly before the Indiana acquisition, the family had also bought a well equipped brewery in Grand Rapids, Michigan, to boost their capacity, bringing up their annual combined total barrelage to 1,000,000. In 1944, the Peter Fox Breweries ranked thirteenth out of the twenty-five leading breweries in the United States, beating out the sales of Miller Brewing Company of Milwaukee which ranked sixteenth.

Soon after purchasing the Marion, Indiana brewery, the brothers also entered into oil production in Oklahoma, with a community interest in some of the wells with Standard Oil of Ohio. Because of wartime restrictions, the fifteen or so wells that the company owned were limited to a production of only 200 barrels of oil per well each day. Frank Fox estimated that the wells were capable of producing 1,500 to 2,000 barrels daily when the restrictions were lifted.

The golden touch of the brothers continued throughout the war years when the Chicago headquarters announced a four for one split of their common stock in 1944, selling at the time for $95.50 per share. Satisfied holders of the brewery's common stock surely agreed with the brewery's famous slogan, "Don't say Fox . . . Say Fox DEEE Luxe!"[5]

War Efforts of Chicago Breweries

For local brewers, taking part in community drives to bolster the war effort was not only a demonstration of their loyalty to the cause of peace; winning the war became a daily part of operating their breweries. Conservation of fuel and collections of scrap metal, glass and paper became paramount in the brewers' war efforts, and, if they garnished a little publicity from their collection drives or fund raisers, so much the better.

One of the first local breweries to make use of an equal blending of patriotism and publicity was the Garden City Brewery. With much fanfare, the brewery purchased a two horse team to make local deliveries. Otto Kudrle, president of the brewery, boasted that reverting to horse-drawn wagons for beer deliveries would aid in saving fuel for the war effort. Not coincidentally, the horses were named Prima and Tor after their flagship Primator brand of beer.[6]

On March 31, 1942, the use of tin for the civilian production of beer cans was prohibited. A few months later, civilian steel for crown caps was reduced to 70% of 1941 allotments. A quick result of these restrictions was the resurgence in the consumption of draft beer as bottled production drastically slowed. "When you order from the tap—you save a cap," became a familiar saying during the war years. A similar slogan, aimed at those who still chose bottled beer, was a bit more direct in its wartime message, "Save caps, kill Japs."

Because of the shortage of bottle caps, the industry introduced the steel conserving but cumbersome, half-gallon picnic bottle. The Peter Hand Brewery followed suit in the use of the larger sized bottles but also took the bold step of dating their half-gallon bottles of Meister Brau non-pasteurized draft beer. The use of larger, freshness dated bottles was certainly a show by brewery management of their war conservation efforts, but also demonstrated a calculated move by the brewery to provide the quicker and much publicized delivery of guaranteed fresh draft beer to retailers and ultimately, appreciative customers. Buying up huge blocks of time on WGN Radio, the brewery ads heralded the fact that bottled Meister Brau beer was now "Dated draft beer—Guaranteed tap fresh!"

What goes around, comes around. Fifty years later, the industry has again begun a campaign of dating beer for freshness, trumpeting the move as some sort of new approach to product freshness.[7]

Another local wartime effort that received favorable reaction from the public was a paper and cardboard collection organized by the Illinois Brewers Association. With a fleet of 500 brewery trucks stopping at taverns, restaurants and hotels throughout the city for the pickup of paper scrap, the successful operation was completed with the handing over of proceeds from the drive to a grateful Mrs. Edward Kelly, wife of the Mayor.[8]

Not to be outdone by any competing Chicago breweries, the Peter Fox Brewing Company was duly noted as having set a Red Cross Drive record for contributions by its employees with each employee averaging $13.50 per person.[9]

One of the most ambitious wartime efforts by any Chicago brewery was the "Jobs for G.I. Joe" program, sponsored by the Atlas Brewing Company, in cooperation with the War Manpower Commission's United States Employment Service. This WBBM Radio production featured a live studio audience with a homey mix of entertainment from The King's Jesters, a CBS singing trio, Jimmy Hillard and his orchestra, and a presentation of job seeking veterans and their stories. Acting as moderator was a young Paul Harvey, himself an ex-soldier. The program was well received by Chicagoans and led to the job placement of many returning veterans, all helped by the politically-connected brewery.[10]

The Challenges of the Post War Years

With peace once again on hand, 550 members of the Small Brewers Committee (S.B.C.) and the allied industries met at the Edgewater Beach Hotel in October of 1945 to prepare for the struggles they knew they would soon face. Wartime restrictions on the use of grain, fuel, steel, glass and other brewing materials had actually offset encroachment by the national breweries on many local markets. As cities rallied during the early and mid-1940s to overcome the enemy and help end the war, the back home efforts of the local breweries during this time were warmly appreciated and remembered by their customers. But with a return to normalcy, smaller breweries prepared for the worst.

New Realities of the Small Brewer

The central focus of the S.B.C. meeting was the developing heavy-handed reaction by the big brewers toward the aspirations of the smaller brewers and the nationals' alleged use of unfair advertising and merchandising to increase sales. The general counsel of the organization, John E. O'Neill, warned of the dangers that small brewers could face. "Unfair competition, lack of fair play, commercial bribery, subsidization, unfair advertising and the dumping of beer on local markets at less than cost," were described by O'Neill as future problems that faced the S.B.C. members from the larger shipping brewers.

O'Neill's predictions initially seemed overstated, but as the months went on after the war, there was an unmistakable shift in the structure of the American brewing industry, later confirmed by the United States Brewers Foundation. Looking at the future state of the brewing industry in the United States, the organization made public their acknowledgment and seeming acceptance of what many smaller and mid-sized breweries had feared. "All individuals do not achieve the same stature, mental or physical. That is equally true in business. It is not necessary nor possible for each brewer to be the largest in order to achieve success, but every brewer can be a successful brewer if he will. It rests with the individual. Size is not the only hallmark of success." The fragmented brewing industry, consisting mostly of family-run operations, would never be the same and the smaller brewers knew it. For many of them, the white flag would soon go up.[11]

The Sins of the Past

Business in general, especially during the post-war boom years, was about growth and consolidation. Bigger wasn't necessarily better, but it was becoming a fact of life.

In the brewing industry, those early brewers who had had the foresight to export their product in years past, continued to expand their markets and their distribution networks. They recognized the importance of mass advertising and were able to accumulate huge fortunes long before the disaster of National Prohibition. While the dry years of the twenties and early thirties shut down the legitimate operations of both big and small breweries, the larger breweries, for the most part, were fiscally and physically maintained by their far-sighted owners.

The Busch family of St. Louis demonstrated a prime example of brewers with vision. Starting with the production of Budweiser Barley Malt Syrup and Budweiser Yeast during the lean years, and the profitable sales of their corner saloon locations during the early days of National Prohibition to petroleum companies for gas stations, the brewery continued to find ways to stay in business. Further shifting their operations to the manufacturing of glucose, corn sugar, corn oil and even ice cream, August A. Busch maintained the Busch family fortune during Prohibition. So sure was he that beer would one day return, that he periodically sent his master brewer to Germany to keep abreast of the latest brewing techniques and innovations during the dry years.[12]

From Repeal on, several financially strong regional breweries such as the Theo. Hamm Brewing Company of St. Paul, Minnesota, the Falstaff Brewery, Pabst, Schlitz and others began carefully chosen programs of national expansion, nurtured by their accumulated wealth earned before Prohibition.

On the other hand, most Chicago brewers were now facing the sins of their fathers and grandfathers. Having been content to operate for years in the vast and ever growing Chicago market, few local brewers from the early boom years of the 1880s and beyond had ever made a serious attempt at expansion and the nurturing of future export sales. While Chicago brewers became wealthy during the pre-Prohibition years, visionary out-of-town brewers such as Busch, the Uihleins of Schlitz and the Hamms of St. Paul became much wealthier, always looking at further expansion and innovation for continued existence.

Local brewmaster, Joe Pickett, at one time a man who could easily have qualified for the title "The Hardest Working Man In The Chicago Beer Business" as he served as brewmaster for three local breweries during the 1940s and '50s, later acknowledged the fatal shortsightedness of Chicago's brewing industry, especially during the post-Prohibition era. "Many Chicago breweries died of their own weaknesses. Many owners were not interested in perpetuity, just in making as much money as possible while putting very little back into their businesses."[13]

Pact with the Devil?

Although brewers nationwide were probably guilty of some sort of larcenous activities during National Prohibition, as Gussie Busch would later proudly boast, the Chicago brewers had raised violations of the Volstead Act and the Eighteenth Amendment to an art. Content to operate under the protection of Capone, Torrio or any other assortment of bootleggers of the era, local brewers were eager and willing to share in the illicit, unreported booty that Chicago's mobsters had provided them. Without the artificial market of gangster-provided accounts, maintained by the dual edged sword of intimidation by mob enforcers and the equally necessary protection that these beer drummers provided them from rival gangs, the Chicago brewing industry was being reduced to a handful of small, debt-ridden family businesses. Forced to compete with each other and the bigger, well-funded breweries, who were flush with cash for new equipment, advertising and further expansion into the lucrative Chicago market and beyond, the local industry began to crumble.

The Early Fifties

1950 was a particularly devastating year for Chicago brewers. After fifty-nine years of operation, the Birk Brothers Brewery closed. Although President Frank Birk's advanced age was given as a major reason for the closing, the North Side brewery, with an annual capacity of 200,000 barrels, had reported sales in 1949 of only 60,000 barrels. The Best Brewing Company, another family-owned business of seventy-one years, and the Garden City Brewing Company, also fell victims to the changing business conditions and tastes of Chicago consumers. The Atlas Brewery and its affiliate, the Schoenhofen-Edelweiss Brewery, were gobbled up by Drewry's Ltd., U.S.A. of South Bend in 1951. Prior to its acquisition, the Atlas had been carrying on a desperate struggle of producing old brands from defunct breweries, a move often seen in troubled breweries trying to keep production up after their own house brands have peaked in sales.[14]

Troubles at Fox

Expansionism, however, actually led to the demise of a once promising local brewery. A few days before Christmas of 1949, the Peter Fox Brewing Company of Chicago suddenly announced the resignations of J. Raymond Fox, director and master brewer, and Kenneth Fox, who served as advertising manager for the local brewing empire. With his unexplained departure in Chicago still looming, the company soon accepted the additional resignation of J. Raymond Fox as director and head of production for Fox DeLuxe Brewing Companies in Michigan and Indiana. For nervous shareholders watching the unfolding drama at Fox, it would only be a matter of time until the other shoe dropped.[15]

A few months later, the brewery headquarters reported the sale of their Oklahoma City plant which was located close to their oil drilling operations and was the last plant acquired during their swift expansion phase. The brewery had proven to be a money losing proposition from the start and had been closed since the fall of 1949. Sold for

$90,000, the brewery proved to be a financial misadventure of $267,650. The brewery at Marion, Indiana fell next in 1951, starting with an asking price of $250,000, later reduced to $150,000. The Indiana brewery had also been closed since late 1949. In December of 1951, vice-president Milton Fox announced that the Grand Rapids, Michigan location would also shut down on December 31. Fox called this latest move an "economy operation" and declined further comment. For all concerned, it was the reason for the mass resignations in 1950.

The local brewery floundered until 1955 when the Chicago plant was finally closed and the entire operation consolidated with the Fox Head Brewery in Waukesha, Wisconsin. The family still remembers the irony of selling to the Wisconsin interests. For years, the family had worked hard to keep the Fox Deluxe name separate from the Fox Head name, ". . . because of apparent mafia links to Fox Head . . ."[16] The once thriving Chicago brewery had jumped on the post-war wagon of unbridled expansion but had lost control and come up flat.[17]

Less Filling, Tastes Great?

In a paradox that still confounds numerous micro-breweries in existence today, Chicago consumers during the 1950s were abandoning the old time beers with their unique flavors, house character and filling richness for the blander, lighter tasting beers of the national brands. Those local brewers who initially refused to reformulate their products for the changing taste of beer drinking Chicagoans were rapidly losing their market, even when the purchasing trends for the less satiating beers of the national breweries reflected repeat and multiple sales. As mass advertising from the nationals relentlessly pounded home the message that their beers were better, image and price became problems for Chicago brewers. "Why should I buy an Edelweiss or an Ambrosia Nectar," must have certainly entered the minds of many local beer drinkers, "when I can enjoy 'The King of Beers' or 'The Beer That Made Milwaukee Famous' for a few pennies more?"

Unable to combat the advertising budgets of the giants, soft local brand loyalties developed. With the resultant poor sales of Chicago brewed beers, the falloff in sales forced local brewers to further lower the prices of their products. In order to lower the price of their beer, however, and maintain a reasonable profit margin, they also had to lower the quality of the beer's ingredients and shorten the lagering period. Those smaller breweries which had tried to hold on to the idea of producing richer tasting beers were now forced to produce cheaper versions of their fading, once premium-brewed brews, the cheaper made beer referred to in the brewing industry as "popular-priced." Realizing there might be an additional market in the cheaper beers that the local breweries were beginning to brew, the nationals began offering their own economy versions, backed by their seemingly inexhaustible war chest of advertising dollars.

The price sensitive sector of local beer drinkers went with the nationals. "Chicago breweries didn't have a chance in a market considered so vital by the big brewing companies," William O'Shea of the Small Brewers Association remarked years later. "The major breweries drew from enormous wealth to heavily advertise their products here and undercut small breweries in Chicago and elsewhere."

Image became everything, and in the eyes of many Chicago beer drinkers, that of local beers was a sometimes justified, negative one. "Unfortunately, most Chicago brands had a 'cheap beer' image, mainly because of the lower retail price and sometimes erratic quality control," noted an executive of a major retail liquor store chain. Customers and retailers started to react to the cheap prices of Chicago beers. With room to carry only a limited amount of beer brands, taverns, restaurants and liquor stores started dropping the cheaper-priced local brews, unwilling to give up the built-in profit margins that the premium-priced national beers afforded them. Sales slid even further as Chicago breweries now accounted for only thirty percent of the beer supplied to the Chicago market during the early 1950s.[18]

Death of Lou Greenberg

On December 8, 1955 Pearl Greenberg decided to stop at the office of her husband Lou, at the Canadian Ace Brewing Company at 3940 South Union in Bridgeport. She soon left for a quick shopping jaunt in the Loop while her husband finished his business for the day. After finishing her shopping and returning to the brewery, her husband continued to dawdle for another hour or so before finally packing up to return to their suite at the Seneca Hotel, which Greenberg owned. A recent pattern had been developing in Greenberg's movements that friends and acquaintances had begun to notice. He seemed reluctant to move around in public without his wife and would leave his brewery office only under cover of darkness.

The mob-backed Greenberg brewery had thrived for years while other Chicago breweries were falling by the wayside. Called before the Senate Kefauver Crime Committee in 1951, Greenberg stated that he "guessed" that he was selling ten million dollars worth of beer each year. His testimony at the time also revealed the reason he had changed the name of the Manhattan Brewery to the Canadian Ace Brewing Company. He explained to the committee that he made the name change in 1951 "because of Manhattan's bad name."[19]

Recently however, reports indicated that sales at the syndicate-controlled South Side brewery were slipping. In response, the Canadian Ace sales force was making a very visible show of force in their territories, pushing some of the bigger taverns and lounges to take on even more product to boost sales. Complaints from some South Side tavern owners indicated that they were being muscled by Canadian Ace beer drummers for larger orders. This new sales campaign might have explained Greenberg's unusually long hours during the last few weeks prior to December of 1955. With Christmas and New Year's Eve approaching, it was one final chance to boost year-end sales.[20]

On their way home, after stopping at a local bakery on 33rd and Wallace, the Greenbergs decided to eat at the Glass Dome Hickory Pit, a small Bridgeport rib joint on Union Avenue, just minutes from the brewery. Arriving about six p.m., the couple remained at the restaurant for about a half hour and walked out the front door towards their car which was parked just a few feet west of the entrance. As Greenberg opened the car door for his wife, two men quickly approached the couple and muttered something to Greenberg as they came up behind him. "No, no," Greenberg almost meekly responded to the men, as two shots rang out. Although wounded, the sixty-five year-old millionaire turned and began to chase the two startled men as they ran east across Union. One of the assailants stopped in the middle of the street and fired three more times at Greenberg. As the fatally wounded man fell to the street, the gunmen fled down a nearby alley.[21]

There were a number of theories proposed as to who killed Greenberg and why, but the murder still remains a mystery. "This was not a professional gangland killing," said Captain Thomas McLaughlin of the Deering police district. "The M.O. was different. Bullets of .38 caliber were used. Mob slayers mow 'em down with submachine guns or heavier weapons," the officer dramatically noted. It certainly, however, couldn't have been robbery since Greenberg was still wearing a $5,000 ring and carrying cash. But the defensive Pearl Greenberg insisted that the slaying must have been the result of a botched robbery attempt. "My husband didn't have an enemy," she said in response to whether or not her husband's death had been a result of extortion or perhaps a shady business deal gone sour.

Because the murder involved a mob figure, police rounded up and questioned the usual suspects, including Tony "Big Tuna" Accardo, Jack "Greasy Thumb" Guzik and up-and-coming mobster Gus Alex. All had credible alibis. Greenberg's death was never solved.

Without Greenberg's mob connections and the realization by the mobsters that the reign of the national breweries was imminent and overwhelming, the Canadian Ace Brewery folded in 1968, even after its acquisitions of the Prima Brewing Company in 1958 and the Pilsen Brewing Company in 1963. It became quite common during the years before its demise to see Canadian Ace Lager or Ale for sale in plastic bags offering eight cans for 88 cents at Chicago discount stores or drug stores with the ad tag of "8 for 88!" The Canadian Ace death was slow and agonizing as the brewery frantically bought or initiated scores of new labels in a futile effort to keep production figures up.[22]

With the end of Greenberg's legacy, Meister Brau, Incorporated, became Chicago's only home-town brewery since the Haas & Sulzer Brewery opened in 1833.

Mob Influences Continue

The investigation of Greenberg's death and the later testimony by Gus Alex, a crime syndicate gambling boss and alleged trigger man for the old Capone gang, brought another glimpse into the murky relationship between breweries in Chicago and the old Capone mob.

Called before a Senate rackets committee in the summer of 1958, Alex disclosed to Committee Chief Counsel Robert Kennedy that he had been a "sales representative" for the Chicago branch of the Blatz Brewing Company of Milwaukee from February 1, 1955 to June 20, 1958. His admission came only after the young Kennedy confronted Alex with the mobster's 1956 tax return which listed $12,000 from Blatz as salary for the year. The brewery had inherited Alex in 1955 from a local Blatz distributorship operated by Stanley Stupner.

Stupner, who had once been involved with a Chicago taxi cab union, was in the sales department of Atlas Brewing Company from 1944 to 1952, when the takeover of the local brewery by Drewry's was completed. During the period of Stupner's employment at Atlas, his position was protected by the brewery's president, Louis S. Kanne.

Investigation revealed that Kanne had once been a substantial shareholder in the old Manhattan Brewery with shares he had purchased from the sister of "Hymie" Weiss after the bootlegger had been slain back in the twenties. Kanne sold his shares in the Manhattan brewery to Lou Greenberg in 1937.

When Stupner left the Atlas Brewery in 1952, he took along Gus Alex to form the local Blatz distributorship. Alex's growing reputation as an understudy of "Greasy Thumb" Jack Guzik, an alleged South Side boss of policy gambling and horse booking, eventually made the papers, alerting Blatz officials that they had a public relations problem on their hands. His services were eventually terminated by Blatz, leaving Alex without the $1000 a month salary he had enjoyed for forty-one months.[23]

About the same time that Gus Alex's involvement in the Chicago brewery trade was being uncovered at the Senate hearings, Fulton D. Thorton, president of the Monarch Brewing Company in Chicago, announced the sale of that brewery, its equipment and trademarks to the Joliet, Illinois-based Bohemian Brewing Company. The Joliet brewery, which had been under the control of syndicate beer baron Joe Fusco since Prohibition days, made public its plan to use the Monarch to expand the marketing area of Bohemian's Van Merritt brand beer.[24]

Eliot Ness' prophecies of twenty years past were still proving true in Chicago.

Notes

1. *The Brewers Digest*, March and April, 1941.

2. *United States Brewers' Association*, Brewery Production Cost Figures, 1941.

3. *The Brewers Digest*, June, 1941, April and December, 1942; *Modern Brewery Age*, July, 1940.

4. Letter to the author from William Fox II, February, 3, 1999. Bill, son of Kenneth Fox who served as advertising manager for the firm, remembers his mother claiming the Capone connection.

5. *The Western Brewer*, July, 1933; *Brewery Age*, September, 1934; *Brewers Digest*, September, 1943, June, August and October, 1944.

6. *Brewers Digest*, April, 1942.

7. *Brewers Digest*, October, 1942.

8. *Brewers Digest*, February, 1944.

9. *Brewers Digest*, April, 1944.

10. *Brewers Digest*, December, 1944.

11. *Brewers Digest*, October 1945; *United States Brewers Foundation*, Seventh Annual Meeting, 1946, p. 21.

12. Peter Hernon and Terry Ganey. *Under the Influence. The Unauthorized Story of the Anheuser-Busch Dynasty.* (New York, NY: Simon & Schuster, 1991) pp. 132–134, 152.

13. *Chicago Tribune*, April 24, 1977.

14. *Modern Brewery Age*, September and November, 1950; Donald Bull, Manfred Friedrich and Robert Gottschalk, *American Breweries.* (Trumbull, CT: Bullworks, 1984) pp. 58, 65.

15. *Modern Brewery Age*, January, 1950; *Brewers Journal*, Chicago, IL, Gibson Publishing, February, 1950

16. Letter to the author from William Fox II, February 11, 1999.

17. *Modern Brewery Age*, March 1950, August, October and December 1951, July, August, and December, 1955.

18. *Chicago Tribune*, April 24, 1977, *Brewers Journal*, April 1950.

19. *Chicago Tribune*, December 9–10, 1955.

20. *Chicago American*, December 9, 1955; *Chicago Tribune*, December 11, 1955.

21. *Chicago Tribune*, December 10–11, 1955; *Chicago American*, December 9–10, 1955.

22. Phil Pospychala and Joe McFarland. *The Great Chicago Beer Cans.* (Libertyville, IL: Silver Fox Productions, 1970) pp. 23–32, *Chicago Tribune*, April 24, 1977.

23. *Chicago Tribune* and *Chicago American*, August 1, 1958.

24. *Brewers Journal*, September, 1958.

Chapter 17

Meister Brau and Peter Hand, 1965–1978

"If one of the bottles should happen to fall . . ."
Old drinking song refrain.

New Directions

In early 1965, a group of private investors, led by Purdue University graduate and investment banker James Howard, purchased the Peter Hand Brewery. Howard, as the founder of Growth Capital, Incorporated, and later, Growth International, had found that an investment portfolio of diverse manufacturing and insurance stocks could prove profitable to investors and shareholders. With his successfully proven business philosophy of diversity, Howard would soon move to imprint his past experiences on the conservative traditions of Chicago's dying brewing industry.

The old brewery on North Avenue, originally founded by Peter Hand, a Prussian immigrant and Civil War veteran, had enjoyed moderate success since its inception in 1891, especially with its popular Meister Brau brand. Soon after its purchase, the company went public with the issuance of 1,200,000 shares of common and 500,000 shares of preferred stock. Howard was eventually named as company president of the newly named Meister Brau, Incorporated.[1]

Following an aggressive program of sales and expansion, MB soon ranked an impressive twenty-fifth in size nationally, with sales of 899,000 barrels during 1967. Because of management's strong emphasis on mass advertising and continued growth, the company was willing to accept the above average high end cost of advertising at $1.33 a barrel. Having seen so many local breweries fail in the last thirty years, Howard and his fellow investors knew that advertising was the key to increased sales, and most importantly, continued existence.

The revitalized company placed a high emphasis on the relationship between local sports fans and beer drinkers, determining that men aged 18 to 34 made up both groups, a demographic trait that might seem fairly obvious today, but was fairly new ground during the sixties. During the next few years, the brewery sponsored Blackhawk hockey games and the Chicago Bulls over WGN Radio. MB also held a one-fifth sponsorship of the Chicago White Sox on the UHF television channels 32 in Chicago and 24 in Milwaukee, a seemingly closed market that the aggressive Meister Brau management was boldly willing to challenge.[2]

Diversification

The years 1967 and 1968 would prove to be fateful years for the brewery as it began to add diversification to its business agenda, a strategy that President Howard had found profitable in his former business role as an investment and finance banker. After buying out Buckeye Brewing in Toledo, Ohio and its formula for a low calorie beer in 1966, the Chicago brewery launched Meister Brau Lite, a low calorie, low carbohydrate beer that was promoted as having a "non-filling" quality. The brewery continued its theme of acquiring low calorie products with its purchase of the O.G. Meyer Candy Company, a Chicago based manufacturer of sugar-free and regular candies. Rounding out this concept was the inclusion of Jero Black Products, a salad dressing, sauce and syrup manufacturer, the Mi-Diet Cookie Company, a subsidiary of Mickleberry's Food Products, Incorporated and the Lite Soap Company of Aurora, Illinois. These purchases were formed into a separate Meister Brau subsidiary known as Lite Food Products, Incorporated.[3]

The brewery also began the Peter Hand Foundation in 1967, which was an Italian-based agribusiness manufacturer of vitamins and nutritional feed products for livestock that also produced vitamins and chemicals for the food, dairy and drug industries. This purchase was complemented by the additional purchases of Medical Chemicals, Corporation of Melrose Park, Illinois, and Lypho-Med, Incorporated, both pharmaceutical operations.[4]

Almost immediately after making these non-brewing related acquisitions, financial problems for the growing conglomerate began to develop. Despite increasing sales to $37,136,987 in 1967, contrasted with 1966 sales of $35,831,007, President Howard reported a loss of almost $79,000. He described the loss as "nonrecurring," blaming start-up costs for the new Meister Brau Lite beer line and the Peter Hand Foundation, plant modernization and expansion costs, depressed prices in the agribusiness sector and record cold weather throughout their beer marketing area. 1968's efforts were reflected in a fall off in gross sales to $29,173,000, but positive earnings of $234,000.

Once again, the brewery reported an increase in sales for 1969. As in 1968, earnings were positive with an increase to $291,903 from sales of $39,313,799. But Howard cited nagging drains on MB's 1969 operations due to continued heavy advertising for Lite beer, a fall off in sales from their Buckeye brand and start-up costs for the Lite Food Products, Inc. division. An unaudited financial report of the company later showed that these earning figures were inflated. As a result, sales figures were later readjusted to $35,640,000 with earnings pegged at only $93,550.[5] The unaudited financial report also revealed additional losses coming from the Burgermeister Brewing Corporation plant in San Francisco, a plant recently leased by Meister Brau, Inc. The losses from the new brewery operation were attributed to normal start-up costs, but the losses at Burgermeister continued into 1970.

As a result of poor earnings, the directors of Meister Brau, Inc. voted to omit the quarterly common stock dividend. More telling than the failure to pay stock dividends was the announcement that Meister Brau was now in the process of refinancing its long term indebtedness with a $13,000,000 loan. Despite the losses, Howard seemed encouraged and predicted that subsequent quarters would prove profitable.[6]

Glory Days at Meister Brau

Even with the initial poor results of its speculative non-brewing ventures, the company seemed to be on the right track with its expanding brewing operations. In early

The Peter Hand Brewery flagship brand, "Old Chicago," tried to nurture loyalty to a home town brand with its label design of Chicago buildings. From the author's collection.

1968, Meister Brau, Inc. launched an unprecedented $1,000,000 regional sales campaign that reintroduced the concept of draft beer in bottles and cans. "The Big 1" campaign saturated radio, TV and Sunday newspaper supplements, "reflecting the acceptance of Meister Brau as number one in taste and the number one take out beer in the Chicago market," boasted Thierry l. McCormick, vice-president for advertising and public relations for Meister Brau's new ad agency, McManus, John & Adams, Incorporated. McCormick also noted that Meister Brau currently enjoyed better than a 19% share of the Chicago home consumption market over its nearest competitor's 11% share.[7]

Looking to expand their market further, the brewery set up six new distributorships in Indiana, Tennessee and Wisconsin and took back control of its Lite beer production and distribution in the East from Ballantine & Sons of Newark, New Jersey.

With a reported first quarter loss for 1969 due to a dock strike and a later fire at their pharmaceutical plant and the added burden of additional start-up costs for the expansion of Lite beer in California, sales backlogs were building up for a potentially strong second half performance. The series of losses certainly didn't slow down Meister Brau's continued ad campaigns. Combining their total television ad expenditures for its growing product line, the brewery spent a total of $215,800 for 1968 for TV. It was a drop in the barrel compared to either national giant Anheuser-Busch whose bill was $2,495,300 for its television ads or the almost $6,000,000 spent by Pabst, but MB's perseverance was showing results, especially in Chicago. Their newspaper ad expenditures were almost as great as AB's at $214,679 and overwhelmed Pabst's newspaper bill of only $47,858. The difference was MB's total media saturation of the local Chicago market and the profitable results that this blanket coverage gave the company.

Chicagoans had accepted the Meister Brau line as their local beer. Ads in the sports section of the *Chicago Tribune* were aimed at those who enjoyed every conceivable game of competition, accompanied, of course, by a cold beer from MB. Saturday night TV viewers were enticed for weeks by springtime Meister Brau Bock Beer commercials during the Channel 2 news with anchorman Fahey Flynn and meteorologist P.J. Hoffstrom. Complementing the bock beer ad campaign was a yearly "Bock Is Beautiful" beauty contest, searching for a Bock Queen to reign over their traditional Bockfest. Consumer reaction was extremely positive to the brewery's annual Lenten announcement that "Meister Brau Bock Beer is back!" and the aggressive weekly sales pitches for their other brands of popular beers during the rest of the year, including the well received Meister Brau Lite.

Meister Brau, Incorporated now ranked last out of the top twenty-five national sales leaders, but in doing so, the little neighborhood brewery had established itself as both Chicago's home town favorite and a growing national brewer.[8] Continuing its drive to become not only successful locally but nationally, Robert E. Ingram, Meister Brau's senior vice-president of marketing, announced an expanded national ad campaign, buttressed by a newly organized national sales organization. Greatly encouraged by 1969's sales of over 1,000,000 barrels, the brewery projected 1970 sales of more than 1.6 million barrels of beer, a large portion of this increase due to the emerging national acceptance of their Lite beer brand. Ingram went on to predict an astonishing sales target of 2.5 million barrels of beer in 1972, noting that ". . . all our forecasts are on target."

Financial Problems Continue

With lingering questions in late 1970 as to Meister Brau's failure to release fully audited returns for 1969, the company was forced to disclose details of its debt restructuring negotiations. MB's efforts to refinance had delayed the fully audited 1969 financial results as U.S. Steel Finance Corporation, a wholly owned subsidiary of United States Steel Corporation, poured over the company books. Meister Brau's rapid expansion in the brewing industry and its efforts to diversify into the profit draining non-brewery related businesses had left the business asset strong, but unable to maintain positive earnings as beer sales increased yearly but losses continued overall.

With the returns for 1969 finally audited and complete, the loan conditions by U.S. Steel Finance were made public. Terms of the new loan agreement indicated just how bad the financial problems at MB had become and how bad they would be if the Chicago based brewery failed to win its gamble of continued expansion. But this philosophy of non-brewery related acquisitions, a keystone to the business strategy of Meister Brau Company's President Howard, had thus far incurred numerous yearly losses and had now forced management to the negotiation table for a hefty cash infusion.

Under the terms of the refinancing agreement, Meister Brau was able to complete certain transactions that were technically prohibited by its old long term financial agreements. Despite the financial restrictions that MB had agreed to when securing their past loans, the company had purchased the Burgermeister plant from the Jos. Schlitz Brewing Company rather than continuing to lease it, and had boldly purchased another candy plant. With the 13 million dollar infusion from U.S. Steel Finance, the Chicago brewery paid $6,000,000 for the Burgermeister plant, $1,000,000 for the candy plant and used $5,400,000 to repay its original loan holders, ending any possibility of problems with them for exceeding the boundaries of their past loan agreements.[9]

It was, however, a deal with the devil. In return for the cash transfusion, Meister Brau agreed to mortgage its brewery properties, pledge inventories and receivables and not surprisingly, agreed to consult with U.S. Steel Finance before making other acquisitions, an annoying restriction that MB had also agreed to with its former lenders, but nonetheless chose to ignore. In addition, the brewery was required to pay 4½% interest over prime with principal amortization of $250,000 per quarter beginning in the second year of the three year loan. The company also agreed to use its best efforts to repay $4,000,000 of the $13,000,000 loan during the first year, either through the selling off of current assets or with the proceeds of additional financing from other sources. With the new debt restructuring agreement and the possibility that the acquisitions of the last few years might yet prove profitable, MB continued its day-to-day operations, stubbornly holding on to its financially draining non-brewery related assets.[10]

Burgermeister Failure

Soon before the bailout agreement went into effect, it became painfully obvious that their most recent acquisitions, including the $6,000,000 Burgermeister plant, would not be the answer to the brewery's growing financial problems, but would only compound them. With reported sales of more than $14,000,000 for the second quarter of 1970, compared to $8,781,107 for the same period of 1969, President, and now Chief Executive Officer Howard disclosed an earnings loss of $154,740 for Meister Brau, Inc., totaling $354,899 for the first fiscal half year. "Our earnings continue to be adversely affected by recent acquisitions," said Howard, and with an all too familiar refrain, he claimed good things on the horizon, ". . . we believe that the company performance in the second half will result in a profitable 1970 year." Perhaps unwilling to change course in the midst of the not yet implemented financial agreement, shareholders reelected Howard and his management team in September of 1970.[11]

Howard's enthusiasm proved unwarranted as he once again reported the Meister Brau phenomenon: 1970 sales had unbelievably rocketed past last year's sales by almost 21 million dollars to $56,116,502 but the result was an earnings deficit of $2.76 per share. Howard's reaction was not surprising. "Some operations may continue at a loss in 1971; however, we expect total company operations will be profitable."[12]

Beginning of the End

With one year of operation completed under the new financing agreement, the hard realities of Meister Brau's financial position had become obvious. As part of the U.S. Steel financing deal, assets were to be liquidated as needed to meet the obligations of the agreement. In late 1971, Meister Brau, Inc. announced that it had closed the San Francisco Burgermeister plant and had sold the brand name and business to the Theo. Hamm Company, now owned by Heublein, Inc., for an undisclosed amount of cash. Meister Brau still retained physical ownership of the West Coast plant.

Howard had made the trek to San Francisco days earlier to personally announce to brewery employees that the brewery was closing after operating at a loss, despite having regained a production level of 750,000 barrels annually. With competition from out of state breweries hampering sales and the fact that Burgie was a popular priced beer, the only beer the plant produced, profit margins had become non-existent. One might question why the validity of relying solely on the production of a single, low profit brand had not been considered before executing the $6,000,000 purchase that Howard and his board of directors had so eagerly pursued.[13]

With some of the proceeds from the Burgermeister deal, MB turned around and purchased Better Brands of Illinois, a major beer and liquor wholesaler. The local distributor handled a variety of popular products including Miller High Life, Carlsberg beer, Tanqueray gin and the latest beer fad drink, Hop-N-Gator. It appeared to be a step in the right direction for a brewery that had strayed so far from its roots. With this new acquisition, it was hoped by the company that MB would be able to further its beer distribution throughout the Chicagoland area. Distribution of MB products, however, was not the problem.[14]

With the good news, however, came the bad. Meister Brau reported a net loss in the spring of 1971 of about 2.1 million dollars on revenue of almost $40,000,000. This time, there was no hopeful prediction by CEO Howard for a profitable year-end statement. The brewery somberly announced that it was now in the process of disposing of certain assets and business operations to improve its financial position. At the same time that the board of directors was supposedly liquidating some of its assets, the Chicago brewery inexplicably turned around and bought the defunct Warsaw Brewing Company of Warsaw, Illinois for $86,000, a brewery that had no real value as an asset for a company now trying to make a national impact. Months after its purchase by MB, the Warsaw brewery remained closed as Howard and his people belatedly decided that it would be too expensive to put the plant back into operation. With that costly observation, Meister Brau disposed of the Warsaw Brewing Company, taking close to a $46,000 loss for its misadventure.

It was the beginning of the end for Chicago's historic brewery and both Howard and his board of directors knew it, or soon would.[15]

It's Miller Time

On June 28, 1972, the *Chicago Tribune* reported that Miller Brewing Company, a recent acquisition of cigarette manufacturer Phillip Morris, Incorporated, had entered into discussions with Meister Brau, Incorporated about the possibility of Miller purchasing some or all of Meister Brau. Indirectly connected with MB through Meister Brau's recent purchase of Better Brands of Illinois, Miller had consistently shown poor sales performance during its post-war years in the Chicagoland market. In addition to poor Chicago sales, a new Fort Worth, Texas plant for Southern distribution of its flagship brew, Miller High Life, was brewing far below capacity. Even the Miller headquarters brewery in Milwaukee was having problems maintaining a reasonable output. The purchase of a good selling Chicago beer brand would certainly help Miller's under-production plight and hopefully boost its sluggish sales in the Midwest; for the ailing Meister Brau, however, the question would still be whether to sell the entire brewery operation, physical plant and all, or perhaps sell one or all of the MB brand names while retaining the brewery plant.

MB had already sold off the Burgie label and batch formula and had recently announced the sale of Kanda Corporation, the candy distribution company that the brewery had purchased just two short years before in one of the transactions that had precipitated the $13,000,000 loan from U.S. Steel. In spite of management's belated realization that the selling off of its many unrelated brewery operations was now a matter of economic survival, the selling of the soul of Meister Brau, the brewery at 1000 West North Avenue, was still out of the question.

On June 29, 1972, Miller Brewing Company confirmed that it had purchased for cash the trade names of Meister Brau, Meister Brau Lite and Buckeye beers and certain assets of Meister Brau, including distributor Better Brands of Illinois which had been recently purchased by MB. Better Brands was Miller's only conduit to the potentially profitable Chicago market. Caught in the middle of Chicago brewery history were 300 hapless MB employees.

CEO James Howard had made a prophetic statement in 1967, predicting a place for regional brewers as the smaller city breweries passed into oblivion. "It's inevitable that the industry should pass from many, purely local operations to fewer more broadly based operations." Unknowingly, Howard had predicted the fate of Chicago's Meister Brau.[16]

Bankruptcy

Two weeks after the sale of Meister Brau's brand names to Miller, the beleaguered brewery filed a petition in Federal Bankruptcy Court for voluntary reorganization. CEO Howard optimistically stated that the purpose of filing Chapter XI was to give the company breathing room in order to propose a rescheduling of debt with the brewery's creditors. Still looking for needed cash, the brewery entered into an agreement with Falstaff Brewing Corporation of St. Louis to sell the San Francisco-based Burgermeister brewery. Falstaff was eager to buy the 20 million barrel capacity plant to accommodate greatly increased sales of its Falstaff Premium on the West Coast. To ensure a high level of production, Ballantine Ale and Ballantine Beer were also scheduled to be brewed at the plant, avoiding the problems that Meister Brau had incurred with its unforgiving one brand production philosophy at the West Coast brewery.[17]

In December of 1972, while still trying to bail out the debt-ridden brewery, Howard was asked about rumors circulating in brewing and financial circles that he was attempting to acquire the Drewry label from G. Heileman Brewing Company. Once brewed in Chicago by Associated Brewing of Detroit, it would have been a sort of homecoming for a recognized brand label. Tight-lipped, Howard would neither confirm nor deny any negotiating for the Drewry label. "I've talked to quite a few brewers," said Howard, and then seemed to tip his hand. "We could operate it (the Chicago plant) profitably at a forty percent capacity"—about 400,000 barrels annually.

In spite of an estimated $2,500,000 needed to resume brewing operations, Howard claimed no problems in raising the needed capital. There was, of course, the little matter of a $1,800,000 pay off to U.S. Steel Finance and more than $6,000,000 in unsecured debt to contend with.

Two months later, on February 9, 1973, Howard was given just five more days by the Bankruptcy Court to come up with a workable solution to MB's financial mess, including the repayment of all outstanding debt. Howard had earlier testified that Meister Brau needed to come up with at least $750,000 in interim financing in order to begin the brewing of two new brands of beer, Peter Hand Old Chicago and Spartan. With a $500,000 loan commitment from a Milwaukee based finance company, the MB CEO now claimed that he and his board of directors could put the company back in the black by May of 1973. Meister Brau's restructuring period was extended. It was the second extension given to Howard by an understanding bankruptcy referee. This new extension, however, had worried creditors objecting to yet another grace period for the beleaguered brewery.[18]

But days later, the ordeal was over. On February 15, 1973, Meister Brau, Incorporated, was declared bankrupt. With its Buckeye Brewery in Toledo, Ohio, the Jero syrup plant and the old brewery on North Avenue in Chicago, the assets of Meister Brau, Incorporated were valued at about $4 million, with a final payment of almost $2 million needed for U.S. Steel Finance and the rest needed to partially satisfy millions of dollars in unsecured debt.

The Peter Hand Brewery

In April, 1973, the Meister Brau plant was put on the auction block by the Federal Bankruptcy Court. The successful bidders were Fred Huber of Huber Brewing Company in Monroe, Wisconsin and Fred Regency, president of a local textile manufacturer. Only one other bidder attempted to beat their high bid of $1.35 million—former Meister Brau CEO James Howard, with an unsuccessful bid of $1.25 million.

A veteran of over twenty years in the beer business, Huber launched an ambitious plan to keep the brewing legacy alive in Chicago. In a local publicity campaign blitz that went on for months, the Wisconsin brewer played hard on the local aspect of the reopened brewery, a tactic that had been successful for Meister Brau's Chicagoland sales. "People will support a local beer," claimed Huber. "By the end of May, we hope to be in production with our first label, Old Chicago Beer," he predicted.

Estimating a first year run of 250,000 barrels, Huber and marketing director Charles DeLorenzo, a holdover from the Howard regime, talked of expanding production with new brand lines as sales would hopefully increase. With the proper blend of community pride and aggressive promotion as the key to their success, DeLorenzo went out on a limb with a first year projection of 300,000 barrels and a peaking out at 450,000 barrels. "Chuck may be a little optimistic," conceded Huber. A few months later, however, Huber was taking the same stance. Estimating the Chicago market at around 5 million

When the Peter Hand Brewery closed in 1978 a brewing tradition of 145 years ended in Chicago. The brewery is seen here circa 1950. Courtesy of Ernie Oest.

barrels a year, the brewer gushed dreamily, "If we can grab 10 percent of the trade, we'll be quite happy!"[19]

But times were changing in Chicago and the issues of loyalty and community pride in the choice of local beer had become moot points. As Peter Hand tried to regain a niche segment of Chicago's beer drinkers, the nationals overwhelming gained control of the local beer market. The Jos. Schlitz Brewing Company had recently celebrated its dislodging of Anheuser-Busch from the position of number one statewide sales leader, with sales of 1,815,000 barrels in Illinois, or 24.1% of the market, with most of the sales coming from Chicago. AB, with 23.3% of the state market, was being pursued by the aggressive G. Heileman of La Crosse, Wisconsin and Miller Brewing Company, which had risen 9.5% in sales since acquiring Meister Brau and, more importantly, the Meister Brau Lite label and formula.

Opening a beer advertising blitz in August of 1972, just months after buying the MB brands, Miller began saturating the Chicago daily papers with full page ads and multiple 30 second TV spots during local sportscasts, targeting the old Meister Brau and Meister Brau Lite crowd. With the deep pockets of Phillip Morris and the formula for the old Meister Brau Lite, now known as the new low calorie, low carbohydrate Lite beer from Miller, the Milwaukee brewery exploited the same market that MB had successfully nurtured . . . sports enthusiasts. They could now, however, take their advertising efforts to a much higher level; they went totally national, not region by region as Meister Brau had. Once again, they pursued the sports crowd. "To push a product that held a great deal of appeal for athletic, fitness-conscious people, Miller bought sports. Any sports. By the time Anheuser-Busch went looking for available sports airtime, Miller owned something like 70 percent of network television sports beer advertising," says author Philip Van Munching in his entertaining and informative book, *Beer Blast.*[20]

Lite beer from Miller, son of Meister Brau Lite, soon became the beer that made Miller famous. In a bit of ironic beer karma, the recently renamed Miller Lite is currently the biggest selling brand of beer in the city of Chicago, with a market share of almost twenty-three percent.[21]

With only one city brewery left, the domination of the local beer market by the nationals and after conceding that Chicago would never again be a brewing center, the Chicago chapter of the Master Brewers Association voted unanimously to dissolve its charter. Roger Sieben, a brewmaster at the new Peter Hand Brewery, explained the reasoning behind the dissolution of the local MBA: "Two years ago we had a meeting and said 'Let's really try to have a proper malt and hops session.' Only eight guys showed up." The apathy of the membership was simply a reflection of the attitude of the Chicago beer drinking public as a whole; local brand loyalty was truly dead. In the business of beer, image was everything . . . and still is.

On September 1, 1978, with sales of less than 100,000 barrels for 1977, and no prospects for a bubbly future, the Peter Hand Brewery closed, ending one hundred and forty-five years of brewing history in Chicago.

For the next nine years, Chicago would be the exclusive playground of out-of-town brewers.

Notes

1. *Brewers Digest*, January, 1968.

2. *Brewers Digest*, February, 1968, July, 1968, and November, 1968. Also see William Oscar Johnson, "Sports and Suds," *Sports Illustrated*, August 8, 1988, 74.

3. *Brewers Digest*, May, 1968, and March, 1969; Philip Van Munching. *Beer Blast.* (New York, NY: Times Books, 1997) p. 31.

4. *Brewers Digest*, November, 1969.

5. *Brewers Digest*, March, 1969, August, 1970; *Modern Brewery Age*, August 3, 1970.

6. Chicago Tribune, March 9, 1968, Brewers Digest, May, 1968; Modern Brewery Age, August 3, 1970.

7. Brewers Digest, June, 1968. The nearest competitor was probably Anheuser-Busch.

8. Brewers Digest, March, 1969, June, 1969, Modern Brewery Age, March, 1969, August, 1969.

9. Brewers Digest, August, 1970

10. Brewers Digest, Ibid.

11. Brewers Digest, October, 1970.

12. Brewers Digest, May, 1971, Modern Brewery Age, April 4, 1971.

13. Brewers Digest, January, 1972.

14. Brewers Digest, February, 1972, March, 1972.

15. Brewers Digest, April, 1972.

16. Chicago Tribune, June 28, 30 and July 11, 1972, Brewers Digest, August, 1972.

17. Brewers Digest, August, 1972, Chicago Tribune, July 12, 1972.

18. Chicago Tribune, December 22, 1972, February 7 and 10, 1973.

19. Chicago Tribune, April 14 and, 19, July 3, 1973.

20. Van Munching, op. cit. p. 64.

21. Chicago Tribune, April 30, 1974, November 30, 1997, March 7, 1998; Brewers Digest, September, 1972.

Epilogue

"Chicago? Al Capone . . . Rat-a-tat-tat!" (tommy-gun sound)

Typical reaction from out-of-towners when a Chicagoan answers the question of where he's from

Legacies

Today, the memory of Chicago's brewing history has become an odd intermingling of generational realities. If you're part of the so-called "Generation X," perhaps asked to recall any known particulars about the history of the Chicago brewing industry, you might remember the ill-fated Sieben's River North Brewery on West Ontario or the forgettable Tap & Growler on Jackson, both failed brewpub concepts.

Baby-boomers might still recall local brand names from the Peter Hand/Meister Brau misfortunes, intertwined with fading memories of Prohibition-era Chicago from the exaggerated Hollywood portrayals of Eliot Ness, Al Capone and the local brewing industry, courtesy of *The Untouchables*, ABC's old television series.

During the course of research for this book, I've had the pleasure of talking with older individuals who can still recall the last days of Prohibition in Chicago and the final days of some of the local, historic breweries. During their youth, the breweries were a part of their lives and a part of their old neighborhoods. These old witnesses are dwindling in number, unfortunately, as they become a fading part of the city's overall history and take their recollections of neighborhood Rathskellers and Sunday afternoons at local brewery beer gardens with them.

This book began as a simple personal curiosity: What ever happened to Chicago's old breweries? The industry's origins, eventual disappearance and undocumented history have proven to me to be more than the preconceived notions of Chicago gangsters wielding deadly machine guns or Al Capone and his gang rolling out barrels of beer during National Prohibition. As I delved into the beginnings and later years of the Chicago breweries, researched their histories and began to chronicle their years of operation, I became more aware of the tangible and intangible elements of the former Chicago brewing industry legacy that still surround us.

The ways that the regulation of beer and its sale and distribution are handled in Chicago are just one example of the industry's intangible legacy with most of these activities influenced by the sins and abuses of the past. Contemporary issues of tavern closing times, special use permits and late morning Sunday openings are still others. The election of November, 1998 demonstrates the rediscovered strength of local option as a means to an end, with the constituencies of more than a score of Chicago precincts voting their neighborhoods dry and almost as many South Side precincts threatening to follow suit in the next local election. Unfortunately, this blanket use of local option is closing many law abiding, family run operations. No longer owned by European ethnics, as were the Chicago saloons before Prohibition, the African-American establishments are being forced out of business because of the regulatory abuses and excesses of a few. This community use of local option has been merely noted by the local press but bodes of future problems for city beer distributors, retailers and even Chicago's small micro-brewery industry, an important issue that will be explored in *The History of Beer & Brewing in Chicago, Volume II*. The parallels between this reemerging phenomenon and the use of local option after 1907 are eerily similar. If history repeats itself, this is only the first step in a new wave of neo-prohibitionism in Chicago.

One tangible legacy of the Chicago brewing industry is faithfully nurtured by a number of organizations that collect, record and trade relics of the city's oldest breweries. Without the cooperation of members of the American Breweriana Association, Incorporated, and the National Association of Breweriana Advertising, this book would have been woefully lacking in illustrations. As I hope I've represented in this book, brewery history is more than a recording of brewery openings and closings. For better or worse, this industry was once an integral part of Chicago's economic, political and social history. Both of these organizations continue to foster this notion. If you'd like more information about the ABA or NABA, you can contact the following individuals:

Stan Galloway, Executive Director
American Breweriana Association, Inc.
P.O.Box 11157
Pueblo, Colorado 81001-0157.

Robert Jaeger
National Association of Breweriana Advertising
2343 Met-To-Wee Lane
Wauwatosa, Wisconsin 53226.

I'm always interested in hearing from anybody with additional information on Chicago brewing history or breweriana. I can be contacted by Email at toddlintown @mediaone.net. Check out *The History of Beer and Brewing in Chicago* Web site as well.

A more tangible legacy, however, and one that might make an enjoyable day trip or two is detailed in the following pages.

Schlitz Tied-Houses

The Schlitz old tied-houses are local curiosities that can still be found throughout the Chicago area. Using an almost modern franchise concept, the buildings exhibit a deliberate similarity in design and function. The Schlitz globe was often seen on an exterior wall. Two of the most beautifully maintained former Schlitz buildings are now known as the Southport Lanes & Billiards at 3325 North Southport Avenue and Schuba's at 3159 North Southport, within walking distance of each other. The Southport Lanes location is particularly interesting since it has two interior murals of wood nymphs dancing through a Teutonic forest, one scene stretched across the top of the backbar, the other over the original four lane, hand set bowling alleys. Other locations of Schlitz tied-houses are at Belmont and Damen, at 21st and Rockwell, at 35th and Western, and 92nd and Ewing.

Brewery Relics

A surprising number of old breweries can still be found throughout the city. Unfortunately, almost all of them have lost their traditional towers. Nonetheless, a few of these relics still exhibit a majestic presence.

NORTH SIDE BREWERIES

1) *Bartholomae & Leicht Brewing Company*—Sedgwick and Huron. In its final form, it was part of Milwaukee and Chicago Breweries, Company, Ltd., a.k.a. the United States Brewing Company. The *Rundbogenstil* in red brick makes it a distinctive structure

Some legacies don't last long. This advertisement for Conrad Seipp's Salvator beer was visible on the old saloon's wall only briefly before being covered by a sign for the tenant, a bakery. Courtesy of Richard Remson.

in the neighborhood. The brewery had an annual capacity of 80,000 barrels. It closed in 1911. The last standing remnant of the old brewery now houses a number of small businesses. Beautiful.

2) *Brand Brewing Company*—2530 Elston Avenue. Another member of the old United States Brewing Company syndicate, the cream colored structure now houses Ted Furman's Golden Prairie Brewery. Built in 1899 and closed in 1935, its original capacity was 100,000 barrels annually. Still in good shape but with an ugly, out of place, modern structure added on to the front of the brewery at a later date. Interesting.

3) *The Home Brewery*—2654-2670 West Elston, just north of the Brand Brewery. An unremarkable structure built in 1910 and closed in 1920, it reflects the economic reality of breweries built at this time in Chicago; form and functionality ruled over ornate design. A stone's throw away from Brand's Brewery, with an unremarkable presence.

4) *Best Brewing Company*—1301–1329 Fletcher Street. Originally built in 1885 as Klockgeter & Company and renamed in 1890–1891 as the Best Brewing Company, the structure has been painstakingly preserved. It's now a condo complex. A brewery with a 150,000 barrel annual capacity, it closed in 1961. A definite "must see" on your tour.

5) *William Pfeifer*—718–742 North Leavitt Street. A.k.a. Pfeifer's Berlin Weiss Beer Company, its biggest claim to fame was that during National Prohibition it served as one of Terry Druggan's and Frankie Lake's breweries. The red brick brewery is still in nice shape and a good example of a small neighborhood brewery. Stop by for a look, at least for its historic bootlegging significance.

6) *City Brewery Company*—764 West Chicago at Hoyne Avenue. Part of the City of Chicago Brewing and Malting Company and later the Chicago Consolidated Brewing and Malting Company. At one time owned by local politician F.J. Dewes and known as the F. J. Dewes Brewery Company, much of the original complex is still visible throughout the neighborhood. Closed in 1906, the original ice and refrigeration plant is still in operation. Sprawling and industrial in design, it's worth a look.

7) *West Side Brewery Company*—916 North Paulina. Once known as the East Side Brewery (go figure). At one time owned by the Conrad Seipp Brewing Company, it became another element of the City of Chicago Consolidated Brewing and Malting Company syndicate during the 1890s. At the turn of the century, the brewery covered almost the entire frontage of the 900 block of North Paulina. All that's now left is what appears to have been the original brew house, minus its single tower and top floors, but still conspicuous at the south end of the block. Recently gutted and rehabbed as lofts, some of the

architectural features remain visible. Had an annual capacity of 150,000 barrels. Decapitated and disemboweled of its neighboring structures, there's not much to look at now but it's nice to know that the remaining part of the plant still serves a useful function.

SOUTH SIDE BREWERIES

8) *Carl Corper Brewing Company*—4160 South Union Avenue. With just the red brick east wall of the brewery still standing in the *Rundbogenstil*, and a warehouse structure in front of it, the brewery holds a bit of Chicago brewing industry significance. In early 1904, after being arrested for operating a brewery without a license and faced with bankruptcy and personal ruin, brewer Corper put a gun to his head and performed the fatal "Dutch Act" in the brewery office. The brewery was later known as the Westminster Brewing Company after National Prohibition and soon after, as the Prima Brewing Company. It's safe to say that it was a part of the Frank Nitti-controlled Manhattan Brewery combine, operated by Lou Greenberg. At one time, it must have been a beautiful structure, as evidenced by the remaining east wall.

9) *The Manhattan Brewery*—39th and Emerald. Arguably the most famous, if not most infamous brewery in Chicago. It was gangster Johnny Torrio's first brewery purchase in Chicago. The brewery's beer drummers were still roughing up South Side tavern owners to take on its products through the late 1950s and early 1960s. Just a section of what I believe *might* be part of the original complex of buildings remains. It's now a meat house, totally unrecognizable as a former brewing structure. Nothing really to look at but it's just a few blocks away from two other more recognizable breweries.

10) *White Eagle Brewery*—3735–3757 South Racine Avenue. The ethnic isolation of Chicago's neighborhoods was reflected in its many churches *and* breweries. The Irish had the Fortune Brothers and Keeley Breweries, the Italians, the Tosetti Brewing Company and the Poles enjoyed the intoxicating efforts of the White Eagle. Closed in 1950. Just north of the Pershing Avenue bridge, the faded white structure is still in good shape. Head two blocks north on Racine for the next brewery.

11) *The Frank McDermott Brewery*—3435–3441 South Racine. A little neighborhood brewery with a bit of history. Founded in 1892 as the Henn & Gabler Brewing Company. Owned by state senator Frank McDermott during National Prohibition, the 75,000 barrel brewery provided beer for the surrounding Bridgeport neighborhood. With competition from the legitimate trade taking its toll after Repeal, it folded in 1937. The brew house tower is gone, but still retains some nice neighborhood brewery features.

12) *Mutual Brewing Company*—22nd & Spaulding Ave. Built in 1907, it openly continued to brew beer until 1924, five years after the Illinois State Search & Seizure Act was in full force. With a Greek-influenced arch over the old entrance and a battered corner-

stone which still gives testimony to its opening day dedication, it's representative of pseudo-classical industrial design. The cornerstone, however, raises the interesting question as to whether it's a time capsule, possibly containing company papers or brewery memorabilia of interest.

13) *Monarch Brewery*—2419–2443 West 21st Street. Founded as the Jos. Hladovec Brewing Company in 1890, it's another example of industrial design. Its most notorious moment was its takeover in 1958 by mobster Joe Fusco and its operation under the name of the Van Merritt Brewing Company. The rear of the brewery is all that remains. Architecturally uninteresting.

14) *Schoenhofen-Edelweiss Company*—1900 West 18th Street. The one-time National Brewing Company became the Schoenhofen Company in 1925 and the Schoenhofen-Edelweiss Company in 1933. Later owned and operated by Drewry's, the modern industrial structure will soon meet with the wrecking ball as will the old neighborhood Bishop's Chili stand, adjoining the brewery, all in the name of urban progress. See it while you still can.

15) *The Edward R. Stege Brewery*—1501 South Ashland. With the main brew house gone, the remainder of the plant, all built in 1890, exhibits a confusing mix of simplified round arches and long boring interludes of modern industrial design. It operated as a Druggan and Lake brewery during the early years of National Prohibition, but closed as a result of Mayor Dever's beer war in late 1923.

16) *Peter Schoenhofen Brewing Company*—18th & Canalport. Originally the Gottfried & Schoenhofen Brewery, the old red brick structure is everything a brewery hunter would want in a brewery building. Over the front entrance are the dates 1860 A.D.–1886. The year 1860 represents the original founding date of the G & S concern on 12th & Jefferson, but the significance of the final date of 1886 is unknown. The structure was built in 1867 and might represent the oldest existing brick structure in Chicago.

Also note the star symbol representing the art of the brewer; it is *not* the Star of David, though claims have been made that King David was a brewer.

The reconditioned warehouse/powerhouse to the east of the original structure was built during the first few boom years of the early 1900s. Water from an on-site 1600 foot deep artesian well now provides water for sale in gallon containers throughout the city. Additional structures of the brewery complex can be found scattered throughout the neighborhood, including what was once the old Stark's Warehouse structure on 16th and Canal, giving evidence of the huge size of the original brewery. Evidence can be seen of refurbishing and reconstruction on a number of the easily recognizable brewery buildings. Absolutely the most impressive and beautiful brewery remains in Chicago.

17) *Independent Brewing Association*—821–825 West Blackhawk at Halsted. The answer by local businessmen to the growing infiltration of British investors into the Chicago brewing industry before the turn of the century. Operated during the early years of National Prohibition as the Primalt Products Company and after Repeal as the Prima Company. The plant had an annual capacity of 150,000 barrels. A goodly number of the sprawling brewery buildings have been nicely restored and are now being used as office buildings. A worthy stop on your brewery tour. The buildings appear to be of Joliet limestone construction.

Map of Breweries

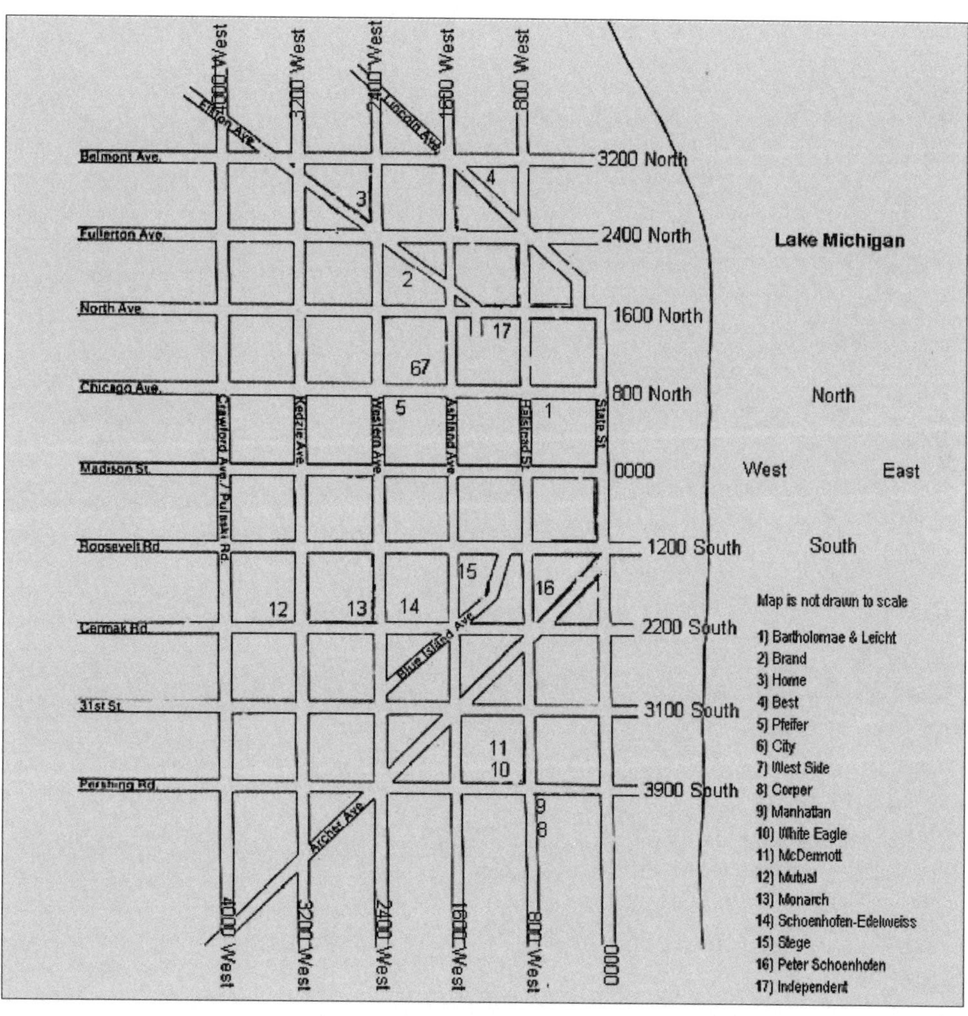

Glossary

Ale—lightly carbonated malted beverage produced from the top fermenting yeast, *Saccharomyces cerevisiae*. Ferments out in 5 to 7 days. A precursor to lager beer.
Barrel house—a low class saloon. Customers usually stood around full barrels of inventory, using the containers as a bar.
Baudelot (German)—used to cool the boiling unfermented wort before pitching the yeast. Usually consist of a series of horizontal tubes, assembled into vertical stands. Replaced the more inefficient coolship for the receiving of hot wort.
Bier Gartens (German)—in Chicago, usually was an outdoor beer drinking area, heavily attended by German families on Sundays. More often than not, the original bier gartens were found in picnic groves or adjacent to a brewery.
Blind pigs—any unlicensed saloon or tavern.
Blue law—prohibits dancing, sports and drinking on Sundays; of Puritanical derivation.
Braumeister (German)—literally, a brewing master. The highest level in the brewing trade.
Comfort station—a public toilet or restroom.
Concert saloons—turn of the century saloon that offered music and entertainment. Prostitution was not uncommon at these establishments.
Coolship or Kuhlshiff (German) – The original piece of equipment used for the receiving of hot wort. It consisted of a shallow, rectangular metal vessel that held the wort until it cooled. It was replaced by the more efficient Baudelot.
Cooper—a person who makes or repairs barrels.
Copper—the metal container in which the wort and hops are boiled. Originally made from copper. Contemporary vessels are usually stainless steel.
Dive—a cheap, disreputable saloon.
Drink of moderation—beer. Originated by beer advocates during the late 1800s to distinguish the gentle affects of a moderate amount of beer consumption from the stronger affects of hard alcohol. The expression is still used in the brewing industry.

Drummer—traveling beer salesman. During National Prohibition, it meant an agent of a bootlegger, who used intimidation and force when necessary to make a sale.
Dry—anti-drink advocate.
Ebullimeter—device used to measure alcoholic content.
Family entrance—side entrance of a saloon. Properly escorted women would be brought into the saloon through this entrance. The almost instinctive habit of husbands to escort their wives through the side entrances of Chicago taverns would prevail through the 1950s.
Free lunch—evolving from a complimentary heated oyster with every beer, the free lunch would later become a spread of meats, vegetables and breads, washed down with a nickel glass of beer.
Golden gate—an original keg tapping device. Virtually obsolete today.
Green beer—unfermented or partially fermented beer, not ready for consumption.
Government tunnel—restricted use tunnel that led from the beer storage tanks to the bottling department.
Home rule—the administration of the affairs of a precinct, ward, city, county or state by the citizens who live in it.
Hop-jack—straining device used to remove hops from the wort.
Kiln—a single, double or triple floor structure that removes moisture from the malt. The color of the malt depends on the length and intensity of the kilning process.
Kraeusen (German)—the introduction of young fermenting beer to beer that has achieved fermentation. The process creates a secondary fermentation which makes for carbonation and a completely fermented product.
Lager Bier (German)—beer produced from the use of the bottom fermenting yeast, *Saccharomyces uvarum*. Usually ferments out in 7 to 14 days and is stored (lagered) in a cool environment for an extended period of time for a final fermentation and rounding out of flavor.
Local option—often used by prohibitionists, it allows constituents in any precinct, ward, city or county to petition for the elimination of the serving of alcohol in any given area. Enforced through referendum.
Malt—barley that has been steeped in warm water to initiate growth. After removal from the water, it is transferred to a compartment with a perforated floor through which warm humidified air is passed. After germination, the malt is transferred to the kiln for the final operation.
Mash—a mixture of water and ground malt from which are derived the necessary sugars for fermentation.
Nativist—a person who favors an American-born individual over an immigrant.
Needle beer—near beer, usually injected with alcohol through the bung of the barrel.
On-premise—the consumption of a drink at a bar or saloon.

Pasteurization—the heating of beer to a temperature of 140°F for a predetermined period of time. Used to ensure microbiological stability of beer.
Picnic bottle—half gallon bottle used during the Second World War.
Pitching—the introduction of yeast to raw, unfermented beer.
Placing the beer—establishing a beer account at a retail location.
Porter—a type of ale, brownish or ruby in color and sweet in taste.
Prohibition—the forbidding by law of the manufacture, sale or consumption of alcohol. National Prohibition.
Racking—removing beer from a barrel or other device, usually for bottling.
Rathskeller (German)—beer tasting room, usually located in the lower level of the brewery.
Set ups—soda pop or seltzer used as an accompaniment to liquor. A "wash."
Shipping brewers—refers to any brewery that exports beer outside of their local market
Small beer—low alcohol beer.
Spendings—an allocated amount of money used by beer salesmen to entice saloon customers to try their product with free drinks.
Steinie—stubby shaped, throw away twelve ounce bottle.
Sternewirth (German)—free beer dispensed to brewery workers, often in lieu of higher pay.
Schwimmers (German)—tear drop or conical shaped metal containers for holding blocks of cooling ice. The containers were placed into the hot wort and allowed to "swim" on the surface of the wort.
Teetotaler—a person who drinks no alcohol.
Tied-house—a saloon owned or controlled by a brewery.
Wet—one who favors the use and manufacture of alcohol.
Wildcat brewery—an unlicensed, clandestine brewery.
Wort—raw, unfermented beer.

Brand Slogans

Following Repeal, advertising became the key element in distinguishing one brand of local beer from another. Slogans could be repeated in everything from radio and television commercial messages to print ads on billboards or packaging. The following list of brand slogans, container tags and coaster messages range from the obscure to the sometimes laughable. But in these short sentences is the genesis of today's beer advertising.

Ambrosia Brewing Company

Ambrosia Nectar Premium Beer	*"Properly Brewed Aged and Mellowed"*
	"For Particular People"

Atlantic Brewing Company

Riviera Special Dark	*"The Kind Dad Use To Drink"*
Barbarossa Beer	*"Premium Beer Brewed With Exactness"*
Tavern Pale Ale	*"Sure It's Different . . . It's Brewed For Me"*
	"The Beer For A Good Head"

Atlas Brewing Company

Atlas Praeger	*"Atlas Praeger, Got It? Atlas Praeger, Get It!"*
	"America's Most Imitated Beer!"
	"Always Better Never Bitter!"
G*E*S Premium Beer	*"Yours For Better Living"*
Premium 9.0.5 Beer	*"Properly Aged In The Brewery Cellars"*

Best Brewing Company

Malt Marrow	*"The Family Treat That Can't Be Beat"*
Hapsburg	*"Made Best by Best"*

Birk Brewing Company

T.A.P Beer	*"Just Like Old Times"*
Trophy Beer	*"Taste How Good Good Beer Can Be!"*

Drewry's Brewery

Drewry's Malt Liquor/Stout	*"A Man's Drink"*
Tropical Extra Fine Ale	*"Taste Tells"*

Garden City Brewery

Old Brew Beer	*"Chicago's Best by Test"*
	"Wow! That's the Beer"

Keeley Brewery

Keeley Beer and Ale	*"Taste Just Right"*

Manhattan (Canadian Ace) Brewery

KC's Best	*"Mellowed And Balanced"*
Lubeck Premium Beer	*"Old World Import Flavor"*
Black Dallas Beer	*"Brewed From The Finest Ingredients For Real Beer Lovers"*

Meister Brau, Incorporated

Meister Brau Lite	*"Non-Filling"*
Meister Brau Beer	*"The Master Brew"*
	"The Custom Brew"
	"Gives you more of what you drink beer for"
	"You can't serve a finer glass of beer!"

Monarch Brewing Company/Van Merritt

Bullfrog Beer	*"Our Old Famous Brand"*
Monarch Beer	*"Brewed Better . . . To Taste Better"*
	"Let Your Taste Decide"
	"Fun for the money!"
Monarch Encore	*"The Mark Of Perfection In Beer"*
Van Merritt	*"C'Mon Man . . . Have A Van"*

Peter Fox Brewing Company

Fox De Luxe Beer	*"Don't Say Fox..Say Fox Deee Luxe!"*
	"The Beer Of Balanced Flavor"
	"Vitamins B And C In Every Drop"
Patrick Henry Malt Liquor	*"Velvet Smooth"*

Peter Hand Brewing Company

Peter Hand's Reserve	*"Sets A New Standard Of Excellence For Both The New World And The Old"*
	"There's So Much In Reserve For You!"
	"The Remarkable American Beer With The Continental Character"

Pilsen Brewing Company

Yusay Pilsen Beer	*"Often Imitated But Never Duplicated"*
	"It's The Right Weigh"
	(Advertised as a non-fattening drink)

Prima Bismarck Brewing Company

Prima Beer	*"The folks at home are thirsty too— Take some Prima Home With You!"*

Schoenhofen-Edelweiss Brewery

Edelweiss	*"A Case Of Good Judgment"*

United States Brewing Company

Rheingold	*"Not a common name. Not a common beer."*
	"Extra Pale like a Liquid Gold it's always the Favorite where Beer is sold"
	"Its popularity sweeps the country"
Chicago Club	*"A real New Brew that's Flavored right. We're sure you'll like it, try it tonite!"*

Appendix of Chicago Breweries

This Appendix is based upon the book, *American Breweries,* by Donald Bull, and used with his permission, for which I am exceedingly grateful. The alphanumeric listing of breweries are arranged in the following manner:

1. The first listing next to each numeric or alphanumeric entry gives the name of the brewery, the original address and the founding and ending date of the brewery.
2. Listings for any brewery entry will change to an alphanumeric entry when one of the following events occur in the history of the brewery:
   a. Name change as a result of incorporation, merger or purchase by another party or brewery.
   b. Address change due to renaming or renumbering of the street.
   c. Address change due to a physical move to another location.
   d. Gap in production due to Prohibition, fire, other natural disaster, or bankruptcy.

1	Albrecht & Finkler, (Home Brewery)	1709 Lincoln Avenue	1901–1902
2	American Brewing Company	922 N. Ashland Avenue	1890–1901
3	Augsberg Brewing Company	3024 W. 30th Street	1934–1934
4	Adam Baierle	34–38 N. Market	1863–1869
5	Banner Brewing Company	1088–1092 Wilcox Avenue	1896–1897
6a	Bartholomae & Leicht, (Eagle Brewery)	684–706 Sedgwick Street	1873–1877
6b	Bartholomae & Leicht Brewing Co.		1877–1889
6c	Bartholomae & Leicht Brewing Co., (United States Brewing Co.)		1889–1890

6d	Bartholomae & Leicht Brewing Co., (Milwaukee and Chicago Breweries Co., Ltd.), (a.k.a. United States Brewing Company)		1890–1911
7	John Behringer	157 Orchard near Willow	1861–1869
8a	Bemis & Rindge		1862–1864
8b	Downer, Bemis & Company	23rd & Kankakee	1864–1866
8c	Downer, Bemis & Company	23rd & South Park Avenue	1866–1869
8d	Downer & Bemis Brewing Co.		1869–1882
8e	Bemis & McAvoy Brewing Co.		1882–1887
8f	McAvoy Brewing Co., (merged with Wacker & Birk)	91 South Park Avenue	1887–1889
8g	McAvoy Brewing Co., (Chicago Breweries, Ltd.)		1889–1920
8h	McAvoy Company (Wacker & Birk Brewing & Malting Co.)		1920–?
9a	Berliner Weiss Beer Brewery, Ferdinand Harke	82 Willow, Rear	1874–1875
9b	Berliner Weiss Beer Brewery, August Harke		1875–1876
10a	Matthias Best	Indiana Avenue near 12th & The Lake	1858–1863
10b	Killian or Christian Schott	Indiana Avenue near North Halleck	1863–1865
10c	Martin Best	721 Indiana Avenue	1865–1866
11a	M. Best	Foot of 14th Street	1852–1854
11b	Conrad Seipp		1854–1855
11c	Conrad Seipp	Foot of 27th Street	1855–1858
11d	Conrad Seipp & Co. (a.k.a. Conrad Seipp)	Lakeshore near Northern, Rio Grande, Hardin Pl.	1858–1860
11e	Seipp & Lehmann		1860–1872
11f	Conrad Seipp	Lakeshore foot of 27th St.	1872–1876
11g	Conrad Seipp Brewing Co., (merged with West Side Brewery Co.)		1876–1890
11h	Conrad Seipp Brewing Co., (City of Chicago Consolidated Brewing & Malting Co., Ltd.)		1890–1933

12a	Binz & LaParle	Cottage Grove, between 27th & 28th Streets	1866–1868
12b	F. Binz Brewery (a.k.a. Michael Keeley Brewery)		1868–1878 1876–1878
12c	Keeley Brewing Co.		1878–1920
12d	Keeley Brewing Co.	516 East 28th Street	1933–1953
13a	Blattner & Seidenschwanz, (a.k.a. Blattner & Co.)	Hinsdale Street between Rush & Pine Streets	c1850–1857
13b	Seidenschwanz & Wacker		1857–1858
13c	Wacker & Seidenschwanz, (a.k.a. Wacker & Co.)	North Franklin near Green Bay, Asylum Place, Dyer & Sophia	1858–1865
13d	Frederick Wacker	848 North Franklin Street, later Webster Avenue	1865–1867
13e	F. Wacker		1867–1872
13f	Wacker & Birk Brewing & Malting Co. (merged with McAvoy Brewing Co)	Des Plaines & Indiana Sts.	1882–1889
13g	Wacker & Birk Brewing & Malting Co. (Chicago Breweries Ltd.)	516 East 28th Street	1889–1918
14a	Bohemian Brewing Co. of Chicago	680–706 Blue Island Avenue	1891–1896
14b	Atlas Brewing Co., (a.k.a. Atlas Brewing Co. of Chicago)		1896–1920 1896–1902
14c	Atlas Beverage Co.		1920–1929
14d	Atlas Brewing Co., (affiliated with Schoenhofen-Edelweiss)		1944–1951
14e	Atlas Brewing Co., (branch of Drewry's Ltd., South Bend, IN)		1951–1962
15	William Bohn	651 37th Street	1893–1993
16a	Brand Brewing Co.	1251 Elston Avenue	1899–1909
16b	Brand Brewing Co., (a.k.a. Producer's Brewing Co.)	2530 Elston Avenue	1901–1922 1916–1920
16c	Brand Co., (a.k.a. Prima Products Co.) (a.k.a. Royal Brewing Co.)		1932–1935 1932 1934
17a	Brand & Hummel Brewing Co.	Avenue L & 100th St.	1880–1887

17b	South Chicago Brewing Co.		1887–1895
17c	South Chicago Brewing Co.	Avenue N & 100th St.	1895–1897
17d	South Chicago Brewing Co., (a.k.a. United Breweries Co., a.k.a. South Chicago Brewery)		1897–1922
18a	Michael Brand	Elston Avenue near West Fullerton	1871–1879
18b	Michael Brand & Co.	Elston Avenue near Snow Street	1878–1879
18c	The Michael Brand Brewing Co.		1886–1889
18d	Unites States Brewing Co. of Chicago (a.k.a. Michael Brand Brewing Co.) (Milwaukee and Chicago Breweries, Ltd.)		1890–1927 1890–1915 1890–1927
18e	United States Brewing Co.		1932–1955
19a	Brewer & Hofmann Brewing Co.	41–55 S. Green St.	1886–1902
19b	George J. Cooke		1905–1910
19c	George J. Cooke Co.	14–30 North Green St.	1910–1922
20a	Brisach & Hessemer	Oak Street near Green Bay	1858–1859
20b	Joseph Brisach	Foot of Oak Street	1859–1860
21	Broadway Brewing Co.	5245 Broadway	1934–1934
22a	Bucher & Hiller	Green Bay Road	1858–1866
22b	George Hiller	9104 N. Clark & Green Bay Road & Wolcott	1866–1868
23a	George Burroughs		c1850
23b	Frederick Burroughs	144 West Lake near Union	c1854–1862
24a	Valentin Busch	31 Cedar St. near Green Bay & Wolcott	1851–1858
24b	Busch & Brand		1858–1873
24c	Busch & Brand Brewing Co.		1873–1879
25a	Calumet Brewing Co., (a.k.a. Calumet Brewery)	10555–10557 Torrence Ave.	1901–1909
25b	Calumet Brewing & Malting Co.	Torrence & 106th Street	1909–1911
25c	Bessemer Brewing Co.		1911–1913
26a	James Carney	39–63 S. Water St.	1840–1855

26b	John O' Neill		1855–1860
27	Castle Brewery Co.	East Chicago Avenue & River Street	1896–1896
28	Chicago Ale & Malt Co.	South Water & Clark	1861–1867
29a	Chicago Brewing Co.	64–80 W. North Street	1888–1898
29b	Chicago Brewing Co., (United Breweries Co.)		1898–1909
29c	Chicago Brewery (United Breweries Co.)	1269 West North	1909–1919
30a	Chicago Union Brewing Co., (a.k.a. Union Brewing Co.) (a.k.a. Patrick O' Neill)	27th St. & Johnson	1867–1885
30b	Cooke & Stenson		1885–1887
30c	Cooke Brewing Co.	Brewery Ave. & 521 East 27th St.	1887–1910
31a	Citizens Brewing Co.	Archer Avenue & Main Streets	1893–1898
31b	Citizens Brewing Co., (United Breweries Co.) (a.k.a. Citizens' Brewery)	Archer Avenue & Throop Street	1898–1920
31c	Bismarck Brewing Co., (a.k.a. Hunter's Brewery Inc.)	2738–2762 S. Archer	1933–1941 1940–1941
31d	Prima-Bismarck Brewing Co.		1941–1951
32a	Columbus Brewing Co.	297 Cornell & Noble	1902–1910
32b	Lutz Brewing Co.		1910–1910
32c	Atlantic Brewing Co.	1401 Cornell & Noble	1910–1912
33a	Corper & Nockin	101–109 Webster Avenue	1886–1891
33b	Birk Bros. Brewing Co.		1891–1909
33c	Birk Bros. Brewing Co.	1315–1325 Webster Ave.	1901–1923
33d	Birk Bros. Brewing Co.	2117 N. Ward at Webster	1933–1936
33e	Birk Bros. Brewing Co.	2117 N. Wayne Street	1936–1950
34a	Carl Corper Brewing & Malting Co.	39th & S. Union	1893–1898
34b	Carl Corper Brewing & Malting Co., (United Breweries Co.)		1898–1900
34c	Carl Corper Brewing Co.	41st & Union	1903–1904

34d	Globe Brewing Co.		1904–1910
34e	Brand Brewing Co., No. 2	4057 S. Union	1910–1913
35	Matthew Cziner	18 Canalport Avenue	1874–1875
36a	Francis J. Dewes	764 W. Chicago	1882–1885
36b	F.J. Dewes Brewery Co.		1885–1890
36c	F.J. Dewes Brewery Co., (City of Chicago Brewing and Malting Co.)		1890–1898
36d	City Brewery Co., (Chicago Consolidated Brewing and Malting Co.) (a.k.a. Malt Sinew Co.)		1898–1906 1901–1906
37a	Arah P. Dickinson	Cass & Michigan	1858–1859
37b	Dickinson & Bemis	Cass & Kinzie	1859–1860
37c	Arah P. Dickinson, (a.k.a. North Star Brewery)		1860–1864
38	Thomas Donovan	Pine & Pearson Sts.	c1860
39	Downer, Bemis & Co., (Ale & Porter Brewery)	16th St. at The Lake	1860–1864
40a	Morgan Doyle	423 Wolcott	1863–1864
40b	Doyle & Brother	State Street	1864–1866
40c	Doyle & Brother (a.k.a. Doyle & Co.)	423 N. State St.	1866–1878 1874–1875
40d	John Devereaux		1878–1879
41a	Eagle Brewing Co.	1469–1479 N. Western Ave.	1901–1909
41b	Eagle Brewing Co.	2608–2631 N. Western Ave.	1909–1927
42	Simon Eichenseher, (a.k.a. Eichenseher & Screiber)	Larrabee between Willow & Center	1858–1866 1863
43a	Endlich & Saladin	164–168 Archer Avenue	1858–1860
43b	William Saladin		1860–1870
43c	Matheus Gottfried		1870–1882
43d	Gottfried Brewing Co.	2249 Archer	1882–1924
44a	Ernst Bros. Brewing Co.	47–67 Larrabee St.	1884–1889
44b	Ernst Bros. Brewery, (Milwaukee and Chicago Breweries) (a.k.a. United States Brewing Co.)		1889–1890

45	Erickson & Berquist	123 S. Sedgwick	1874–1875
46	Julius Fachenbach	449 W. Fullerton	1898–1902
47a	Ernst Fecker, Jr, (ale & porter brewery)	863–869 Dudley St.	1894–1895
47b	Geo. J. Stadler Brewing Co.	863–869 Winchester Ave.	1895–1899
47c	Stenson Brewing Co.		1899–1903
47d	Stenson Brewing Co	1748 N. Winchester	1909–1923
47e	Stenson Brewing Co.		1933–1943
48a	The Fecker Brewing Co. (lager brewery)	871–875 Dudley St.	1890–1895
48b	The Fecker Brewing Co.	871–875 Winchester	1895–1898
48c	The Fecker Brewing Co., (United Breweries Co.)		1898–1901
49	F.C. Feigel	721 Indiana Avenue	1875–1876
50	August Fischer	20 S. Des Plaines Ave.	1888–1888
51	William Fleming	Hinsdale St. near Green Bay Road	1858–1876
52a	William Fleming & Co.	Wolcott near Church	1861–1863
52b	Excelsior Brewery, William Fleming, (a.k.a. Fleming & Conway)	110 Grand Haven	1863–1869 1863–1864
53a	Fortune & Co.	62 Oakwood	1864–1865
53b	Schmidt & Katz		1865–1866
53c	Schmidt, Katz & Leverns		1866–1867
53d	Schmidt, Katz & Co.		1867–1869
54a	Fortune Bros.	138–144 W. Van Buren	1857–1881
54b	Fortune Brothers Brewing Co.	225 Des Plaines	1881–1920
54c	Fortune Bros. Brewing Co.	725 W. Van Buren	1936–1948
55a	E. Funk & Co.	144–146 Willow St.	1874–1877
55b	Ernst Funk		1877–1884
55c	Ernst Funk	50 Clyde Street	1884–1891
55d	Ernst Funk	50 Osgood Street	1891–1909
55e	Ernst Funk	1921 Osgood St.	1909–1911
56a	Gambrinus Brewing Co.	1525–1547 Fillmore	1900–1909
56b	Gambrinus Brewing Co.	3032–3058 Fillmore	1909–1922

56c	Gambrinus Brewing Co.		1933–1935
56d	Gambrinus Co., Inc.		1935–1936
56e	Patrick Henry Brewing Co., Inc.		1936–1939
57	Garden City Brewing Co.	868 Hoyne	1890–1890
58a	Garden City Brewing Co.	21st Pl. & S. Albany	1901–1902
58b	Garden City Brewery		1902–1925
58c	Garden City Brewery	2111–2123 S. Albany	1933–1951
59	Jacob Gauch	Indiana St. between Pine & St. Clair	c1845
60	Joseph Geeman	Clybourne near Larrabee	1862–1865
61a	Gillen, Schmidt & Co.	404–416 E. 25th Street	1878–1880
61b	Henry F. Gehring, (a.k.a. Bavarian Brewing Co.)		1880–1884
61c	Bavarian Brewing Co., (a.k.a. O'Donnell & Duer)		1884–1891
61d	Cantwell & Ryan Eagle Brewing Co.		1891–1893
61e	Cantwell Eagle Brewing Co.		1893–1897
62a	Gottfried & Schoenhofen	178 W. 12th Street	1860–1864
62b	Gottfried & Schoenhofen	34–50 [illegible], 18th & Canalport	1864–1867
62c	Peter Schoenhofen		1867–1879
62d	Peter Schoenhofen Brewing Co., (merged with National Brewing)		1879–1925
63	Gutsch Brothers	160–169 West Lake St.	1859–1865
64	Haas & Powell	27–31 W. Madison	1870–1871
65a	Haas & Sulzer Brewery		1833–c1836
65b	William Haas & Co.	Pine & Chicago Ave.	c1836–1841
65c	Lill & Diversey, (a.k.a. The Chicago Brewery) (a.k.a. Lill's Chicago Brewery)		 1841–1871 1867–1869
66a	Peter Hand Brewery Co., (a.k.a. Peter Hand Brewing Co.)	37–59 Sheffield Ave.	1891–1909 1891–1891
66b	Peter Hand Brewery Co.	1612–1632 Sheffield Ave.	1909–1920
66c	Peter Hand Brewery Co.		1933–1967
66d	Meister Brau, Inc., (a.k.a. Warsaw Brewing Co.)	1000 W. North Ave.	1967–1972 1971–1972

66e	Peter Hand Brewing Co.		1973–1978
67	Thomas G. Hanson	28 Chicago Ave.	1862–1867
68	Healy & Regitz	129–131 Fullerton Ave.	1887–1888
69a	Henn & Gabler Brewing Co.	35th & Ullman Street	1892–1895
69b	Henn & Gabler Brewing Co.	34th & Court St.	1895–1898
69c	Henn & Gabler Brewery, (North Western Brewery) (United Breweries Co.)		1898–1901
69d	Northwestern Brewery Co. No. 2, (United Breweries Co.) (a.k.a. Henn & Gabler Brewery)		1901–1908
70	Matthew Hitz	Green Bay & Cedar	1855–1862
71a	Jos. Hladovec Brewing Co.	1090–1118 W. 21st St.	1890–1892
71b	Monarch Brewing Co.		1892–1898
71c	Monarch Brewing Co., (a.k.a. Monarch Brewery) (United Breweries)		1898–1904 1898–1909
71d	Monarch Brewery	2419–2443 W. 21st St.	1910–1922
71e	Monarch Beverage Co.		1923–1932
71f	Monarch Brewing Co., Inc.		1932–1936
71g	Monarch Brewing Co.		1936–1958
71h	Van Merritt Brewing Co. (a.k.a. Bohemian Brewing Co.) (a.k.a. House of Augsburg) (a.k.a. Monarch Brewing Co.)		1958–1967 1958–1967 1959–1967 1958–1967
72a	John L. Hoerber	216–224 West 12th St.	1864–1882
72b	Bartholomay & Burgweger Brewing Co		1882–1887
72c	William Ruehl Brewing Co.		1887–1898
72d	William Ruehl Brewing Co., (a.k.a. Ruehl Brewery) (United Breweries Co.)		1898–1907
73a	John L. Hoerber	186 Griswold Street	1858–1864
73b	Hoerber & Gastriech		1864–1865
73c	John L. Hoerber		1865–1865
73d	Michael Sieben	186–188 Pacific Avenue	1865–1876

74a	John L. Hoerber	646–662 Hinam	1882–1885
74b	John L. Hoerber Brewing Co.	646–662 W. 21st Place	1885–1909
74c	John L. Hoerber Brewing Co.	1617–1629 W. 21st Place	1909–1927
74d	The Hoerber Brewing Co.		1934–1941
75a	Hofmann Bros. Brewing Co.	107 W. Monroe	1896–1909
75b	Hofmann Bros. Brewing Co.	2606–2626 W. Monroe	1909–1925
75c	Peter Fox Brewing Co.		1933–1955
76	Home Brewery	2654–2670 Elston Ave.	1910–1920
77	Home Brewing Co.	1294 W. 61st Street	1895–1895
78	Home Weiss Beer Brewery, (a.k.a. Home Brewery)	2702 N. 40th Street	1913–1916
79a	Huck & Schneider	Chicago Ave. & Division	1847–1855
79b	John A. Huck, (Eagle Brewery)	Wolcott near Division	1855–1860
79c	Huck's Chicago Brewing Co.		1860–1869
79d	John A. Huck Brewing Co.	445–449 N. State	1869–1871
80a	Illinois Brewing & Malting Co.	38th & S. Centre Ave.	1901–1910
80b	White Eagle Brewing Co.	3735 S. Centre Ave.	1910–1913
80c	White Eagle Brewing Co.	3735–3757 S. Racine Ave.	1913–1925
80d	Mid-West Products Co.		1926–1932
80e	White Eagle Brewing Co.		1933–1950
81a	Independent Brewing Association, (a.k.a. Prima Tonic Co.)	585–612 N. Halsted	1901–1909 1905–1907
81b	Independent Brewing Association	1440–1472 N. Halsted	1909–1915
81c	Independent Brewing Association	821–825 Blackhawk	1915–1920
81d	Primalt Products Co.		1920–1925
81e	The Prima Co., (merged with Bismarck Brewing Co.)		1933–1938
82a	Joseph Jerusalem	Foot of Elm St.	1868–1871
82b	Joseph Jerusalem	357–365 Rush St.	1872–1887
82c	Ulrike Jerusalem	562–564 N. Halsted	1888–1891
82d	Gustav Eberlein		1891–1903
82e	Ulrike Eberlein, (a.k.a. Eberlein Weiss Beer Brewery)		1903–1908 1904–1908

83a	Joseph Junk	3700–3710 S. Halsted	1883–1887
83b	Magdalena Junk, (a.k.a. Junk's Brewery)		1887–1904 1890–1892
83c	Jos. Junk Brewing Co.		1904–1909
83d	South Side Brewing Co.		1909–1921
83e	South Side Ice & Beverage Co.		1922–1926
83f	South Side Brewing Co, (a.k.a. Frederick Bros. Brewing Co.)		1934–1937 1934–1937
83g	Ambrosia Brewing Co., (a.k.a. Frederick Bros. Brewing Co.)		1937–1959 1937–1941
83h	Atlantic Brewing Co., plant 2	827 W. 37th Place	1959–1965
84	Henry Kassens	Hyde Park	1884–1884
85	George Keller		1867–1869
86a	Kerber & Stege	583 N. Clark	1864–1866
86b	Herman Spanknebel		1866–1867
86c	Edward Stege		1867–1868
87a	Klockgeter & Co.	1317 Fletcher	1885–1886
87b	Kagebein & Folstaff, (Lakeview Brewery)		1886–1889
87c	Alvin Greiner		1889–1891
87d	Best Brewing Co. of Chicago, (a.k.a. Best Brewing Co.)		1891–1915
87e	Best Brewing Co. of Chicago	1301–1329 Fletcher	1915–1928
87f	Best Brewing Co. of Chicago (a.k.a. Best Brewing Co.) (a.k.a. National Brewing Co.)		1932–1950 1933–1934 1933–1935
87g	Best Brewing Corp., (a.k.a. Malt Marrow Brewing Co.)		1950–1961
88	William Knight	Hubbard between Lincoln & Roby	1861–1863
89	Koch & Poggensee	455–457 W. North	1905–1906
90a	Koch & Reyber	Hyde Park	1888–?
90b	Louis Wagner		?–1891
91	Koller Brewing Co., Inc.	39th & Racine	1933–1953
92	A.G. Kurth	1049 N. Oakley Ave.	1888–1888

92a	Louis Lamm	941–943 N. Western	1897–1891
92b	Germania Brewing Co.		1898–1899
92c	Germania Brewing Co.	588 N. California	1899–1900
93	Ludwick & Co.	31 Green Bay Road	1858–1863
94a	Charles B. Mader	347 Milwaukee Ave.	1884–1888
94b	Mader & Bartelme		1888–1890
94c	Charles B. Mader		1890–1893
94d	C.B. Mader & Co.		1893–1895
94e	Siegler & Schiemann Brewing Co.		1895–1897
94f	Imperial Brewing & Bottling Co.		1897–1898
94g	Globe Brewing Co.		1898–1901
94h	Charles B. Mader		1901–1902
94i	Chicago Consolidated Bottling Co.		1902–1904
94j	Koch & Poggensee		1904–1907
95a	Manhattan Brewing Co.	3901 S. Emerald Ave.	1893–1933
	(a.k.a. Malt Maid Products Co.)		1923–1932
	(a.k.a. Malt Maid Co.)		1923–1932
	(a.k.a. Fort Dearborn Products Co.)		1925
95b	Manhattan Brewing Co.	3900–3950 S. Union	1933–1947
95c	Canadian Ace Brewing Co.		1947–1968
	(a.k.a. Ace Brewing Co.)		1958–1962
	(a.k.a. Ace Hi Brewing Co.)		1958–1962
	(a.k.a. Allied Brewing Co.)		1954–1957
	(a.k.a. Berlin Brewing Co.)		1964–1965
	(a.k.a. Bismarck Brewing Co.)		1963–1968
	(a.k.a. Cold Brau Brewing Co.)		?
	(a.k.a. Crest Brewing Co.)		1961–1964
	(a.k.a. Empire Brewing Co.)		1959–1963
	(a.k.a. Essex Brewing Co.)		1957–1961
	(a.k.a. Essex Brewing, Ltd.)		1957–1961
	(a.k.a. Gipps Brewing Co.)		1956–1963
	(a.k.a. Gold Brau Brewing Co.)		1958–1968
	(a.k.a. Hapsburg Brewing Co.)		1964–1967
	(a.k.a. Jester Brewing Co.)		1953–1957
	(a.k.a. Kings Brewing Co.)		1959–1962
	(a.k.a. Koening Brau Brewing Co.)		1955–1967
	(a.k.a. Kol Brewing Co.)		
	(a.k.a. Leisy Brewing Co.)		1960–1964

	(a.k.a. Lubeck Brewing Co.)		1960–1964
	(a.k.a. Malt Maroow Brewing Co.)		
	(a.k.a. 9-0-5 Brewing Co.)		1962–1965
	(a.k.a. Old Missouri Brewing Co.)		
	(a.k.a. Old Vienna Brewing Co.)		1962–1964
	(a.k.a. Pilsen Brewing Co.)		1962–1968
	(a.k.a. Prima Brewing Co.)		1955–1964
	(a.k.a. Prima-Bismarck Brewing Co.)		1956–1960
	(a.k.a. Royal Brewing Co.)		1964–1966
	(a.k.a. Schultz Brewing Co.)		
	(a.k.a. Star Union Brewing Co.)		1963–1968
	(a.k.a. Superior Brewing Co.)		1963–1965
	(a.k.a. Tudor Brewing Co.)		
	(a.k.a. United States Brewing Co.)		
	(a.k.a Westminster Brewing Co.)		1858–1962
	(a.k.a. Westminster Brewery, Ltd.)		1958–1962
	(a.k.a. Windsor Brewing Co.)		1956–1960
96	MacDonald Brewery	1300–1308 McKinley Ave.	1935–1935
97	Frank McDermott Brewing Co.	3435–3441 S. Racine	1925–1937
	(a.k.a. Beverly Brewing Co.)		1937
	(a.k.a. Hunters Brewery, Inc.)		1934
	(a.k.a. Frank McDermott)		
98	Metropolitan Weiss Beer Brewing Co.	3802 S. Armour Ave.	1898–1898
99a	Mette & Vogt	471 E. 26th St.	1888–1889
99b	John Vogt	467–473 26th St.	1889–1892
99c	Vogt & Sweeney,		1892–1895
	(a.k.a. Vogt & Sweeney Brewing Co.)		1892–1895
99d	Mullen Brewing Co,		1895–1904
	(a.k.a. James J. Mullen)		1895
100a	George Metz,	401–403 Wolcott	c1850–1869
	(a.k.a. Union Brewery)		
	(a.k.a. George Metz & Killian Schott)		1862–1863
	(a.k.a. Metz & Brand)		1863–1864
100b	Metz & Steges,	401–403 N. State	1869–1875
	(a.k.a. Union Brewery)		
100c	George Metz, Jr.		1875–1877
101a	Miller & Son	State St. between Goethe & Division	1863–1870

101b	Seipp & Lehmann		1870–1871
102a	H.B. Miller & Son	Wolcott & Grand Haven Strip	1865–1865
102b	H.B. Miller & Son	420–440 N. State St.	1866–1868
103	John B. Miller	Larrabee between North & Blackhawk	1859–1862
104	Timothy Mitchell	Hyde Park	1862–1864
105	Moser Bros.	62–64 Hulburt	1866–1868
106a	Mueller Bros.	1131–1137 Fulton	1887–1890
106b	The Star Brewery Co.,		1890–1897
	(a.k.a. Star Brewery)		
	(a.k.a. The Star Brewery of Chicago)		1896–1898
106c	The Star Brewery,		1898–1902
	(branch of United Breweries Co.)		
	(a.k.a. Star Brewery of Chicago)		1898–1900
107a	Mueller Brothers	28 S. Des Plaines	1884–1888
107b	Mueller Bros. Brewing Co.		1888–1890
108a	A.&G.H. Mueller,	152 W. Randolph	1859–1862
	(a.k.a. Mueller Bros.)		
108b	Mueller Bros.	308 W. Madison	1862–1865
109a	Simon Munger	212 W. Chicago Ave.	1888–?
109b	Henry P. Caldwell		? –1891
110a	John Nangle	Lydia between Union & Halsted	1861–1864
110b	John Nangle	154 N. Rueben	1864–1868
111a	National Brewing Co.	846–860 W. 18th St.	c1889–1909
	(a.k.a. National Malt Tonic Co.)		1900–1909
111b	National Brewing Co.,	1900–1910 W. 18th St.	1900–1910
111c	Schoenhofen Co.,		1925–1933
	(a.k.a. National Brewing Co.)		1925–1933
	(a.k.a. National Malt Tonic Co.)		1925–1928
111d	Schoenhofen Edelweiss Co.	1900–1956 W. 18th St.	1933–1944
111e	Schoenhofen Edelweiss Co.,		1944–1951
	(affiliated with Atlas Brewing Co.)		
111f	Schoenhofen Edelweiss Co.,		1951–1966
	(branch of Drewery's, Ltd., South Bend, IN)		
	(a.k.a. Atlas Brewing Co.)		1951–1966
	(a.k.a. Barbarossa Brewing Co.)		1959–1966

	(a.k.a. Drewery's Ltd., USA)		1962–1966
	(a.k.a. Great Lakes Brewing Co.)		1957–1964
	(a.k.a. 9-0-5 Brewing Co.)		1960–1962
	(a.k.a. Prost Brewing Co.)		1961–1965
	(a.k.a. Trophy Brewing Co.)		1960–1964
111g	Schoenhofen Edelweiss Co.,		1966–1971
	(branch of Associated Brewing Co., Detroit, MI)		
	(a.k.a. Associated Brewing Co.)		1970–1971
	(a.k.a. B.B. Brewing Co.)		1966–1971
	(a.k.a. Drewery's Ltd., USA)		1966–1971
112a	Mutual Brewing Co.	3324 W. 22nd St.	1907–1924
	(a.k.a. The New Brewery)		1907
112b	Mutual Ice & Beverage Co.	22nd & Troy	1933–1933
113	Non-Alcoholic Beer Co.	54 Clybourne Ave.	1893–1893
114a	North Western Brewing Co.	781–831 Clybourne Ave.	1888–1898
114b	North Western Brewing Co.,		1898–1909
	(United Breweries Co.)		
	(a.k.a. North Western Brewery)		
114c	North Western Brewery,	2270–2332 Clybourne Ave.	1909–1921
	(a.k.a. North Western)		1918–1921
115a	O'Donnell & Duer,	3937 S. Wallace	1892–1904
	(a.k.a. Bavarian Brewing Co.)		
115b	Muller Brewing Co.		1904–1917
115c	National Brewing Co.		1917–1918
116a	Chas. F. Ogren	West Division & Wood Sts.	1886–1888
116b	Chas F. Ogren	625–629 Shober St.	1888–1892
116c	Chas. F. Ogren Brewing Co.		1892–1895
116d	Chas. F. Ogren Brewing Co.,	625–629 N. Irving Ave.	1895–1909
	(a.k.a. Ogren Brewing)		1908
	(a.k.a. Charles F. Ogren & Co.)		1898–1909
116e	Charles F. Ogren	1222–1228 N. Irving Ave.	1909–1913
	(a.k.a. Ogren Brewing Co.)		
117	Old Abbey Brewery Corp.	4539–4541 Armitage Ave.	1936–1941
118a	John O'Neill Brewery	Cedar St.	? –1860
118b	Dickinson & Bemis		1860–1862
119	John Parker,	115–117 Dearborn	c1854–1856
	(Garden City Brewery)		

120a	William Pfeifer	499 Milwaukee Ave.	1888–1891
120b	William Pfeifer	339–347 Leavitt St.	1892–1909
	(a.k.a. Berlin Weiss Beer Co.)		1892–1905
	(a.k.a. William Pfeifer Weiss Beer Co.)		1892–1905
	(a.k.a. Pfeifer's Berlin Weiss Beer Co.)		1905–1909
121c	William Pfeifer,	718–742 N. Leavitt St.	1909–1918
	(a.k.a. Pfeifer's Berlin Weiss Beer Co.)		
121d	Superior Brewing Co.,		1933–1941
	(a.k.a. Hunter's Brewery, Inc.)		c1936
122a	John Pforr	147–149 Fullerton Ave.	1888–1892
122b	Catherine Pforr		1892–1895
122c	Catherine Pforr,	74 Perry Street	1895–1897
	(a.k.a. John Pforr)		
122d	John Pforr,		
	(a.k.a. Catherine Pforr)		1898–1900
	(a.k.a. Catherine Pforr Estate)		1901–1903
	(a.k.a. J. Pforr & Co.)		1903–1904
	(a.k.a. Pforr Weiss Beer Brewery)		1904–1908
122e	Edw. J. Birk & Bro.	2341 Perry St.	1910–1912
123a	Phoenix Brewing Co.	53–63 W. Division St.	1896–1898
123b	Phoenix Brewing Co.,		1898–1901
	(United Breweries Co.)		
124a	Pilsen Brewing Co.	368 W. 26th St.	1903–1909
124b	Pilsen Brewing Co.	3043–3065 W. 26th St.	1909–1920
124c	Pilsen Brewery Co.,		1933–1962
	(a.k.a. Pilsen Products Co.)		1933–1936
125a	Pohl Bros.	27–35 Cooper St.	1881–1882
125b	Pohl & Henry		1882–1884
125c	Paul Pohl		1884–1905
125d	Paul Pohl Brewing Co.	2335–2344 Cooper St.	1905–1913
125e	Tabor Brewing Co.		1913–1915
125f	North American Brewing Co.,		1915–1932
	(a.k.a. Bosworth Products Co.)		1927–1932
125g	Bosworth Products Co.	2336 Bosworth Ave.	1932–1933
125h	Atlantic Brewing Co.,	1545–1549 W. Fullerton	1933–1965
	(a.k.a. Champagne Velvet Brewing Co.)		1960–1965

	(a.k.a. C.V. Brewing Co.)		1960–1965
	(a.k.a. Excell Brewing Co.)		
	(a.k.a. Red Top Brewing Co.)		1960–1964
	(a.k.a. Savoy Brewing Co.)		
	(a.k.a. Tuxedo Brewing Co.)		
126	Quist & Carlson	895 Sheffield Ave.	1908–1908
127a	Jacob Rehm & Co.	333–337 W. 12th St	1865–1866
127b	Rehm & Bartholomae		1866–1868
127c	Bartholomae & Co.		1868–1873
127d	Bartholomae & Roesing		1873–1888
127e	Bartholomae & Roesing Brewing & Malting Co.		1888–1890
127f	Bartholomae & Roesing Brewing & Malting Co., (Milwaukee and Chicago Breweries Co., Ltd.), (a.k.a. United States Brewing Co.)		1890–1909
127g	Bartholomae & Roesing Brewing & Malting Co., (Milwaukee and Chicago Breweries Co., Ltd.)	908–920 W. 12th St.	1890–1909
128	Joseph Reidelberger	Green Bay Rd. near Franklin	1864–1865
129	Reiser & Portmann	223 Michigan St.	1859–1860
130	Riverside Brewing Co.	4511 S. Kedzie	1938–1938
131a	Henry F.L. Rodemeyer	368–370 Ohio St.	1858–1859
131b	Schock, Devry & Co.		1859–1860
132a	Charles Rooth	336 S. State St.	1859–1860
132b	Thies & Bouland		1860–1862
133a	Ruehl Bros. Brewing Co.	2646 Harvard St.	1901–1915
133b	Ruehl Bros. Brewing Co.	2630–2660 Arthington St.	1915–1925
133c	Roosevelt Brewing Co.		1933–1938
134a	J.S. Saberton	Wolcott & Church	1854–1857
	(a.k.a. Saberton Brewery)		
	(a.k.a. Truman Downer)		
	(a.k.a. North Star Brewery)		1854–1857
	(a.k.a. J.A. Irvin)		1855
	(a.k.a. Isaac Irvin)		1856

134b Arah P. Dickinson, (North Star Brewery) (a.k.a. Dickinson & Downer, North Star Brewery)		1857–1858
134c James McDonald		1859–1860
134d J.S. Saberton		1861–1864
135a J.J. Sands, (Columbia Brewery)	Pearson & Pine Sts.	1855–1863
135b Sand's Ale Brewing Co., (Columbia Brewery a.k.a Hiram Wheeler & Sons)		1863–1871
136a Scanlon & Prinderville	251 Kinzie	1862–1864
136b John Scanlon		1864–1867
137 Scheffel & Co.	18–20 Hawthorne Ave.	1891–1899
138 Schmidt & Bender	509–511 Larrabee	1866–1870
139 Schoenhofen Edelweiss (branch of Drewry's)	2132–2146 S. Laflin	1954–1962
140 Fred. Seibt	785 N. Halsted	1882–1884
141a Michael Sieben	172–180 Clybourne	1896–1898
141b Michael Sieben, (United Breweries Co., a.k.a. Sieben Brewery)		1898–1905
142a Michael Sieben	335–345 Larrabee	1876–1895
142b Excelsior Brewing Co.		1895–1898
142c M. Sieben's Brewery	1454–1478 Larrabee	1911–1914
142d Sieben's Brewery Co.		1914–1920
142e Mid-City Brewery Co., (a.k.a. The George Frank Brewery)		1920–1924
142f Sieben's Brewery Co.		1933–1967
143a Siebert & Schmidt, (a.k.a. Siebert & Co.)	22 N. Clark	1860–1864
143b Siebert & Schmidt	Asylum Pl. near N. Clark & Green Bay Rd.	1864–1866
143c K.G. Schmidt	9–35 Grant Pl.	1866–1871
143d Schmidt & Glade		1871–1882

143e	K.G. Schmidt Brewing Co.		1882–1890
143f	K.G. Schmidt Brewing Co., (Milwaukee and Chicago Breweries Co., Ltd.) (a.k.a. United States Brewing Co.)		1890–1909
143g	K.G. Schmidt Brewing Co.	415–445 Grant Pl.	1909–1917
144	Siebert & Woelffer	32–38 Chicago Ave.	1866–1868
145a	The Standard Brewery	12th & S. Campbell	1892–1920
145b	The Standard Products Co.		1920–1923
146a	Edward R. Stege	15th & S. Ashland Ave.	1890–1905
146b	Edward R. Stege Brewery	1508 S. Ashland Ave.	1905–1923
147	John Stutz	245 Cottage Grove Ave.	1865–1867
148a	N.P. Svenson	18 Huron	1866–1867
148b	Henderson & Vedell		1867–1868
149	Ernst Tosetti Brewing Co.	Wright, Butler & 40th Sts.	1886–1915
150a	Adolph Wagner	70–72 Clyde	1886–1887
150b	Katherine Wagner		1897–1898
150c	Robert Seyer		1890–1890
150d	Columbia Weiss Beer Brewing Co.	70–72 Osgood St.	1893–1896
150e	Martin J. Schnitzins, (Columbia Weiss Beer Brewery)		1896–1905
151	E.A. Wagner & Co.	80 Willow St.	1882–1882
152	Louis Wagner	567 96th St.	1895–1897
153	Ludwig Wagner	942 N. Clark	1867–1883
154a	Frank Walther Brewing Co., (a.k.a. Frank Walther)	402–416 Paulina	1878–1881
154b	East Side Brewery Co., (a.k.a. West Side Brewery)		1881–1890
154c	West Side Brewery Co., (City of Chicago Consolidated Brewing) (a.k.a. The Malt Sinew Co.)	916 N. Paulina	1890–1919 1907
155a	Westminster Brewing Co.	4160–4182 S. Union	1935–1938

155b	Prima Brewing Co., (Prima Co.) (a.k.a. Old Missouri Sales Co.)		1938–1941
156a	White Eagle Brewing Co.	18th St. & S. Ashland Ave.	1900–1909
156b	White Eagle Brewing Co.	1703 S. Ashland	1909–1910

Acknowledgments

Research for this book was facilitated by the staff of many Chicago institutions including the Chicago Historical Society, the Newberry Library, the John Crerar and Regenstein Libraries at the University of Chicago and the Harold Washington Library in Chicago. Thanks also go to Beverly Watkins of the National Archives—Great Lakes Region in Chicago; Glenn E. Humphreys, Special Collections Librarian at the Sulzer Regional Library; Tim Waters at the Museum of Science and Industry; Bill Siebel, Chairman and CEO of the Siebel Institute of Technology; Stan Galloway, Executive Director and Bob Pirie of the American Breweriana Association in Pueblo, Colorado. Stan took time away from his job to write the Foreword for this book for which I am extremely grateful.

I also want to thank Susan K. Appel, associate professor of art history at Illinois State University (Normal, IL), a specialist in the study of brewery architecture, who took the time to read and comment on the manuscript.

Ed Chensky of Riverside, Illinois was kind enough to spend a Saturday morning regaling me with his recollections and insights of life in the Pilsen area during the years before and after Repeal in Chicago.

George G. Weiss, step-grandson of Gottfried Brewery owner John H. Weiss, William Fox II, son of advertising director Kenneth Fox of Fox DeLuxe, and Edwin A. Seipp, Jr., great-grandson of the innovative advertiser, promoter and brewer Conrad Seipp, were all kind enough to answer my written queries. Valerie Turner, a descendant of brewer Michael Diversy, helped solve the mystery of the spelling of "Diversey" versus "Diversy," a little thing perhaps, but useful in clearing up what was an annoying inconsistency.

A letter to the editor of the *Chicago Tribune Magazine*, clarifying some issues about Chicago's old brewery trade, brought a generous offer from Larry Anderson of Naperville, Illinois to send me assorted bits of Breweriana from the old Stege Brewery. Many pictures of local breweries during the early 1950s were provided by "Uncle" Ernie Oest for inclusion in this book. Ernie, an American Breweriana Association member and former owner of a brewery memorabilia museum at Port Jefferson Station, New York, has been a collector of brewery knickknacks for longer than the life span of some of Chicago's less enduring breweries. Richard Remson also helped with a picture of a beautiful pre-Prohibition ad for Seipp's Salvator beer painted on the side of what was once an old saloon in Chicago. Uncovered after years of being blocked by an adjoining building, the sign was painted over in just days after eighty years in hiding. A last minute picture contribution from Steve Bernard saved me from dragging out my dusty collection of bottles from Chicago's breweries.

Herman and Jan Berghoff, owners of the Berghoff Restaurant, a Chicago institution on West Adams., were kind enough to provide time from their busy schedules for background information and photographs on the family's relationship to beer and brewing in Chicago.

Almost forgotten after five years of research is University of Illinois professor Jon Binder of the Merry Gangsters Literary Society who steered me, early on, towards the relationships between Johnny Torrio and Al Capone and the Chicago brewing industry during National Prohibition.

I am also grateful to Don Bull, co-author of *American Breweries*, P.O. Box 596, Wirtz, VA 24184, for permission to use the list of Chicago's breweries in the Appendix of this book. His list of breweries throughout the United States is an invaluable research tool for any brewery-historian. Don has a number of books about collectibles and beer-related items for sale and would be happy to hear from you. Bob Kay provided many of the labels shown here and has a business offering a wide assortment of beer labels to collectors. He can be reached at P.O. Box 1805, Batavia, IL 60510, or email him at beerlabel@aol.com. Phil Pospychala, co-author of *The Great Chicago Beer Cans*, was extremely helpful in adding coasters, labels and other odds and ends. Phil can be reached at 15745 W. Birchwood Lane, Libertyville, IL 60048. His book gives an interesting look at the history of Chicago's breweries and is a great reference for anyone specializing in the collecting of Chicago cans or who wants to delve further into Chicago brewery history. Bob Brockmann helped round everything out with a nice assortment of trays and some beautiful pre-Prohibition lithographs.

Fil Graff, editor of the National Association of Breweriana Advertising's magazine, *The Breweriana Collector*, contributed a number of fine photographs of breweriana memorabilia.

Lastly is my never ending thanks to my remarkable and understanding wife, Daria, who never blinked an eye when I said I was going to write a book about beer and brewing in Chicago. Convincing her, however, that I was really working as I sat staring at a blank screen with a Goose Island Honker's Ale at my side, took some determined effort. I also have to thank my two boys, Nikolas and Francis, who served as beer runners throughout the editing of this book. I needed it.

Bibliography

Background Materials

Ahern, M.L., *The Political History of Chicago.* Chicago, IL: Donohue & Henneberry, 1886.

Allsop, Kenneth, *The Bootleggers and Their Era.* Garden City, NY: Doubleday, 1961.

Anderson, Will, *The Beer Book, an Illustrated Guide to American Breweriana.* Princeton, NJ: The Pyne Press, 1976.

Andreas, A.T., *History of Chicago,* Volumes 1–3. New York, NY: Arno Press, 1975 (reprint).

_______, *History of Cook County Illinois.* Chicago: A.T. Andreas, Publisher, 1884.

Asbury, Herbert, *Gem of the Prairie.* DeKalb, IL: Northern Illinois University Press, 1986 (reprint).

Bergreen, Laurence, *Capone. The Man And The Era.* New York, NY: Simon & Schuster, 1994.

Broderick, Harold M., editor, *The Practical Brewer, A Manual for the Brewing Industry.* Madison, WI: Master Brewers Association of the Americas, Ninth Printing, 1991.

Brooks, H. Allen, *The Prairie School.* New York: W. W. Norton & Co., Inc, 1976.

Calkins, Raymond, *Substitutes for the Saloon. An Investigation Made for the Committee of Fifty under the Direction of Francis G. Peabody, Elgin R. L. Gould, and William M. Sloane.* New York: Houghton Mifflin Company, 1901.

_______, *Chicago Blue Book of Selected Names of Chicago and Suburban Towns.* Chicago, IL: The Chicago Directory Company, 1893–1915.

Demaris, Ovid. *Captive City.* New York, NY: Lyle Stuart, Inc., 1969.

Duis, Perry R., *The Saloon. Public Drinking in Chicago and Boston, 1880–1920.* Urbana, IL: University of Illinois Press, 1983.

Dunne, Finley Peter, *Dissertations by Mr. Dooley.* New York, NY: Harper & Brothers, Publishers, 1906.

Farr, Finis, *Chicago, A Personal History of America's Most American City.* New Rochelle, NY: Arlington House, 1973.

Flinn, John J., *History of the Chicago Police.* Chicago, Il: under the auspices of the Police Book Fund, 1887.

Harrison, Carter H., *Carter H. Harrison.* Chicago, IL: Ralph Fletcher Seymour, Publisher, 1944.

_______, *Stormy Years*. Indianapolis, IN: The Bobbs-Merrill Company, 1935.

Hernon, Peter and Terry Ganey, *Under the Influence. The Unauthorized Story of the Anheuser-Busch Dynasty*. New York, NY: Simon & Schuster, 1991.

_______, *History of Chicago; Its Commercial and Manufacturing Interests and Industry*. Chicago, IL: Church, Goodwin & Cushing, 1862.

Hofmeister, Rudolph, *The Germans of Chicago*. Champaign, IL: Stipes Publishing, 1976.

Keil, Hartmut, *German Workers' Culture in the United States 1850 to 1920*. Washington, D.C., and London: Smithsonian Institution Press, 1988.

Keil, Hartmut and John B. Jentz, editors. *German Workers in Industrial Chicago, 1850–1910: A Comparative Perspective*. DeKalb, IL: Northern Illinois University Press, 1983.

Keil, Harmut and John B. Jentz, editors, *German Workers in Chicago: A Documentary History*. Champaign, IL: University of Illinois Press, 1988.

Kobler, John, *Capone, The Life and World of Al Capone*. New York, NY: G.P. Putnam's Sons, 1971.

Kogan, Herman and Robert Cromie, *The Great Fire, Chicago, 1871*. New York, NY: G.P. Putnam's Sons, 1971.

Landesco, John, *Organized Crime in Chicago*. Chicago and London: The University of Chicago Press, 1929.

Leonard, William, *The Lill Story in the History of Chicago*. Chicago, IL: Lill Coal & Oil Company pamphlet, 1958.

Lowe, David, *Lost Chicago*. Boston, MA: Houghton Mifflin Company, 1975.

Lyle, John H., *The Dry and Lawless Years*. Englewood Cliffs, NJ: Prentice-Hall, Incorporated, 1960.

Mezzrow, Mezz and Bernard Wolfe, *Really The Blues*. Garden City, NY: Doubleday, 1972.

Moses, John and Joseph Kirkland, *History of Chicago*. Chicago, IL: Munsell & Company, Publishers, 1895.

Murray, George, *The Legacy of Al Capone*. New York, NY: G.P. Putnam's Sons, 1975.

Ness, Eliot, *The Untouchables*. New York, NY: Julian Messner, a division of Pocket Books, Incorporated, 1966.

Pegram, Thomas R., *Battling Demon Rum. The Struggle for a Dry America, 1800–1933*. Chicago, IL: Ivan R. Dee, 1998.

Peterson, Virgil W., *Barbarians in Our Midst*. Boston, MA: Atlantic, Little, Brown Books, 1952.

Pierce, Bessie Louise, *A History of Chicago*, Volumes 1–2. London: Alfred A. Knopf, 1940, 1957.

Schmidt, John R., *"The Mayor Who Cleaned Up Chicago." A Political Biography Of William E. Dever*. DeKalb, IL: Northern Illinois University Press, 1989.

Seeger, Eugen, *Chicago, The Wonder City*. Chicago, IL, 1893.

Sheahan, James W. and Upton, George P., *The Great Conflagration. Chicago*, Chicago, IL: Union Publishing, 1872.

Sullivan, Edward D., *Rattling the Cup on Chicago Crime*. New York: The Vanguard Press, 1929.

Wendt, Lloyd and Herman Kogan, *Lords of the Levee*. Cornwall, N.Y.: Cornwall Press, The Bobbs-Merrill Company, 1943.

Wilson, Samuel Paynter, *"Chicago" and its Cess-pools of Infamy*. Chicago. Third Edition, 1910.

Magazine Articles

Angle, Paul, "Michael Diversey and Beer in Chicago," *Chicago History* 8 (Spring, 1969) 321–6.

Appel, Susan K., "Chicago and the Rise of Brewery Architecture," *Chicago History* 24 (Spring, 1995) 4–19.

George, John E., "The Saloon Question in Chicago," *Economic Studies* 2 (American Economics Association, 1897) 57–110.

Johnson, William Oscar. "Sports and Suds," *Sports Illustrated*, August 8, 1988, 68–82.

Melendy, Royal L. "The Saloon in Chicago," *American Journal of Sociology* 6 (1900–01) 289–306 and 433–464.

Renner, R. Wilson, "In a Perfect Ferment: Chicago, The Know-Nothings, and the Riot For Lager Beer," *Chicago History* 5 (Summer1976) 161–170.

Brewery Trade Journals

American Brewers Review, Chicago.

The Brewer and Maltster and Beverageur, Chicago.

The Brewers' Digest, Chicago.

The Brewers' Journal, Chicago.

Brewery Age, Chicago.

Modern Brewery, New York.

Modern Brewery Age, Chicago.

The Western Brewer, Chicago.

Brewery-Related Publications

A Handbook of Facts and Figures. New York: United Brewers Industrial Foundation, 1937.

American Breweriana Journal of the American Breweriana Association, Incorporated, Pueblo, Colorado.

Arnold, John P., *Origins and History of Beer and Brewing*. Chicago, IL: Alumni Association of the Wahl-Henius Institute of Fermentology, 1911.

Arnold, John P., and Max Henius. *History of the Brewing Industry and Brewing Science in America*. Chicago, IL: Privately printed, 1933.

Baron, Stanley Wade, *Brewed In America. A History of Beer and Ale in the United States*. New York, NY: Arno Press, 1962.

Bull, Donald, Manfred Friedrich, and Robert Gottschalk, *American Breweries*. Trumbull, CT: Bullworks, 1984.

Cochran, Thomas Childs, *The Pabst Brewing Company*. Westport, CT: Greenwood Press, 1975.

Kuhlman, Kurt M., "The Best Brewing Company," *The Breweriana Collector, Journal of the National Association Breweriana Advertising.* 74 (Summer 1991), 8–13.

One Hundred Years of Brewing, Chicago & New York: H. S. Rich, 1903.

Pospychala, Phil and Joe McFarland, *The Great Chicago Beer Cans.* Libertyville, IL: Silver Fox Productions, 1970.

Schlueter, Herman, *The Brewing Industry and the Brewery Workers' Movement in America.* Cincinnati, Ohio: International Union of United Brewery Workers, 1919.

Tenth Anniversary Reunion of Chicago. Chicago: Blakely Printing Company, 1901.

The First Fifty Years of the Pilsen Brewing Company 1903–1953. Chicago: Pilsen Brewing Company pamphlet, 1953.

Van Munching, Philip, *Beer Blast.* New York, NY: Random House, 1997.

Collections, Archives, Diaries

Application For City Retailer's License Alcoholic Liquor, City of Chicago, Form C Z 502-Corporate Form.

Saloon Applications. Archives of Lake View City, 1872–1889. Chicago, IL. Library of Northeastern University.

Charles Schaffner Collection, 1902–1917. Chicago, IL, Agreement and Lease, Box 321, 1902–1917, Chicago Historical Society.

Chicago City Council Proceedings Files, 1833–1871. Springfield, IL: Illinois State Archives.

Manuscript Collection of William B. Ogden. William B. Letter Book, Chicago Historical Society.

John Herbert Weiss Papers [manuscript], 1900–1904, Chicago Historical Society.

Inaugural Addresses of The Mayors of Chicago, 1840–1995, edited by Tiwana Shaw, Ellen O'Brien, and Lyle Benedict, Chicago, IL: Chicago Public Library, Municipal Reference Collection, 1998.

Indictment of Capone. District Court of The United States of America for the Northern District of Illinois, Eastern Division, June Term, 1931.

Journal of the Proceedings of the City Council of the City of Chicago. Chicago, IL: Chicago Public Library, Municipal Reference Collection, 1933–1934.

List of Licensed Saloons in The City of Chicago. Chicago, July 1, 1908, Chicago Public Library, Municipal Reference Collection.

A Memoir of Edward G. Uihlein, 1917. Translated by Rosina L. Lippi and Jill D. Carlisle, Chicago Historical Society.

Records of the Alien Property Administration, Schoenhofen Family. National Archives, Trust Files, 2662, 2752, 3436, and 4922.

Record of the Seventh Brewers' Congress. U.S. Brewers' Association, 1867.

Report of The Special Investigating Committee of the City Council, March 7, 1904. Chicago Public Library, Municipal Reference Collection.

Taft Papers, Library of Congress.

Testimony of Prohibition Agents John Showalter and Andrew Hermanson. United States of America, Northern District of Illinois, Eastern Division, State of Illinois, County of Cook, May 20, 1924.

United States Brewers Foundation. Seventh Annual Meeting, 1946.

United States of America vs. Stenson Brewing Company, Number 6721, District Court of the U.S. Northern District of Illinois, Eastern Division.

Newspapers

Chicago American
Chicago Daily Democrat
Chicago Daily News
Chicago Herald
Chicago Herald and Examiner
Chicago Journal
Chicago Record-Herald
Chicago Sun-Times
Chicago Times
Chicago Tribune
Milwaukee Daily News
Milwaukee Sentinel
Nation's Restaurant News
New York Times
St. Louis Globe

Index

Page numbers in bold type indicate black and white illustrations.
"CS" indicates illustrations in the color supplement.